Hinduism and Modernity

RELIGION IN THE MODERN WORLD

Series Editors: Paul Heelas and Linda Woodhead, *University of Lancaster*

Editorial Adviser: David Martin, *Emeritus Professor, London School of Economics*

Founding Editors: John Clayton, *University of Boston*, and Ninian Smart, *formerly University of California – Santa Barbara*

The **Religion in the Modern World** series makes accessible to a wide audience some of the most important work in the study of religion today. The series invites leading scholars to present clear and non-technical contributions to contemporary thinking about religion in the modern world. Although the series is geared primarily to the needs of college and university students, the volumes in **Religion in the Modern World** will prove invaluable to readers with some background in Religious Studies who wish to keep up with recent thinking in the subject, as well as to the general reader who is seeking to learn more about the transformations of religion in our time.

Published:

Don Cupitt – *Mysticism After Modernity*
Paul Heelas, with the assistance of David Martin and Paul Morris – *Religion, Modernity and Postmodernity*
Linda Woodhead and Paul Heelas – *Religion in Modern Times*
David Martin – *Pentecostalism: The World Their Parish*
Steve Bruce – *God is Dead*
David Smith – *Hinduism and Modernity*

Forthcoming:

Juan Campo – *Pilgrimages in Modernity*
Bronislaw Szerszynski – *The Sacralization of Nature: Nature and the Sacred in the Global Age*
Peter Berger – *Questions of Faith*

Hinduism and Modernity

David Smith

Blackwell
Publishing

350 Main Street, Malden, MA 02148-5018, USA
108 Cowley Road, Oxford OX4 1JF, UK
550 Swanston Street, Carlton South, Victoria 3053, Australia
Kurfürstendamm 57, 10707 Berlin, Germany

First published 2003 by Blackwell Publishing Ltd

Library of Congress Cataloging-in-Publication Data

Smith, David (David James), 1944–
    Hinduism and modernity / David Smith.
        p. cm. — (Religion in the modern world)
    Includes bibliographical references and index.
    ISBN 0–631–20861–5 (hardback : alk. paper) — ISBN 0–631–20862–3
(pbk. : alk. paper)
    1. Hinduism.   2. Hinduism and culture.   3. India—Religion—20th century.
I. Title.   II. Series.

BL1202 .S63 2003
294.5—dc21

2002074759

A catalogue record for this title is available from the British Library.

Set in 10 on 12.5 pt Galliard
by Ace Filmsetting Ltd, Frome, Somerset
Printed and bound in the United Kingdom
by MPG Books Ltd, Bodmin, Cornwall

For further information on
Blackwell Publishing, visit our website:
http://www.blackwellpublishing.com

namo gurubhyaḥ

For J., A., W., M., D.

Dare to reason for yourself!

> Horace, Gassendi, Kant

You, the individual self, are the Universal Self.
tat tvam asi

> *Chhandogya Upanishad*

For the learned,
every country is one's own country,
and every town one's own town.

> *Tirukkural*

Contents

Preface

This book is a product of Lancaster University, where colleagues past and present in Religious Studies, Sociology and the Institute for Cultural Research have done much to further understanding of modernity and postmodernity. Notwithstanding scepticism on my part in respect of both modernity and postmodernity – especially postmodernity, which I suspect relates to what it is like to be a well-to-do resident of a metropolis at any point in the history of civilization – the work of my colleagues prompted me to attempt a presentation of Hinduism in relation to modernity.

By modernity I mean not modern times, but the theorization of modern times, the quasi-theological sociological reductionism which is a reified caricature of modern times. Modernity means rationalization, the autonomous individual, capitalism and the nation-state. Modernity, product of the Enlightenment, is generally brought into sharper focus by the contrast with what are called 'traditional societies', and somewhat blurred by the further contrast with the agglomeration of qualities known as postmodernity.

By Hinduism I mean of course the religion (or religions) of Hindus, religion that is a prime example of tradition, the product of 'a civilization which in its origins is probably as ancient as either the Egyptian or the Sumerian, but unlike them is yet functioning as a vital factor in the lives of nearly a fifth of the entire population of the world'. Thus Radhakrishnan described Hinduism in 1941.[1] In this book Hinduism is discussed both in terms of its historical scope and more particularly as it is manifested today.

In the chapter by Radhakrishnan I have just cited, he asks, 'What is the spirit of Hinduism? What are its essential principles?' These are not fashionable questions, for essentialism is now seen, rightly, to be dangerous. But essentialism is an important part of Hinduism. 'The brahminical scriptures of the Buddha's day, the Brahmanas and the early Upanisads, were mainly concerned with a search for the essences of things: of man, of sacrifice, of the universe. Indeed, brahminical philosophy continued in this essentialist mode down the centuries.'[2] Whereas the Buddha taught an active practice of liberation from rebirth, the Upanishads teach meditation upon the inner essence that is consciousness. The Hindu essence implies techniques to reach it, just as eating salt implies the process of extracting salt from water, but the goal is highlighted rather than the path. The essence as a point of focus is what counts in Hinduism. The image of the deity expresses the spiritual essence for the worshipper, who concentrates upon that essence, establishes contact with it, and absorbs it into himself. A common metaphor for essence is butter produced from milk. The essence of the male is the semen slowly distilled within, so easily lost. The essence of the female is her female power, her *shakti*, expressed in her milk and her menstrual blood. The brahman is the essence of the caste system, the mouth of the originary cosmic giant. Gold, the essential metal, hoarded over the millennia in India, and displayed as jewellery, is a physical expression of the essence of life. Everything behaves in accordance with its essential quality. Life is the expression of inner substance, of milk and semen; the spiritual is the expression of the inner essence, formless consciousness.

The answer to the question 'What is Hinduism?' depends on the degree of accuracy demanded, on the degree of zoom. What Hinduism is could be answered by a photograph from outer space of the tens of millions of Hindus assembled in the 2001 Kumbhamela at the confluence of the three rivers: Ganga, Yamuna, and the mythical Sarasvati. That huge body of people purifying itself of its sins by bathing in holy water, mass action on a unique scale, that mark on the surface of the earth visible from outer space is for a brief time the visible essence of Hinduism. If we zoom in, we are confronted by individual faces, life histories, each of which would have to be plumbed were there to be a complete understanding of Hinduism today. The same applies to the extensive variety of texts. I take Hinduism in the largest sense – even though viewed here primarily in its articulation by the Sanskrit tradition – englobing also its borderlands of Dalits and Muslims, against which it has reacted and with which it has coalesced, borderlands in the absence of which it cannot, so to speak, be its proper self; and also a Hinduism that has broken free of India and come to the West!

Modernity, not unlike Hinduism, has become a single, reified entity, that casts a long shadow. Modernity is the encrustation of modern times with a kind of secular theology. Modernity has an ethics, a logic, and an ontology. It fulfils itself in globalization. Hegel's *Phenomenology of the Spirit* is 'modernity's Sermon on the Mount'.[3] And so on. It is not my purpose to study the ideology of modernity in any depth. I shall give merely the briefest outline of modernity; but I do set out what part India and Hinduism have played in the formation of that ideology, and also consider what further effect Hinduism might have upon it.

Hinduism and modernity are opposite poles that are in some ways parallel entities. Imaginary in so far as they are held to be single entities, their changing shapes are not always dissimilar. Both Hinduism and modernity, to some extent and in differing ways, are subject to sustained critiques by feminism and postcolonialism. This book seeks to map the intellectual scene within which Hinduism may be situated. Like the reader inescapably within the confines of my own time, I look at Hinduism through the eyes of modernity, but attempt also to look back at modernity through the eyes of Hinduism.

The opening chapter of this book introduces modernity and shows the part – the small part – that India and Hinduism played in its formation. The second chapter considers the transposition of tradition into modernity in India via the image of the Juggernaut. The third chapter introduces the traditional literature of Hinduism and its modern developments.

The second part of the book takes a longer look at the reception of Hinduism: through the eyes of Islam (chapter 4), through the eyes of Europe (chapter 5), and contemporary revisionism of Orientalism and postcolonialism (chapter 6).

The third part of the book examines basic aspects of classical Hinduism and contrasts these with modernity. Here the core of Hinduism and its most distinctive features – though caste is only lightly touched upon – are set against parallel features of modernity. In order to present the Hindu equivalent of modernity's view of the self, four chapters are necessary. I begin with 'woman caste' (chapter 7), for Hinduism emphasizes, or at least does not seek to deny, woman's biological difference from man. The power Hinduism attributes to women, especially to mothers, leads naturally to Hindu goddesses (chapter 9), the area where Hinduism differs most notably from other 'world religions'. In this chapter mention is made of the attempt by the women's movement to make use of Hindu goddesses outside Hinduism. I then consider the divine in Hinduism more generally (chapter 10), looking at the whole notion of image worship, in addition to surveying the pantheon. The chapter concludes with a conspectus of multiple gods and polytheism, from the Enlightenment to the present.

We now have sufficient context to present the Hindu view of the Self (chapter 10). Here we start from a poster print of Shiva and his family, a print that is presented as a family photograph. The gods mirror the human family, and the human family mirrors the gods. Gods, other divine beings, and film stars present life on a bolder canvas that instructs and encourages. In the South, images of politicians and film stars appear on giant posters beside the road, just like the giant images favoured by Buddhism and Jainism in the past. Human events become superhuman. Human beings are able to attain superhuman powers. Hinduism inculcates superhuman possibilities, and superhuman realities.

The last part looks at specific aspects of Hinduism in the modern world: at the phenomenon of godmen and godwomen in India and in the West (chapter 11), and at politics, nationalism and the Hindu–Muslim divide in India (chapter 12). The chapter on politics is the one chapter fully and solely concerned with Hinduism in India today.

India today is referred to through the book, but here we face the current situation of Hinduism in India. This might be thought regrettable, but in fact our journey is made easier by postponing till the last moment confrontation with the dire reality of Hinduism's current political situation. It is here that Hinduism and modernity finally meet in the manifestations of Hindu nationalism, dissolving into the Hindutva which haunts India today.

Acknowledgements

This book owes much to many people: colleagues, friends, and family, along with all the cited authorities. The staff of Lancaster University library have as always been most helpful, especially Ms Thelma Goodman and now Dr Jenny Brine and their colleagues in the Interlibrary Loan Department. Sources of inspiration have been Chandrashekharendra Sarasvati, A. K. Ramanujan, the Dikshitas of Chidambaram, and *para shakti*, my wife.

Part I

Hinduism and Modernity Explained

Chapter One

Modernity and Hinduism

Hail to Ganesha, the God of Beginnings, the Remover of Obstacles.

The most powerful institutions over time are those whose membranes give the impression they are impermeable, but are the most porous.[1]

The Ganesha milk miracle

On the morning of Thursday, 21 September 1995, a miracle took place in a Delhi temple. The image of elephant-headed Ganesha drank up the milk offered to him in worship. News of this event spread throughout India and was reported world-wide the next day. Hindus in every continent, in temples and in homes reported that their Ganesha too was drinking the milk offered to him. A barrister reported from Malaysia that the plastic Ganesha on his car dashboard had exhibited the same thirst. The London *Guardian* of 23 September reported it as 'probably the first example of global religious fervour propagated by mass telecommunications'.

This world-wide Hinduism was counterbalanced by the modernity of the national press in India which generally declared it to be no miracle, to be indeed a waste of time and milk – under such headlines as 'Ganesh Hysteria Peters Out', 'Have the Gods had their Fill?' and 'Temples Deserted, Rationalists Prove Capillary Action Works Always'. The usual editorial line was that such superstitious credulity was incompatible with the secular and scientific orientation of independent India. Among English-language publications it was left to the Hawaii-published *Hinduism Today* to lament that 'in India, which has taught mankind so much about religious tolerance, it is a surprise to see such an anti-Hindu bias. Years of British "divide and rule" policy, Christian missionary attacks and Marxist influence have created this atmosphere of bias. Lord Ganesha, Guardian of Dharma and Remover of Obstacles, has now revealed this anomalous situation to the entire world.'[2] That is, Ganesha had deliberately exposed the anti-Hindu bias of the Indian press. Here we see at once the global scope of Hinduism today, the strength of traditional belief, the rational scepticism of the Indian press, and the embattled attitude of the new fundamentalism.[3]

Ganesha became the first god to span the world instantaneously. What occurred was not simply world-wide reporting of a miracle, but the instantaneous world-wide occurrence of multiple instances of the same miracle. This miracle contrasts with the popular myth wherein the chubby Ganesha opts out of the hassle of circumnavigating the globe: when Shiva offers his two sons a mango as prize for the first to race round the world, six-headed Skanda dashes off on his peacock, while Ganesha merely ambles round his parents to claim the mango, explaining that they are the universe in themselves.

Hinduism and modernity

Like six-headed Skanda, modernity encircles the globe. Ganesha, with his elephant trunk, pot belly, and plate of sweets, most bizarre of gods to Western eyes, sums up in himself the chaotic variety of Hinduism. Shiva got his sons to run a race. I venture to set Hinduism against modernity: I propose a consideration of Hinduism and modernity by means of which each will cast light on the other. Skanda, of course, is no less profoundly Hindu than Ganesha, an 'ejaculation' of Shiva's semen while Ganesha is made from a fold of Parvati's sari; Skanda's origins lie deep in south India. But the rivalry of the two brothers justifies for the moment my metaphor.

Both Hinduism and modernity are somewhat arbitrary intellectual constructs. Modernity is not a word used in ordinary speech. Modernity is not simply the modern world or modern times; it is the theorization of the modern world. Hinduism too, though an older term than modernity, began as an extraneous, external term for the indigenous religions of India other than the reform movements that became separate, clearly self-identified, religions: Buddhism, Jainism, and Sikhism. Hinduism comprises Vaishnavism, Shaivism, and Shaktism, themselves refracted in turn into more distinct groupings. Both terms – Hinduism and modernity – constitute theorizations.

Our point of focus is not India and the West today, though that combination is the background of our investigation, the theatre in which this performance proceeds, the stage that Hinduism and modernity tread. Hinduism is the religion of 80 per cent of Indians, but it has only recently been sharply defined. Modernity is the time in which we all live, but here it is used in the sense of a coherent body of doctrine, a kind of sociological theology, a reified entity. Hinduism as a unit is set out in a stream of mainly Western books; it is mainly Western scholarship that has set out for inspection Hinduism as a 'world religion'. Modernity is conjoined with endless subjects in hundreds of book titles; its hard core is provided by studies of such authors as Max Weber and Walter Benjamin. The world has become disenchanted, art has lost its aura. For Weber the peculiar conditions of the modern world were to be explained by the uniqueness of Europe; for Benjamin, messianic materialist, modernity is the landscape of the metropolis. For Weber, modern bureaucracy has created an iron cage for mankind; for Benjamin, mankind is seduced by the bright lights of arcades of shops in the big city. These two cult figures for current definers of modernity serve to delimit our view of modernity.[4]

For modernity, the self is autonomous and God is dead. The death of God is 'the inescapable "fact" of modern life'.[5] For Hinduism, new gods jostle for place with old ones. For Hinduism, the self is hierarchical, people differ widely, and almost everyone is subordinate to someone else; yet it is open to the Hindu to abandon the social self and become a spiritual self. The clearest contrast between Hinduism and modernity is perhaps that the latter claims to be a unique period in history, while the former has the longest history of any living culture.

Modernity is global but, as the opening of this chapter shows, Hinduism is now by no means restricted to the single subcontinent that was its origin. Hinduism is closely connected with Jainism and Sikhism, and also with Buddhism, another 'world' religion. Hindu nationalists would see the three as aspects of Hinduism; certainly all three subsist within the penumbra stemming from ancient Hinduism. There is not space here to discuss these other religions in detail, despite their importance, though I will return to them in the final chapter. Modernity dissolves – at its edges at least – into postmodernity, its light becoming darkness when truth becomes relative. In the final analysis nothing is clear. We shall, however, stay in the light as far as is possible.

Both Hinduism and modernity are contentious terms, threatened and threatening. Hinduism as Hindutva, that is to say, Hindu nationalism, has become the battle-cry of fundamentalists and fascists, modernity the boast of the still imperializing West. Some Hindus feel threatened by Islam and left-wing thinkers; modernity is threatened by postmodernity and by all forms of fundamentalism. Hinduism is threatened by modernity, and modernity is threatened by Hinduism. As Al-Azmeh says, 'Naming is not an innocent activity . . . [it] lies at the very heart of ideology . . . concrete images put forward as factually paradigmatic . . . serve as iconic controllers of identities and take on general values generated by a truncated and telescoped history.'[6] Hinduism and modernity, first merely coinages, have taken on their own momentum – in their power, their mightiness, their volume, they have become juggernauts.

Why compare Hinduism and modernity?

Hinduism is not the most obvious religion to juxtapose with modernity. It is remote from those religions usually considered in relation to modernity: Christianity, Judaism and Islam. Judaism has a most intimate relationship with modernity. Gillian Rose's essays on Judaism and modernity treat modernity as an in-house concern of Jewish thought, as indeed it has largely been. Thinkers of Jewish ori-

gin have had a dominant role in the formation of modernity. Hinduism, by contrast, is an outsider. For Emmanuel Levinas, 'Europe *is* the Bible and Greece.'[7]
For Chief Rabbi Herzog, Greeks and Jews are the 'master-builders of the gigantic
temple of civilization . . . Civilization exhibits two forces – religion and science –
contending for mastery over the human mind. Science is ultimately traceable to
the contribution made by the Hellenic race, Israel, on the other hand, has brought
into the world the light of religion in its highest and purest form.'[8]

Christianity, Islam and Judaism are religions of a book (*the* book, is the way
they put it), and are largely defined by their respective central codified texts,
though they have their borders, their heterodox traditions, their badlands.
Hinduism is a religion of many books and of no book, of myriad oral teachings and ritual practices. There is no overall religious authority to define and
exclude. The watchwords are both unity and multiplicity, not either/or, but a
dynamic fuzzy logic allowing endless manipulation of the hierarchy that dissolves into universal oneness.

The relativity of truth that Hinduism accepts is well shown by the Indian
story of the blind men and the elephant. Each man touched one part of the
elephant, and declared the elephant to be what he experienced. Every account
was accurate as far as it went, but none of the men had any idea of what an
elephant really was. All human truth is relative. However, until recently Hinduism has lacked desire to define itself, to proclaim the unity of the elephant of the
story. Taking the long view, a complete survey of all forms of religion that
claimed to be Christian would scarcely be less diffuse, contradictory, and bizarre than the forms of Hinduism. Indeed such a total body of forms of Christianity would conceivably be less coherent than Hinduism. It is fashionable for
good political reasons to deny the unity of Hinduism, but its multiple forms are
more mutually accessible than are the disparate sects of other religions.

My title is chosen to articulate the working assumption of a potentially
revealing duality of opposites. Hinduism is the best, or at least the largest,
single instance of traditional culture. As such it can stand as the type, the very
image of tradition, as modernity's opposite, this polarity taking its place in the
line of such oppositions as ancient and modern, Matthew Arnold's Hebraic
and Hellenic, and Nietzsche's Dionysian and Apollonian (There is more truth
in this the more we ignore the impact of modernity upon India.)

The definition of modernity

I take modernity as the single destination to which 'all lines of developmental
traffic lead', the Eurocentric, Euro-American-centric view, and treat only cur-
sorily the impact of modernity on India. Such writers as Breckenridge and
Appadurai affirm that modernity is a global experience 'as varied as magic,
marriage, or madness':[9]

Every national society now creates its own ways of playing with modernity . . .
As far as this sort of play with the 'means of modernity' is concerned, the advanced capitalist countries may have a head start, but they are no longer gate-
keepers. The genie is out of the bottle . . . particular societies become locations
not of pristine cultures, but rather of complex and specific negotiations between
history and globality.[10]

For the most part I shall restrict myself to the genie before it left the bottle.
What I am dealing with here is Western modernity, above all and indeed
almost entirely a codified and reified Western modernity, which I call simply
modernity.

How then is modernity best defined? 'There are few terms which seem
to unleash such a flood of words and debates as that of "modernity".'[11]
Perhaps the simplest formulation is that modernity is what succeeds the
pre-modern, and which may or may not be succeeded in turn by the postmodern, but that gives us two more terms to deal with, each predicated on
the modern. Modernity is the Enlightenment project, with its certainties
of reason and progress; it is the detraditionalizing of the traditions which
preceded it. According to Charles Taylor, as summarized by Felski, modernity is 'a general philosophical distinction between traditional societies,
which are structured around the omnipresence of divine authority, and a
modern secularized universe predicated upon an individuated and self-con-
scious subjectivity'.[12]

When did modernity begin? That is a hard question. As Cahoone points
out,

> any century from the sixteenth through the nineteenth could be, and has been,
> named as the first 'modern' century. The Copernican system, for example, argu-
> ably a cornerstone of modernity, dates from the sixteenth century, while demo-
> cratic government, which can claim to be the essence of modern politics, did
> not become the dominant Western political form until very recently.[13]

According to their interests, writers speak of modernity as social structure,
or psychological experience, or philosophical project, and tend to assume that
all aspects share a common time-frame, and that as modernity spreads elsewhere in the world all the aspects will be found together. A confidently precise definition, based on Max Weber's understanding of the spirit of capitalism,
is provided by Bryan Turner:

> modernity is an effect of the processes of social rationalization which had their
> origins in the asceticism of the Protestant sects, in the ethic of world mastery of
> the seventeenth century, in the evolution of positivistic experimental sciences
> (especially Dutch and English experimental medicine), in Enlightenment ra-
> tionalism and in the slow and uneven formation of a general secular culture.[14]

It is fashionable to speak of 'the project of modernity' rather than simply 'modernity', for modernity is credited with an agenda, it has a plan, a trajectory almost as if it were a rocket, a rocket that must fall to earth eventually. The contemporary German philosopher Habermas expresses the general view: 'the project of modernity' was 'formulated in the eighteenth century by the philosophers of the Enlightenment'. It 'consisted in their efforts to develop objective science, universal morality and law, and autonomous art according to their inner logic . . . The Enlightenment philosophers wanted to utilize this accumulation of specialized culture for the enrichment of everyday life – that is to say, for the rational organization of everyday social life.'[15] In the words of Ernest Gellner, 'The creed of the Enlightenment *philosophes* was a kind of social programme, a vision of a rational order on earth which would also be a happy one.'[16] The canonical eighteenth-century French text on the idea of progress was *Sketch of a Historical Survey of the Progressions of the Human Mind* by Condorcet (1743–94), wherein it is shown that, thanks to scientific knowledge, mankind will continuously develop in health and happiness, its conduct ever more rational. Karl Marx was to argue that, through rational awareness of the working of society, people could free themselves from the blind, irrational forces that had hitherto governed their lives. Liberalism and socialism, the major ideologies of the West in the twentieth century, spring from the Enlightenment and share its belief that reason and freedom will prevail.

The lineage of modernity

Each of the European nations has it own lineage of modernity. Here I will pick out only the very greatest figures. I begin with Francis Bacon (1561–1626), herald of the Enlightenment according to Voltaire and D'Alembert, whose doctrine can be summed up as utility and progress:

> To make men perfect was no part of Bacon's plan. His humble aim was to make imperfect men comfortable . . . the aim of the Platonic philosophy was to exalt man into a god. The aim of the Baconian philosophy was to provide man with what he requires while he continues to be man. The aim of the Platonic philosophy was to raise us far above vulgar wants. The aim of the Baconian philosophy was to supply our vulgar wants.[17]

Bacon gave a visionary account of the experimental science of the future.

Modern philosophy – the 'philosophy of subjectivity'[18] – is usually said to begin with Descartes (1596–1650), who established the priority of internal subjectivity. His delight at achieving the famous insight *cogito ergo sum* led him to offer thanks to the Black Madonna at Loreto. However, his *Discourse on Method* reduced knowledge to the measurable, and his stress on reasoning led him to fear the Inquisition of the Catholic Church which had recently forced Galileo to recant his proof of Copernicus's claim that the earth goes round the sun. It is all too easy today to overlook the power of the Inquisition, and thus to exaggerate the religious sensibilities of philosophers whose very lives were threatened by it and wished to put it off the scent. Goya, a profoundly modern painter, had reason to fear the Spanish Inquisition even in the nineteenth century.

A junior contemporary of Descartes was François Bernier (1620–88), a minor figure in European intellectual history, but who is nevertheless important in the present book, and he will be referred to frequently in the early chapters. Bernier is usually described as a traveller, but his account of seventeenth-century India is based on a 10-year stay, mainly in Delhi, and his letters from India are treatises of great intellectual weight. I shall carefully consider his accounts of Hinduism and Mughal India. His formulation of Oriental despotism has resonated to the present day. A doctor of medicine, he was a disciple of Descartes's opponent Gassendi (d. 1655), who wished to revive the philosophy of Epicurus – atomism, the advocacy of pleasure over pain and liberation from the bonds of religious superstition. Despite being a canon of the Church, Gassendi's motto was 'Dare to reason for yourself!'[19] The followers of both Descartes and Gassendi are mentioned in a skit by Bernier, who speaks in mock alarm of their attempting to assist 'an obscure person, who goes by the name of Reason' 'to make forcible entry into the schools of our University' in order to expel the Aristotle of the theologians.[20] It was perhaps Bernier's attack on the influential astrologer Morin that made it advisable for him to leave France, and led him to India in 1659. Returning in 1669, he later had the same patroness as La Fontaine, whose highly successful *Fables* told of speaking animals modelled on and partly retold from sources originating from the Hindu *Panchatantra*, introduced to him by Bernier. Descartes stressed the separation of mind and body: only the mind could attain certainty; the body was a machine. In his view, animals did not have souls, but were merely machines.

The flow of information about India and other Eastern countries had been steadily increasing from the Middle Ages onwards, as has been set out by Donald Lach in his masterly *Asia in the Making of Europe*.[21] Much information was obtained by Jesuits. A Portuguese translation of the *Jnaneshvari*, Marathi paraphrase of the *Bhagavad Gita*, was made as early as the sixteenth century, but remains unpublished. It was only in the Enlightenment that the significance of this information began to be taken on board by philosophers. At first the stream of pagan Indian thought, that is Hindu thought, was held to be extremely ancient and correspondingly pure. Voltaire used Indian paganism to attack Christianity, ironically using as proof of Hindu wisdom the *Ezour Veda*, a Sanskrit text faked by Jesuits in support of their own belief. One of the most widely read texts of the Enlightenment was Raynal's treatise on colonialism, *The Philosophical History of the Two Indies*, surveying the whole range of European colonization. Raynal in his day was as famous as Rousseau, and, no less than Rousseau, an oracle of the coming French Revolution:

> Religion was everywhere an invention of skilful politicians who sought in the sky the force they lacked themselves, and brought down terror. Their reveries were generally accepted in all their absurdity. It was only by the progress of civilization and the enlightenment that we have become emboldened to examine them and begun to blush at belief.[22]

Raynal (1713–96) and others, such as his fellow countryman Anquetil-Duperron (1731–1805) and the Dutchman Jacob Haafner (1754–1809) who both wrote accounts of their travels in India,[23] are now praised for their opposition to colonialism, but this opposition was perhaps prompted by the fact that their own national interests were pre-empted by Britain. As we shall see at the end of this chapter and in chapter 6 on Orientalism, postcolonialism and feminism point up the contrast between the Enlightenment stress on reason and freedom and the beginning of European colonialism.

At least from the time of Spinoza (1632–77), atheism was an important element of the Enlightenment. A distinction may be made between the radical, atheistic, enlightenment of Spinoza and others, and the moderate, mainstream Enlightenment which included most of the well-known figures of the period. But the distinction is rather between the plain speakers and the cautious. A widely distributed text prior to Raynal's best-seller was the anonymous work sometimes attributed to Spinoza called *The Three Impostors*. Moses, Jesus, and Muhammad are investigated to 'judge afterwards who are the best founded: those who revered them as Holy men and Gods, or those who treated them as schemers and impostors'. The text takes the latter view:

> Although there was a multitude of divinities, those who worshipped them, whom we call pagans, had no general system of religion. Each republic, each state and city, each particular place had its own rites and thought of the divinity as fancy dictated. Following this came legislators [i.e. Moses, Jesus, and Muhammad] more cunning than the first legislators, and who employed methods more studied and more certain by giving out laws, forms of worship, and rituals which were fit to feed the fanaticism they wished to establish.[24]

I shall now consider to what extent the four greatest names in the formation of modernity used India and Hinduism as reference points. Each of them used Hinduism as an occasional background against which to illuminate their study of the mechanisms of their own 'modern' world.

Immanuel Kant (1724–1804)

When in 1784 a newspaper posed the question 'What is Enlightenment?'
Kant declared:

> Enlightenment is man's emergence from his self-imposed immaturity. Immatu-
> rity is the inability to use one's understanding without guidance from another.
> This immaturity is self-imposed when its cause lies not in lack of understanding,
> but in lack of resolve and courage to use it without guidance from another.
> Sapere Aude! ['Dare to reason for yourself!'] 'Have courage to use your own
> understanding!'–that is the motto of enlightenment.[25]

In *Religion within the Bounds of Mere Reason* (1793), Kant contrasted 'the religion of the priests' with the 'heroic opinion' of contemporary philosophers.
The former, he said, claimed 'that the world began with something good: with
the Golden Age . . . But then they make this happiness disappear like a dream,
and they spitefully hasten the decline into evil . . . so that now . . . we live in the
final age'; the latter claimed that 'the world steadfastly (though hardly noticeably) forges ahead in the very opposite direction, namely from bad to better;
that at least there is in the human being the predisposition to move in this
direction'. For the pessimistic view, that 'the Last Day and the destruction of
the world are knocking at the door', Kant instances India: 'in certain regions of
India the Judge and Destroyer of the world . . . Shiva . . . already is worshipped
as the God now holding power, after Vishnu, the Sustainer of the World, grown
weary of the office he had received from Brahma the Creator, resigned it centuries ago'.[26] The roles of the gods are correctly expressed here by Kant, but
setting them in a historical sequence is a misreading prompted by the Jesuit
forgery, the *Ezour Veda*. The three gods are always contemporaries, though
each can be the first-born or last-born in relation to the others.

In defining the Enlightenment in 1784 Kant wrote not only for the general
public but also for his sovereign, Frederick the Great, who exemplified the
responsible freedom Kant believed to be synonymous with the spirit of true
Enlightenment. For Kant, the emperor was 'truly enlightened in his ability to
permit freedom in matters of religion and personal conscience while remaining constant with respect to the necessity of maintaining a sense of duty and
obedience amongst his subjects regarding matters of social and cultural order'.[27] For Kant, maturity meant freedom of conscience with respect to matters speculative and theoretical, and duty with respect to social obligations (as
it happens, this position resembles that of Hinduism). German thinkers were
under greater political constraint than their French and British counterparts.
It is all the more interesting that Kant, threatened with censorship from 1786
by Frederick's repressive successor, never praised the tolerance of Hindus,
tolerance he referred to in the series of geographical lectures he gave over
many years:

It is a doctrine of the Indians (Hindus) that every nation has a religion of its own. Hence they compel no one to accept theirs. Whenever Christian missionaries tell about Christ, his teachings, his life etc., they listen attentively and raise no objections. But afterwards, when they begin to narrate about their religion, and the missionaries get indignant over it and censure them, as to how they can believe such untruths, then the Indians resent it saying that they believed . . . everything they had said, even though they could not prove their stories, why then could they not likewise believe them?[28]

G. W. F. Hegel (1770–1831)

Kant remained sceptical about moral progress, saying that 'the history of all times attests far too powerfully against it'.[29] It was Hegel who argued the implementation of reason in history. Whereas Kant called on individuals to dare to reason for themselves, Hegel claimed that it was the Spirit that called to the self.[30] 'That world history is governed by an ultimate design, that it is a rational process – whose rationality is not that of a particular subject, but a divine and absolute reason – that is a proposition whose truth we must assume; its proof lies in the study of world history itself, which is the image and the enactment of reason.'[31] In Ernest Gellner's words,

[Hegel's generation] had trouble with the old deity, but was eager to find something it could worship . . . The old deity, simultaneously personified and hidden, was taken to be a code term for a guiding impersonal culture-spirit which guides and bestows meaning on history . . . The impersonal Agency was the Spirit of the Age, or rather, it successively manifested itself in a whole *series* of such Spirits. It was really only a spirit with a succession of incarnations. Each of them was but its temporary avatar. But it could also be identified with the Author and Producer of the great historical drama itself, *and* it could constitute its ultimate culmination . . . the God of the philosophers and the God of Abraham had, at long last, become one and the same.[32]

For Hegel, India was a land of 'sunrise', of early origins and 'childhood'.[33] His lectures on religion put all religions into a temporal sequence of development in which Hinduism comes very near the beginning, as a religion of fantasy. India is 'the character of Spirit in a state of Dream'. Hegel was concerned to refute the post-Enlightenment German Romantics who held that the human race began in a state of innocence, and that traces of an immediate vision of God could be found in, for instance, the earliest Indian religion.[34] But his own view was hardly less romantic when he described India as 'a Fairy region, an enchanted World'. We are far from the informed anthropological understanding of Kant, but then that understanding did not inform Kant's own philosophy, and Kant would have agreed with Hegel that the relationship between Orient and Occident was a relationship of subordination, the Orient having been superseded by the Occident[35] – 'it is the necessary fate of Asiatic Empires to be subjected to Europeans'.[36] We see here an early statement of what Said and Inden call Orientalism, which is considered in detail in chapter 6 below. Hegel's dialectic of the self and the other, manifested for instance in the interrelationship of master and slave, came to have great importance in the revision of the Enlightenment that took place in the second half of the twentieth century.[37]

When Habermas tells us that 'Hegel was the first philosopher to develop a clear concept of modernity,'[38] we must remember that this clarity of concept is brought about by the imputation of unclarity to other cultures. If we have to go back to Hegel to understand the 'internal relationship between modernity and rationality' this is because it was Hegel who was the most extreme in denying rationality to other cultures. Yet not much in Hegel is clear. In the *Phenomenology of Spirit*, he defines 'the True' as 'the Bacchanalian revel in which no member is not drunk'.

Karl Marx (1818–1883)

Marx was greatly influenced by Hegel, but stood him on his head, taking his method but rejecting his mysticism. He completely accepted and continued to develop the notion of the progressive development of humanity. However, for Marx religion had no part to play in this development. The Judaeo-Christian God, gravely weakened by Hegel, who dissolved him into Spirit, now vanishes. What for Hegel is the cunning of the Spirit realizing its goals in history through the human struggle becomes for Marx the dialectical operation of the 'material' laws of history, expressed in the forces of production (the workers) overturning the relations of production (capitalism) by revolutionary struggle. No less confident than Hegel in the unbounded human capacity for progress, for Marx not just Hinduism but all religion was a fantasy projected by a humanity that hitherto had found no fulfilment in this world. Religion, he thought, was the 'opium of the people'. Marx may have had in mind Hegel's comparison of the Hindu's view of the world to an opium dream (though, conversely, opium was the religion of the poor in Europe).

Marx, writing in England in the midst of the Industrial Revolution, in the home of capitalism, was deeply influenced in his view of things by the society in which he found himself. The terrible conditions to which the majority of industrial workers were reduced, their lack of satisfaction in their work, their alienation from their employers and from the end product of their labour – as reported to him by his friend Engels – impressed him so much that his philosophy focused on this level of society. It was from here, from the proletariat, that change was going to come, and it was this level of society that would reap all the benefits that Marx's doctrine would in due course bring. Engels's close observation of the textile industry and other rapidly changing technologies crucially dominated Marx's thinking. As with Kant and Hegel, India was present on the periphery of his intellectual horizon, serving as a contrast to better define the modern society in which he found himself, and which was in itself the future of humanity. Unlike Europe and America, Indian society was, Marx believed, unchanging; above all, the Indian village was unchanging. An understanding of the socio-economic condition of society was now the crucial factor in any system of thought, and Indian thought was the product of a static society. India's institutions were bizarre and in summary form contemptible: the phallic linga, the idle monk, the Jagannath temple with its devotee-crushing car, and the dancing-girl prostitutes.[39]

Max Weber (1864–1920)

Marx's attention to society was continued by the sociologist Max Weber. With him, Hegelian optimism vanished, and the claim for scientific objectivity was the all more convincing. Sociology took over from philosophy as the dominant intellectual method for understanding the world, other than the natural sciences. As with the three previous thinkers, Weber saw the world in terms of an ever-increasing rationality, but for him the future scenario was now considerably less rosy. Rationalization meant disenchantment. Increasing bureaucratization would mean the world was ever greyer; that it would become an iron cage for mankind. Increasing rationalization was intimately connected with capitalism. Much of Weber's intellectual effort was tied to a social explanation of the origins of capitalism. He found these origins to lie solely in the West. It was in Europe and America that Protestantism had created the right psychological and intellectual climate for the rise of capitalism, and thus the distinctive and indeed unique character of modern times. Having first demonstrated the link between Protestantism and capitalism, Weber proceeded to support his case by demonstrating to his own satisfaction both the absence of capitalism and the absence of any equivalent of the Protestant ethic in the civilizations of China and India.[40]

Primary modernity: a summary

Modernity, then, is nothing less than reason. Thanks to reason, it is argued by all theorists of modernity, Europe developed industrial economies; thanks to reason, Europe developed capitalism. Democracy and secularization come by the same route, but the key historical proof of the fact of modernity is provided by the twin forces of capitalism and industrialization. It is important to understand that what I have set out as the lineage of modernity is a retrospective lineage. Whereas Marx and Weber thought in terms of the nature of capitalism, and Kant and Hegel thought in terms of the nature of the life of the mind, and all four thought in terms of the nature of reason, their successors have reformulated the problem under the name of modernity. Thus when we look back what strikes our eye, inevitably, is relevance to the present. Hegel, for instance, is described as '*the* philosopher of modernity', and Weber's primary concern is the nature of modernity, although at the time when he was writing nobody used that term.

Nietzsche and Freud: modernity becomes fragile

I have here presented what might be called the core of modernity or 'primary modernity', but there remain to be mentioned two great Germanic writers who, though they did not produce modernity, profoundly modified it. Friedrich Nietzsche (1844–1900) and Sigmund Freud (1856–1939) constitute *secondary modernity*. Every Enlightenment thinker in some sense wiped the slate clean, making a new beginning from rational first principles, but Nietzsche wiped away more vigorously than most, and made a new beginning with the will to power rather than with reason. He proclaimed the death of God and the transvaluation of all values. Freud, rather than providing a clean slate, showed beneath the rational self the unclean unconscious. Freud saw himself as working in the Enlightenment project as a positivist scientist, but also as the archaeologist of the psyche. His importance, but also the ambiguity of his position in intellectual history, is brought out in the comment of F. A. Hayek, 'I believe men will look back on our age as an age of superstition, chiefly connected with the names of Karl Marx and Sigmund Freud.'[41]

Both Marx and Freud made use of the concept of fetishism, 'ironically throwing back at their own societies the term used to encapsulate primitive, irrational, beliefs'. For both, European rationality had not entirely purged society of the irrational: fetishism was 'a refusal, or blockage, of the mind, or a phobic inability of the psyche, to understand a symbolic system of value, one within the social and the other within the psychoanalytic sphere'.[42]

As modernity took shape, from Kant to Hegel and on to Marx and Weber, there was increasing use of India as an example of what modernity was not. Nietzsche and Freud, however, looked to ancient Greece rather than to India. Nietzsche was influenced by Schopenhauer, who enthused over the Upanishads, and Freud corresponded with Rolland, who promoted Ramakrishna and Vivekananda, but neither felt any need to situate himself in relation to India. Nietzsche was more familiar with Indian thought than was Freud – not least because of his early friendship with the great European proponent of Vedanta, Paul Deussen – and he refers to India occasionally; but it had little or no effect upon his thought, unless his idea of eternal recurrence is seen as a personal version of reincarnation.[43] Freud had almost nothing to say about India, yet I will refer to him frequently in several chapters, for some of Freud's theories fit

Hinduism fairly well[44] (among the Greek and Egyptian statuettes that crowded Freud's desk was an ivory statue of Vishnu, made prominent by its whiteness). Let us note here simply the most fundamental insight of psychoanalysis, 'that the wish, the emotion, and the fantasy are as important as the act in man's experience'.[45] Both Nietzsche and Freud put a stop to the forward march of the Enlightenment by circling back to ancient culture for inspiration, and by the blatant imposition of their own personalities upon their readings of reality. Each claimed to be a unique teacher of the true nature of reality, to be in fact a guru.

Foucault and feminism: modernity attacked

Primary modernity provides the intellectual horizon of modern times. Secondary modernity, even though Nietzsche and Freud are widely repudiated and ignored, nevertheless profoundly affects the view of the self in intellectual circles in the West. We must also take note of *tertiary modernity*, represented by the ideas of a group of more recent thinkers, whose views and insights are not so deeply embedded in modern consciousness, but which nevertheless hold sway with many people. We have in fact the anti-modernity that is called *postmodernity*. Foucault's place in current thinking about modernity, and certainly in academic thinking about modern times in general, is perhaps even more important than that of Freud. The autonomous individual of the Enlightenment, the value-free search for truth inculcated by Weber, although already dissolved by Marx and Nietzsche, are washed away without trace if Foucault is successful in forcing us to admit that 'Power and knowledge directly imply one another . . . there is no power relation without the correlative constitution of a field of knowledge, nor any knowledge that does not presuppose and constitute at the same time power relations.'[46] Closely linked and influential is Gramsci's notion of hegemony, the dominance of the colonizer over the colonized and the predominance of the idea of the nation over the actual inhabitants of the land. The 'subaltern historians' of India, led by Ranajit Guha, giving voice to the voiceless (in the hope of a future hegemony to be exercised by workers and peasants), are inspired by Gramsci. Aijaz Ahmad usefully applies Gramsci's reflections on Italian history to Hindu fundamentalism;[47] Italy's unification in the nineteenth century was not dissimilar to that of India in the twentieth century.

Starting from Nietzsche's 'will to power', Foucault saw all knowledge as the manifestation of power and thus provided the basis for Edward Said's study of Orientalism, reinterpreted to mean arrogant and ignorant exploitation of the Orient. But Foucault himself exhibited elements of Said's redefinition of Orientalism. His initial programme attributed only 'primitive truth' to the East: 'In the universality of western *ratio*, there is that portion which is the East . . . the East as offered up to the colonizing reason of the West, but indefinitely inaccessible . . . even though the West ought to search there for what is its primitive truth. It will be necessary to write the history of this great division, through the whole length of western becoming.'[48] But Foucault did not rise to this 'necessity'.

Feminism

Foucault is highly influential in the women's movement, which likewise seeks to undermine the confidence of modernity. Mary Wollstonecraft is the first of a long line of thinkers, but feminism played what in retrospect looks like a remarkably slight role in formative definitions of modernity. As Janet Wolff says, 'The literature of modernity describes the experience of men . . . It is not at all clear what a feminist sociology would look like.'[49] But feminism has redefined the past and present, and is radically changing the future. Feminism has joined with postcolonialism against the common enemy, imperialism/ patriarchy, the double-headed monster into which the Enlightenment has now been transformed. The phallocentric primacy of reason bears the brunt of the fierce attack from feminists and the colonized. The biological fact of two human sexes is dismissed as a fetish, as a homophobic fantasy; human history is swept aside for the sake of individual fulfilment and satisfaction. There are two basic positions in modern feminism. First, women are the same as men – any current differences are temporary and are socially constructed.[50] Biology lies;[51] and anyway, the future will free us from biology.[52] Alternatively, woman is fundamentally different from man and represents a different and higher order of being; women are conned by patriarchy. All men are rapists by their very nature.[53] Patriarchy oppresses women. Not only are pornography and prostitution oppression of women; religion, marriage, motherhood, and heterosexuality are oppression, the imposition of male power on women.[54]

The Enlightenment sought to map and understand the world. Count de Brosses (1709–77) collected, under the heading of 'fetish', details of strange forms of worship reported by travellers outside Europe. The term fetish was applied by Marx to the new attitude to commodities – the physical products of labour – brought about by capitalism. The term was also taken up by Freud, and given a monocausal explanation. Men worshipped fetishes because they were shocked as children to discover that their mothers did not have penises: the fetish is a penis substitute. In their different ways Marx and Freud brought the fetish back to modern man. Feminism and colonial discourse theory make great play of fetishism, claiming that contrary beliefs to their own are instances of fetish worship, in one way or another. Modernity and the supremacy of reason which it exemplifies turns out to be a relatively brief moment in time, and indeed an illusory moment: the *philosophes*, the thinkers of the Enlightenment, are now seen to be tyrants who fetishized their phallocratic reason.

Postcolonialism

The trajectory of modernity runs parallel with that of European colonialism, and according to postcolonialism colonialism is inseparable from modernity. Postcolonialist writers such as Spivak, Bhabha and Hall act 'as a virus, infecting and changing modernity from within, . . . precipitating the kind of self-questioning that undermines its authority and self-assurance'.[55] Eighty-four per cent of the world's land mass was under colonial rule as late as the 1930s, and the same area is now postcolonial. Colonialism was the midwife to European capitalism, and now modernity, complicit with imperialism, stands accused by the mushrooming discipline of postcolonialism. 'The central figure of . . . Enlightenment discourses, the humane, knowing subject, now stands revealed as a white male colonialist.'[56] Imperialist attitudes are hunted out and exposed. Endless studies of Kipling and of Forster's *A Passage to India* are complemented by generalizations from reading Flaubert on North Africa, and general travel literature. Certainly history and literary history have to be rewritten, and the evil empire exposed, but a clear and full account is called for rather than endless theorization on the basis of minute instances. Postcolonialism is a thriving academic empire; an idea whose time to rule has come. Gellner, no lover of psychoanalysis, tells us that, within a span of less than half a century, psychoanalysis has conquered the world, 'becoming the dominant idiom for the discussion of the human personality and of human relations'.[57] Marxism once held sway. Now, the past is a foreign country that has been colonized by postcolonialism.[58]

Conclusion

In this chapter I have looked at the outlines of modernity, and noted what little part India and Hinduism had to play in its development. There are of course major contemporary Indian thinkers, definers or critics of modernity, who have ignored Hinduism, or who have given no special weight to it, as for instance the dazzling literary theorist Gayatri Spivak, a major practitioner of postcolonialism. As E. P. Thompson once wrote, 'There is not a thought that is being thought in the West or East which is not active in some Indian mind.'[59] My concern here is to lay bare the basic parameters of modernity and Hinduism, rather than attempt to show the contribution of India to the modern world. A separate matter is the influence of Hinduism on the rest of the world and modern times which has not affected the formation of modernity. The well-known influence of Hinduism on German Romanticism, of Hinduism and Buddhism on Schopenhauer, or the 'Hindu invasion of America', did not affect the formulation of modernity any more than did the earlier spread of Hinduism and Buddhism to South-East Asia, or than what has been called the 'Indianization of China'.[60] The slowness of the once expected Oriental Renaissance is discussed in my final chapter.

The modernity of the Enlightenment in its secondary and tertiary modes has become in some senses a monster. Setting aside the universal light of reason, a mythology, an iconography has been invented, where humanity is threatened and overwhelmed by giant forms – fetishism, phallocentrism, patriarchy, imperialism, and so on. The art historian T. J. Clarke sees modernity as 'a great emptying and sanitizing of the imagination',[61] but mankind is still subject to invisible forces – invisible at least to most people – even though their names and forms have changed. Anything and everything modern has at one time been put forward as a symbol of modernity, from the bicycle to the Eiffel Tower, from the camera to the computer, but the grand narrative has never been a grand picture. On the admission of its thinkers, the images of modernity are confused and confusing fetishes. The art historian Donald Kuspit has confidently declared that

> In a sense, all modern artists are like either Francis Bacon or René Descartes, 17th-century thinkers who claimed respectively to observe the world with empirical freshness and to uncover, unaided, a self fundamental to itself. In the Modernist movement, both world and self came to exist experimentally, that is, as hypotheses for which there was no final proof. Thus art relinquished the security of the traditional, absolute sense of world and self, was free to take the risks of being modern.

But he concludes that 'the modern is impossible to specify. It has no core.'[62]

Modernity is largely the creation of the West, but the West is by no means coterminous with modernity: Christianity and Judaism persist there, and Noam Chomsky has recently remarked that 'the United States is a major fundamentalist country . . . For example, 40 per cent of the population in the United States believe that the world was created 6,000 years ago. Around 85 per cent believe in miracles or have even seen them! . . . About half the population thinks there are extra-terrestrials among us . . . aliens.'[63] Washbrook rightly notes that tradition has been reinvigorated by modernity: 'Bourgeois Europe in the nineteenth century actually generated one of the greatest religious revivals in world-history – at least before that of the United States in the twentieth century'; he argues that Victorian Britain was the first instance of modern society but nevertheless partook of 'neo-Gothic architectural fantasies, pre-Raphaelite artistic dreams, monarchical cults, Romanesque militarism and occultist spiritualism'.[64]

Despite massive contradictions between it and political, social and religious realities, and multiple intellectual assaults, in which feminism leads and is perhaps the most effective opponent, the leaning tower of modernity dominates the intellectual scene, and, for people in general, postmodernity remains in the shadows. It is beside and against the complex and multiform shape of modernity that Hinduism is going to be set in the chapters that follow.

Chapter Two

India and the Juggernaut of Modernity

To someone from India the problem of modernity has always been more complex – contradictory, conflictual and distressing – than to someone from the West.[1]

The modern belongs everywhere. It may have started in the West for it owes its inception to a special set of historical circumstances. But there is nothing specifically Western about the printing press, the printed book, the newspaper, the periodical, the novel, or the short story. Nor about the railway, the steamship, the telegraph, the motor car, or the aeroplane.[2]

The Juggernaut of Puri

The temple of Jagannath at Puri, visible from the sea on the voyage to Calcutta from Europe, was for long the most famous Hindu site for Westerners. In the seventeenth century Bernier compared the incredible concourse of people there to the Mecca of his day. The great temple car at Puri, with its 16 solid wheels each seven feet high, hauled a mile by 4,000 devotees, supposedly longing to be crushed beneath those wheels, was the key emblem of Hinduism for the West. The unmanoeuvrable, scarcely mobile, vehicle, set in motion only by a horde of passionate devotees, was the very epitome of senseless tradition. The term 'juggernaut' came to mean unstoppable vehicle, and as such eventually became applicable to modernity, whose progress is supposed to be unstoppable, and indeed to crush all those who oppose it. Yet at the same time, tradition, at least in India, is also showing itself to be unstoppable; so great is its momentum.

Wooden temple cars are periodically rebuilt and replaced – the Jagannath car is unique in being made anew each year – but stone versions, immobile but sometimes with stone wheels that turn without touching the ground, go back to the tenth century in South India. The whole thirteenth-century

Temple of the Sun at Konarak is conceived as a chariot, fittingly, since the sun god drives his seven-horsed chariot around the sky. But all Hindu temples are *vimanas* ('extensions of space' and also 'celestial vehicles'), flying the gods through space. They were created as statements of divine power made self-empowerment by mighty conquering kings who fought against each other, and against the Muslims; kings whose careers were often out of control. The 1999 film *Devi* uses digital morphing and animation to show traditional snake goddesses arriving out of the clouds in a huge, snake-shaped space craft to perform linga worship in the human world. Its vast underside is watched from beneath by astonished earthlings, as in *ET, Judgement Day*, and other science fiction films. Spaceships and war chariots are highly manoeuvrable, whereas temple cars lack steering and brakes.

Juggernaut as lorry or wagon

In Britain, big lorries are called juggernauts. The term is not so used in India, but lorries there crush and maim extensively, taking the lead among the causes of the 60,000 road deaths each year in India. The trunk roads of India are daily littered with smashed lorries. Overworked drivers pushed to the limit and beyond by greedy employers take stimulants and depressants to ease their path and shorten their day. Most Hindu professional drivers have shrines on their dashboards, small plastic images, garlanded, and with a stick of incense burning beneath them. Passengers on a long-distance bus journey might well join the driver in shouting out a prayer to a deity as the bus starts up. At the same time belief in karma and the power of the stars is nowhere more manifest than on the road.

The annual death toll on the grand trunk road across northern India from New Delhi to Calcutta is more than 1,000. Journalist Steve Coll described his 900-mile journey along this road in 1989: 'Its shoulders reveal an almost surreal display of wreckage: trucks lying smashed and upside down in ditches every thirty to thirty-five miles, buses wrapped around trees, vans hanging from bridges, cars squashed like bugs.' Sections of the road are controlled by bandits who hijack trucks several times a month, sometimes killing the drivers. Corrupt policemen demand bribes at every checkpoint and throw drivers in jail if they don't oblige. And in rural areas, if a cow or pedestrian is run over, mobs of villagers attack and burn trucks, and lynch their drivers in revenge. 'All along the road we saw the carcasses of crashed vehicles, resting like fossils in the exact position in which their accident left them. Repairing smashed trucks can take a long time. Often, drivers refuse to leave their vehicles unattended, fearing that bandits or corrupt police will loot the cargo. So the wreckage sits, week after week.'[3]

Modernity as juggernaut

Anthony Giddens says that living 'in the "world" produced by high modernity has the feeling of riding a juggernaut'; he speaks of the ' erratic, runaway character of modernity', of its 'juggernaut-like nature'.[4] The wooden temple cars of tradition move slowly. The stone ones with their stone wheels and stone horses don't move at all: parts of the temple structure they are simulations of simulations, models of the wooden cars which are models of aerial chariots and cosmic mountains. This imaginary motion contrasts with the horrendous velocity of the juggernauts of high- and post-modernity. Martin Fuchs, introducing essays on modernity in India, also writes of modernity as juggernaut. He sees modernity as a project 'that is not only of 'alien' origin, but that drags one into its domain and marginalizes one at the same time, that objectifies and victimizes in a double manner'.[5] The juggernaut comes from somewhere else, and destroys incidentally whatever gets in its way, going we know not whither. Perhaps the most powerful transformation of this symbol into its opposite, from epitome of tradition[6] to embodiment of modernity, comes from David Harvey's use of the juggernaut train in Zola's 1890 novel *La Bête humaine*. Harvey makes the train a symbol of modernity:

> Engineer and fireman, locked in mortal combat out of their own petty jealousies, tumble from the train to be severed limb from limb beneath its juggernaut wheels. The train, driverless and ever accelerating, rushes toward Paris, while the soldiers it carries, intoxicated and drunk with excitement at the prospect of the grand war with Prussia to come, bellow the loudest and bawdiest of songs with all their energy and might. It was, of course, the Second Empire careering toward war with Prussia and the tragedy of the Commune that Zola sought to symbolize. But the image has perhaps a broader application. The urbanization of capital on a global scale charts a path toward a total but also violently unstable urbanization of civil society. The urbanization of capital intoxicates and befuddles us with fetishisms, rendering us powerless to understand let alone intervene coherently in that trajectory.[7]

There is much to unpack in the last three sentences. While the original Jagannath car carried images of the gods that people worshipped, the modernity that is capitalism as it proceeds along its trajectory befuddles us with fetishisms, with factitious, fabricated images. The temple car characteristic of the lumbering, unmanoeuvrable, dangerous quality of Hinduism is transferred to its opposite, modernity, which is fast, unmanoeuvrable, and no less dangerous. Here, in Harvey's modernity of late capitalism, the calm advance envisaged by the Enlightenment is long gone. Marx spoke of the juggernaut of capitalism: 'all means for the development of production . . .

drag [the labourer's] wife and child beneath the wheels of the Juggernaut of capital'. He was glad when the House of Commons refused 'to throw children of 13 under the Juggernaut Car of capital for more than 8 hours a day'.[8] It was in the subsequent decade that Marx formulated his notion of commodity fetishism, while the commodity culture of capitalism became manifest in grandiose shops and arcades of shops. According to Marx's new analysis, commodities, trivial in themselves, the products of men's hands, are charged with meaning because of 'the peculiar social character of the labour that produces them':

> There it is a definite social relation between men, that assumes, in their eyes, the fantastic form of a relation between things. In order, therefore, to find an analogy, we must have recourse to the mist-enveloped regions of the religious world. In that world the productions of the human brain appear as independent beings endowed with life, and entering into relation both with one another and the human race. So it is in the world of commodities with the products of men's hands. This I call the Fetishism which attaches itself to the products of labour, so soon as they are produced as commodities, and which is therefore inseparable from the production of commodities.[9]

In the religious world men make images and worship them, giving them a form of life; under capitalism – strange as it may at first sight seem – the things that men make undergo a somewhat parallel process. Social relations are converted into things, are commodified by capitalism's command over wage labour and land rents. This becoming transcendent on the part of the commodity, as in the case of a mere wooden table, says Marx, is 'far more wonderful than "table-turning" ever was'; he was referring to the domestic conjuring of his day, when mediums summoned spirits of the dead who seemed to prove their presence by moving the table.

> It is an enchanted, perverted, topsy-turvy world, in which Mr Capital and Mrs The Earth do their ghost-walking as social characters and at the same time directly as mere things. It is the great merit of classical economy to have destroyed this false appearance and illusion . . . this personification of things and conversion of production relations into entities, this religion of everyday life.[10]

Walter Benjamin, one of the most quoted definers of modernity, repeatedly asserted that the fetish character of the commodity was the key to modernity. For Benjamin, the enchanted world of the commodity was nowhere more evident than in the shopping arcades of Paris, arcades where space was extended by mirrors with 'the ambiguous twinkle of nirvana'. In Britain, France and Germany, entrances to arcades, museums, even railway stations, were thresholds of the dream world of the nineteenth century, the 'primal landscape' where the commodity reigned unchecked.[11]

The juggernaut of colonialism

For India, the juggernaut of modernity was also the juggernaut of colonialism. In his essay on number and the colonial imagination, Appadurai speaks of the 'colonial juggernaut', the 'incapacities and contradictions of the colonial juggernaut'. That is to say, 'the colonial project of essentializing, enumerating, and appropriating the social landscape' was not wholly successful. In one vitriolic paragraph he encapsulates the current post-colonialist view of the role of the British Raj:

> It is enumeration, in association with new forms of categorization, that creates the link between the orientalizing thrust of the British state, which saw India as a museum or zoo of difference and of differences, and the project of reform, which involved cleaning up the sleazy, flabby, frail, feminine, obsequious bodies of natives into clean, virile, muscular, moral, and loyal bodies that could be moved into the subjectivities proper to colonialism . . . With Gandhi, we have a revolt of the Indian body, a reawakening of Indian selves, and a reconstitution of the loyal body into the unruly and sign-ridden body of mass nationalist protest . . . But the fact that Gandhi had to die after watching bodies defined as 'Hindu' and 'Muslim' burn and defile one another reminds us that his success against the colonial project of enumeration, and its idea of the body politic, was not, and is not, complete.[12]

Here the brief metaphor of colonialism as juggernaut is implicitly extended, as the British ride roughshod over the Oriental reality, crushing their helpless subjects. What Appadurai is excoriating is the census, the counting up and categorizing of the colonial subjects, subjects who are so demeaned by their rulers that they are treated not merely as outdated things belonging only in a museum, but even worse, as animals in a zoo. The colonialists claimed that these censuses were needed to enable modern government, and so that reforms could bring India into the modern world. Appadurai says that, in British eyes, Indians were sleazy, that is to say that they had different sexual mores to the British, took little exercise, were not strong; men were indeed like women, and ingratiated themselves with the British. What the British wanted to do with Indians was to make them like themselves, so that they would think more or less like Englishmen, and enjoy their colonized status. All this the British sought to accomplish by counting up and listing the complexities of Indian society. Gandhi awoke Indians to their true Indianness, made them reject their loyalty to the British colonial overlord and, from the British perspective, made them again unruly and differentiated by their own various divisions ('sign-ridden'). But these divisions were precisely the result of colonial enumeration, of the censuses. It was the fault of the British that Indians saw themselves as 'Hindu' and 'Muslim', because those categories would not have persisted had it not been for the colonial juggernaut.

However, this leaves out of the account the alliance between the British and Indian elites. David Ludden uses more balanced imagery. If the 'juggernaut of Western modernity' rolled over traditional communities 'that were mauled, transformed, modernised, or shocked into rebellion and resistance' 'caste, patriarchy, and religious identity' were conspicuous survivals.[13]

The novelist E. M. Forster was aware how one can become the other – aware, indeed, of the ultimate nullity of colonialism: 'The triumphant machine of civilisation may suddenly hitch and be immobilised into a car of stone, and at such moments the destiny of the English seems to resemble their predecessors', who also entered the country with intent to refashion it, but were in the end worked into its pattern and covered with dust.'[14] The strange transposition of the juggernaut of colonialism or modernity into its source, the juggernaut of tradition, highlights an ambiguity in the root concepts, and brings out the inner complicity between the twin themes of this study. Hinduism and modernity are mutual reflections that at times lose themselves in each other. However, not only was the juggernaut of colonialism liable to stall, but its drivers were not as dedicated as the devotees who pull Jagannath's car. The colonialists in India were not the settlers their etymology (*colonus*, Latin for 'farmer') implies. Kipling, in his poem 'The Galley Slave' written in 1886, compares his compatriots in India to 'slaves' pulling the oars stoically in a 'galley' that one fine day they will leave, if they have the luck to survive.

Technology: the magic of the Raj

If India was free at first from Marx's magic of the commodity fetish, a secret unconscious magic that outdid the table-turning and ghost-walking, the local Western magic, of Marx's London, it was nevertheless the land of magic as it is generally understood. In Kipling's 'In the House of Suddhoo', a tenant cheats his foolish old landlord by delivering news of his sick son's state of health as if by magic when in fact an accomplice has telegraphed the details.[15] 'Does the great queen empress permit the use of white magic?' wonders the simple old man. The elaborate conjuring culminates in the ventriloquistic use of a 'native baby's head' floating in a bowl of water. The 'magic' of the Raj (as described by Kipling in *Kim*) is electricity across telegraph wires; that of India is deceit and exploitation. However, the telegraph would have been known to most inhabitants of Lahore by the late 1880s, the date of Kipling's story.

By the early 1850s the East India Company had spent £110,250 on telegraph lines linking the three presidencies, as the regions under British rule were called. The railway, telegraph and penny post system made the subcontinent a single country and its inhabitants a single nation. In 1865 a cable link was established between Britain and India. The railway was the embodiment of the advance of industrialism around the world. Americans were proclaiming machines as divinely ordained instruments for building the nation and strengthening its moral resolve. In 1852 a Frenchman saw the railway as replacing religion, or at least as comparable to religion in that both bound people together:

> One can compare the zeal and ardor displayed by the civilized nations of today in their establishment of railroads with that which, several centuries ago, went into the building of cathedrals . . . If it is true, as we hear, that the word 'religion' comes from *religare*, 'to bind' . . . then the railroads have more to do with the religious spirit than one might suppose. There has never existed a more powerful instrument for . . . rallying the scattered populations.[16]

In 1853 Marx predicted that railways would lead to the industrialization of the subcontinent, and in the same year Charles Trevelyan told a Commons committee that railways would be 'the great destroyer of caste, and the greatest missionary of all . . . The steam engine . . . was overturning prejudices, uprooting habits and changing customs as tenaciously held and dearly loved as life itself. A sacred Brahmin now sits in a third class carriage in contact with a Dome [untouchable] and, preferring a saving in money to his caste exclusiveness, drops his prejudice.'[17] Vain hopes, for the British shipped out rolling stock from England rather than manufacturing it in India; caste was unaffected by rail travel (and strengthened by censuses).

The Raj itself was far from being a fully fledged form of modernity, as its very name – the Royal Government – suggests. It is only in the last 50 years that the prestige of Graeco-Roman civilization has finally disappeared. Educated Britain, like the rest of Europe, was haunted by the Roman empire. Such Latin texts as Virgil's *Aeneid*, the epic of the founding of Rome, and Caesar's *Gallic Wars*, an account of the Roman colonization of France, Germany and Britain, had a dominant position in European education. When a rail network across India was first mooted, it was seen as a monument that would enable Britain to surpass previous empires: 'The honour, dignity, and the glory of Imperial Britain are concerned in it . . . a magnificent system of railway communications would present a series of public monuments vastly surpassing real grandeur, the aqueducts of Rome, the pyramids of Egypt, the great wall of China, the temples palaces and mausoleums of the Great Moguls – monuments not merely of intelligence and power, but of utility and beneficence.' In reality, the Indian railway network was built primarily for strategic reasons – for moving troops, and to connect the main centres of agricultural exports.[18] The same expenditure on irrigation would have been of far greater benefit for the people of India – the £2 million spent on the Ganges and Punjab irrigation canals quickly generated higher revenues – but the money for the railway was easily raised on the British capital market, which was successfully raising capital for railways all over the world. This was the only massive investment in India by the British – indeed 'the largest single unit of international investment in the nineteenth century'[19] – and gave a generous return to British shareholders, the East India Company guaranteeing the service of the debt.

'Nothing symbolized Britain's power in India so completely as the railway station', declare Richards and MacKenzie; 'Stations were to the British what the motte and bailey and great stone keeps were to the Normans.' This parallel is literally correct after the Mutiny prompted the fortification of stations. Lahore station, built like a castle, is the foremost example of this architecture. The same authors comment on an *Illustrated London News* illustration of the arrival there of the governor general in 1864:

> Huge crowds have gathered, elephants are drawn up, banners are borne aloft, and pennants and flags fly from the entrance and corner towers. It is like a medieval chivalric scene, and the Governor-General emerges from the fortified station like a king or great lord across the drawbridge of his castle. Here the station was setting the tone for a new British self-image, one more related to the power of medieval romance than classical imperial rule.[20]

Opened – with an almost Hindu sense of the importance of the propitious moment – on Queen Victoria's Jubilee Day in 1887, Victoria terminus in Mumbai remains a commanding presence in the city, a true 'steam cathedral'[21] until electric trains took over. 'The finest Victorian Gothic building in India . . . a monumental affirmation of Victorian civic and imperial pride and an effective measure of the economic stature of the city. Crowned by a huge dome and interwoven with eclectic Indo-Saracenic details, it is an exuberant display of polychromatic stone, decorated tiles, marble and stained glass.'[22] It was renamed Chatrapati (Emperor) Shivaji terminus on March 4, 1996, but is still crowned by Thomas Earp's 16-foot-high sculpture of Progress.

Three of India's four great cities were created by the British: Madras (now Chennai), Calcutta (now Kolkotta), and Bombay (now Mumbai). It was in these cities that modernity developed in India in the nineteenth century. We may also note that the British settlement in Calcutta began close to Kalighat temple, the temple of Kali, the patron deity of the city, and Mumbai, the fishermen's goddess, whose name became Bombay in British pronunciation, had her temple on the very site of Victoria terminus. The fourth city, Delhi, the seat of power of earlier empires, was adopted as capital by the British in 1911, and New Delhi was inaugurated in 1931.

The British Raj, says Khilnani, 'created a masquerade of the modern city, designed to flaunt the superior rationality and power of the Raj, but deficient in productive capacities. The modernity of the colonial city had a sedate grandeur to it, but it remained external to the life of the society – few bothered about it.'[23] It is certainly true that few bother about it now, but in architectural terms at least, the British achievement was magnificent. Madras, Calcutta and Bombay were truly modern cities, with buildings of great beauty. Delhi was indeed a masquerade, in that the British empire was – for those who had the eyes to see it plainly – a sham by the time its monuments were set out in Delhi; the earlier cities were masquerades only in the sense that any architecture that takes its inspiration from earlier models is so. As with the railway, the British Raj had as its model the overwhelming precedent of the Roman empire. Take Madras, the first of the great British cities in India to be founded. Work began on Fort St George, Madras, in 1640. Within 60 years it was a city of 300,000 people, half the size of London. Well-off British residents subsequently enjoyed a classical architecture that expressed late eighteenth- and early nineteenth-century English values just as well as London's squares, or the crescents and terraces of Bath:

> The transformation of Madras from an Oriental milieu into a classical vision was no fortuitous transposition of contemporary European taste, but a conscious attempt to identify the expanding British Empire in India with the civilising influence and moral values associated with classical architecture. One of the more obvious demonstrations was the provision of statuary to prominent public figures.[24]

And Calcutta was the city of palaces. All three cities had begun as British forts, and the elegant houses of the British, paid for by their spoils, were near the forts. But in time the troops and civilians moved out into cantonments, separating themselves more emphatically from the natives.

But this is just buildings. What of the life of the mind? In a controversial paper Barun De argues that modernity has only just arrived in India: 'alien rule and modernity are never compatible'. The British weakened the handicraft economies which had been emerging from the eighteenth-century decentralization of the Mughal empire. They established a minimal number of educational institutions and social regulations and made their subjects conversant with British business, administrative and technological practice. But this very limited modernization was unstable and 'put the nineteenth and early twentieth centuries at the end of a medieval period of uncertainty, instead of the beginning of the modern period, which still awaits us in the Third World'.[25]

The normal view is, rather, that it was in Bengal that the first significant intellectual encounter took place between East and West, an encounter 'that presaged the dawn of a modern mentality'. The English-educated *bhadralok* (upper classes) rejoiced in 'a new mentality' – 'rational, scientific, iconoclastic, humanistic and romantic'.[26] Tapan Raychaudhuri has noted that the 'first and only community of followers of Comte's Religion of Humanity with its full paraphernalia of man-oriented rituals was established in the city of Calcutta'.[27]

Moving forward to the twentieth century, let us turn to Ahmedabad, an instance of a manufacturing city that became modernized largely without British help; it was Indian entrepreneurs who financed the textile mills that made the city the Manchester of India. It was here that Gandhi established himself on his return from South Africa:

> I had a predilection for Ahmedabad. Being a Gujarati I thought I should be able to render the greatest service to the country through the Gujarati language. And then, as Ahmedabad was an ancient centre of handloom weaving, it was likely to be the most favourable field for the revival of the cottage industry of hand-spinning. There was also the hope that, the city being the capital of Gujarat, monetary help from its wealthy citizens would be more available here than elsewhere.[28]

It was here, supported by rich Indian mill owners, that Gandhi developed his opposition to modern civilization. By 1909 he had already taken the view that it was not the British people who ruled India, 'but modern civilization rules India through its railways, telegraph, telephone, etc.'. The cities founded by the British – Bombay, Calcutta, and Madras – were 'the real plague-spots of Modern India . . . India's salvation consists in unlearning what she has learnt during the past fifty years. The railways, telegraphs, hospitals, lawyers, doctors, and such like have all to go, and the so-called upper classes have to learn to live consciously, religiously, and deliberately the simple peasant life, knowing it to be a life giving true happiness.[29] Staff in hand, Gandhi walked across India:

> Man is so made by nature as to require him to restrict his movements as far as his hands and feet will take him. If we did not rush about from place to place by means of railways and such other maddening conveniences, much of the confusion that arises would be obviated . . . God set a limit to a man's locomotive ambition in the construction of his body. Man immediately proceeded to discover means of overriding the limit . . . I am so constructed that I can only serve my immediate neighbours, but in my conceit, I pretend to have discovered that I must with my body serve every individual in the Universe. In thus attempting the impossible, man comes in contact with different religions and is utterly confounded. According to this reasoning, it must be apparent to you that railways are a most dangerous institution. Man has gone further away from his Maker.[30]
>
> Every time I get into a railway car, or use a motor-bus, I know that I am doing violence to my sense of what is right . . . When there was no rapid locomotion teachers and preachers went on foot, braving all dangers, not for recruiting their health, but for the sake of humanity. Then were Benares and other places of pilgrimage holy cities; whereas to-day they are an abomination.[31]

In Gandhi's view the very idea of reforming the world was 'simple impertinence'. Material comfort was not conducive to more growth. Improved transport was the least of India's problems. Medical science was 'the concentrated essence of black magic', hospitals 'the instruments of the Devil'.

Gandhi's sympathies lay with simple villagers; he wished to return to the ideals of ancient India as enshrined in Rama's perfectly ordered kingdom, Ramrajya,[32] whose capital Ayodhya, on the bank of the Sarayu river, was where Rama, the ideal king, was born. Ayodhya was the ideal city: on a great highway, with ramparts, a moat and flags flying from its towers, it was set out on level ground, like a chessboard, twelve leagues long and three leagues wide, with well-ordered avenues; its houses were close to one another, without a gap between them. It had every weapon and implement, and every sort of artisan; everyone had personal jewellery and everyone knew his place. Such is the Valmiki *Ramayana*'s description of Ayodhya.

This ideal city looked like heaven. Everything about it is impossibly ideal, but it is also true that every city approaches this ideal, in that every city is relatively rich, and its citizens better off than the surrounding peasantry. All resources are gathered into the city and every trade and profession is practised there. This concentration of expertise and specialization, this mingling of races and nations that is a feature of every metropolis, may be considered as an approximation of the general features of modernity. Modernity is the city and the city is modernity. But Ayodhya is the Hindu ideal city. Every city is an ideal in some respects. The Ayodhya of today is probably in fact a Gupta reconstruction of the fifth century. The incursion of the Huns from the west, and flood damage to the imperial capital, Pataliputra (Patna), caused the Guptas to make a new capital to the west. But with continuing threats from the west, the court soon moved again to the east, to Kanauj, and finally Muslims established Delhi as the capital of the Sultanate.

Ayodhya took on renewed significance in the 1980s with the revival of interest in Rama kindled by the television serialization of the *Ramayana* and the rise of Hindu nationalism. But the archaeological record is relatively slight. Pataliputra, the capital of North India for hundreds of years – from its remains by far the largest city in ancient South Asia – remains unexcavated, though it is known that the massive timber ramparts referred to by Megasthenes in the third century BC are preserved below the modern water table.[33] The power of Ayodhya as metaphor far exceeds the historical record. It is not inconceivable that the poet of the *Ramayana* had Pataliputra in his mind's eye when he described the ideal city of Rama: both are rectangular rather than following the square plan prescribed by the manual of statecraft, the *Arthashastra*.

When the Indian epics came off the page and on to television, their vigour and speed were expressed in the re-creations of the Bronze Age war chariots that thundered their dusty way across the screen. In the *Katha Upanishad* the self is described as the passenger of the chariot of the body, a frequently cited metaphor. A common household adornment today is the sculptured plaque of Krishna instructing Arjuna in the teachings of the *Bhagavad Gita* – the

Lord singing his Song – while they both stand in Arjuna's war chariot, Krishna being the driver. Within a year of these television serializations, a real-life chariot set out to conquer India. The right-wing BJP Party came to power through its motorized chariot rides across India: a Toyota van was decorated with the outer form of a golden chariot, providing the striking phrase 'Toyota Hinduism'.[34]

Chapter Three

Hinduism Ancient and Modern

The ponderous progress of the Jagannath temple car transmutes into the head-long velocity of the juggernaut of modernity. But speed is dear to Sanskrit literature, where kings and warriors dash about in their chariots, and the earliest texts of Hinduism, the Vedas, describe the gods riding about in their spoke-wheeled chariots.[1] The *Katha Upanishad* compares the self (*atman*) to the rider in the chariot, the mind to the driver, and the senses to the horses, whereas Buddhism deconstructs the chariot that is the self: as no single part is the chariot but the chariot is nothing but its parts, so too the self (*King Milinda's Questions*). The chariots of the epic heroes feature largely in the televised version of the *Mahabharata*. The speeding chariot of the king Dushyanta is vividly described by him at the beginning of Kalidasa's play *Shakuntala*, as he bursts upon the tranquillity of a famous sage's hermitage. Chariots are sky-borne too: the sun's chariot is pulled by the seven horses of the days of the week; the demon Ravana carries off Sita in his aerial chariot. Sanskrit texts, in fact, speak of aeroplanes, in that this is the translation sometimes given for 'sky-going chariot'. But the chariot of archaeology is currently a vexed question, since Hindu fundamentalists are keen to revise the notion of an Aryan, Indo-European, incursion into India around 1500 BC in favour of an already long-established Hindu civilization in the Indus Valley. Key proof for such a hypothesis would be the presence of horse-drawn chariots, such as are described in the Veda, in that civilization.

Other great religions have extensive literatures but tend to rejoice in a single sacred text. Hinduism has many sacred texts. The four Vedas are the holiest text for most Hindus, but few can read them. The 'Great Epic of India', the *Mahabharata*, is called the Fifth Veda, and has been vividly alive for Hindus for more than two millennia. It contains the *Bhagavad Gita*, which in the twentieth century was elevated to the status of a kind of New Testament of

Hinduism. Then there is the *Ramayana*, whose god, Rama, has risen to new heights of popularity among Hindu fundamentalists in the last two decades. There is the *Bhagavata Purana*, the gospel of Krishna worship, written around 800, and the central text for followers of the Hare Krishna movement, as for many others. But just as there are nominally 330 million gods in India, there are many sacred texts. There are Sanskrit texts – all those mentioned above were written in Sanskrit; there are versions of those texts in modern Indian languages, from the tenth century onwards; there are new texts in the modern languages; and there are visual texts. A key aspect of the divine in Hinduism is that, apart from the ineffable absolute, it is fully visible. Each deity has one or more well-known forms, and can be present in accurate representations in temples and in home shrines. This detailed imagery can be a powerful theological statement, as in the iconographic programme of the huge temple gateways of Chidambaram.

India is linguistically very varied, while at the same time Hinduism has the benefit of a single primary sacred language, Sanskrit, that has remained unchanged and relatively well understood by the educated for 3,000 years. Its traditional geography placed India as the central island in a world made up of concentric land masses alternating with concentric oceans. From the centre of India rises up the golden mountain Meru, higher than the sun and moon. This self-confidence survived many invasions, and Hinduism readily absorbed aspects of other religions without feeling the need to acknowledge their existence.

The essential features of Hinduism may be stated as follows. Hinduism is polytheistic, monotheistic, and monistic. Many gods and goddesses are worshipped. Vishnu, Shiva and Devi are the principal deities, but they have many forms, and there are many more minor deities. Worshippers usually have one special deity, their 'chosen deity' whom they may see as supreme. At the same time, those Hindus who are philosophically inclined will be aware of the monistic philosophy of Shankara, and may declare that all gods are one, are Brahman, the one true reality, besides which all else is illusion. I pass over here for the sake of simplicity other Hindu theological options, which have many teachers, and extensive literatures.

Many Hindus believe in reincarnation, though devotion to a deity may be said to lead straight to heaven. Actions in previous lives will determine one's condition in this life. One's actions now determine one's rebirth, though devotion to a deity may cause the effect of previous actions (one's karma) to be overridden. The higher one's caste, the more likely one is to believe that one's position now is a result of one's actions in previous lives.

Living beings form a hierarchy, from the highest god to the lowest creature. In the hierarchy of human beings, some are semi-divine, some are divine. There exist spiritual techniques such as yoga which allow human beings to acquire godlike powers, or to become gods. Some gurus are godmen or godwomen, and may be worshipped as divinities. The social order is made up of a hierarchy of castes. It is often said that the one formal definition of a Hindu is that an individual should be born within a caste. One can escape from caste by becoming an ascetic, symbolically ending the life of a house-holder, and devote oneself to escape from rebirth.

Hinduism sets out very clearly a hierarchy of four goals for human beings. These are:

- sensory gratification (*kama*)
- material well-being (*artha*)
- religious behaviour (*dharma*), which leads to heaven or higher rebirth
- salvation, escape from rebirth (*moksha*).

All four are legitimate goals. The fourth, and highest (*moksha*), involves the fourth life-stage, that of the renouncer, though, as has been said, this life-stage can in fact be undertaken at any time of life. The more spiritually ad-vanced the individual, the earlier it will be done. The renouncer leaves the caste system and dies to ordinary life: he alone is a complete individual, an autonomous self.

The Veda (from *c.*1400 BC)

Leaving aside the undeciphered pictographic writings of the Indus Valley civi-lization (*c.*3000–2000 BC), which may or may not relate to Hinduism, the oldest text of Hinduism is the Veda. Scholars date the earliest part of the Veda, the thousand hymns of the *Rig Veda*, to around 1400 BC, though the Hindu tradition continues to affirm the eternality of the whole Veda, the Veda appearing anew as each world cycle recommences. 'Veda' may refer just to the four collection (*Samhitas*) of Vedic hymns (the four Vedas) or to them plus the totality of texts that accreted around them.

The Vedic texts themselves do not mention the periodic creation of the universe, nor do they refer to reincarnation except in their latest part, the Upanishads. Written in Sanskrit by poet-priests (brahmans), the oldest part sings the praises of the warrior gods of a military elite worshipped by sacrifi-cing by fire animals and a holy hallucinogenic plant (soma). Of these gods, only Shiva (here a fierce outsider deity) and Vishnu (a solar deity), each re-ferred to in a handful of hymns, remain of importance. Goddesses are scarcely mentioned. The *Rig Veda*, two other early collections based on it, and a fourth collection of magical and philosophical hymns are followed by the second part of the Veda, the *Brahmanas*, extensive prose texts working out a detailed theology of sacrifice, wherein sacrifice is seen as more important than the gods themselves. The third and final part of the Veda is the Upanishads, mystical texts which internalize the speculations of the sacrificial texts. The Upanishads influence the *Bhagavad Gita* and form the basis of the various forms of Vedanta philosophy.

The four collections of Vedic hymns, each collection with its own attendant sacrificial texts and Upanishads, were preserved for several hundred years before being written down, and the oral tradition has continued to the present day. Generations of male brahmans have learned one or more of these collections by heart, passing them down from generation to generation with complete exactitude. The possession of the Vedas gave the brahmans great prestige, and they asserted that their status was higher than that of kings. They were gods among men. Most of the vast literature in Sanskrit supports that claim, for it was written by the brahmans with that end in view. It was brahmans who stage-managed the great sacrifices for great men, and who developed the mysticism of the Upanishads into the philosophies of the Vedanta.

The Vedic hymns were never an open book, and in due course their preservation became more important than the understanding of them. They increasingly became an esoteric text, giving power to the learned few. But particular verses have been in continuous use, in for example in marriage and funeral rituals. Here I will discuss two extracts which have been in daily use up to the present day: the Gayatri verse, and the Hymn to the Cosmic Man.

The Gayatri verse

Orthodox initiated Hindu men recite the Gayatri, a single verse from the *Rig Veda* (3.62.10) at sunrise every day: 'That excellent glory of Savitar ['the solar stimulator'], the god we meditate on, may he stimulate our spiritual vision.' This is the most famous of all the verses of the Veda. It is a mantra, a word which first meant simply a verse from the Veda and then came to mean any supernaturally charged utterance in Sanskrit, whether or not from the Veda. In the 10 Sanskrit words of the Gayatri is the notion of the all-pervading power of the sun that corresponds to and acts upon the human intellect. This cosmic linkage is further linked to the power of speech: the mantra, God and the world are mutually interlinked. Power over speech gives the brahman power over the world. Here we see the enormous condensing power of Sanskrit, this turning of poetry into a crystal that passes unchanged down the centuries, retaining with precision its shape and power.

The Hymn to the Cosmic Man

Another hymn of far-reaching significance, from the very latest part of the *Rig Veda*, is the only one to refer to the caste system. Here the human body, that most natural of symbols for totality, is the model for the hierarchy and the integration of the caste system. This hymn supposes there is a cosmic man who is sacrificed to create the world. There is a clear echo here of human sacrifice. The brahman priests are said to be the mouth of the cosmic man; the warriors are his arms, the 'people' are his thighs, and the peasants are his feet. All are necessary, each to the other, but their value, their status, varies. All this is set in the context of sacrifice: sacrifice is the ultimate action, the ultimate causation, so it is sacrifice, sacrifice of the cosmic man, that has brought about the fundamental structure of human society, and sacrifice to the gods that produces the gods, along with mankind. Here we see a brahman myth constructed by the brahmans that has been successful over the millennia in justifying and helping to maintain their own position. It is still used in many ritual situations, including the rituals for those who drop out of the caste system in order to become ascetics.

Subsequent history of the Veda

Nearly all the Vedic gods had faded away by the time of the Upanishads. The chief Vedic god, Indra, became merely the god of rain, leader of the subsidiary gods; he reappears in a different guise in Tibetan Buddhism, where his thunderbolt is prominent. Vedic ritual was early reworked by Vaishnava and Shaiva ritualists and brought into temples where oblations of butter have been offered to fire for well over 1,000 years. Schools for teaching the memorization of the Veda continue in various parts of India. In the Hindu diaspora the need has been felt for an equivalent to the Koran of the Muslims and the Adi Granth of the Sikhs, and a large single-volume edition of the Veda has been produced for temples. It is, however, enshrined and worshipped rather than read.

The Veda was deliberately kept secret from lower castes and foreigners by the brahmans. Western interest in the Veda began in the Enlightenment, and Voltaire was excited by the *Ezour Veda* forged by Jesuits. After Sir William Jones (1746–94) realized that Sanskrit was similar in structure and vocabulary to Latin and Greek there arose the notion of an Indo-European or Indo-Germanic language family that had developed from a single language, presumably spoken by a single people, that had spread over Europe and India. From the Vedic accounts of what seemed to be the conquest of an aboriginal people, it was assumed that the Veda gave a direct account of the invasion carried out by the Indo-Europeans.

Max Müller produced the first printed edition of the Veda in Oxford, publication taking from 1849 to 1873. German scholars led the way in Vedic scholarship. The Vedic people's name for themselves, 'the noble' (*arya*), was taken up by the Nazis as an indirect result of Vedic scholarship in Germany. Veneration of the Veda and ignorance of its content caused some credulous Hindus to attribute German scientific advances to German knowledge of the Veda.

A nineteenth-century movement that continues to the present day, the Arya Samaj, founded by a brahman, Dayananda Sarasvati (1824–83), holds that the *Rig Veda* is the key to Hindu reform. Dayananda's first detailed examination of the Veda was via Müller's translation.[2] His own subsequent interpretations of the mantras were idiosyncratic, for he discovered in them not only pure monotheism but the historical basis of Western science and technology, as for instance telecommunications and aeronautics.[3] In the words of Aurobindo (1872–1950), it was 'a master-glance of practical intuition' on Dayananda's part to go back to the 'very root of Indian life and culture [the Veda], to derive from the flower of its first birth the seed for a radical new birth'; 'this scripture . . . degraded by misunderstanding to the level of an ancient document of barbarism . . . Dayananda looked beyond and perceived that our true original seed was the Veda'.[4]

For Dayananda, the Vedas were as canonical for Hindus as the Bible and the Koran for Christians and Muslims, but they were also scientifically true. Modern science corroborated the Vedic understanding of the universe; in fact, the Vedas were the source of science. A breakaway group was led by Guru Datta Vidyarthi (d. 1890), who found there to be no mythology at all in the Vedas, but only exact, scientific, descriptions of natural processes: they were documents of science, not religion. Aurobindo himself saw the Veda as vast piece of symbolism representing the passions of the soul and its striving after higher spiritual planes.

In the 1920s the Indus Valley civilization was discovered, and subsequent archaeological investigations continue to add to our knowledge of what is now known to have been the most extensive ancient civilization prior to the Romans. In the last decade this civilization has become a key issue for many educated Hindus. Edwin Bryant notes that in 1989 Western scholars had no idea that the theory of Aryan migration into India was contested: 'It has since exploded into full view in all South Asian Internet conferences, whether historical, religious, or Indological, usually to the point of . . . exasperation for all'.[5] The general Hindu view now is that the Indus Valley civilization was the work of the Vedic Indians; India was not invaded at that time. Indeed, many Hindus now believe that the Indo-European linguistic area came about through conquest by Sanskrit-speaking Hindus from the Indus Valley.

It is justly said that the whole idea of a self-supposed racially superior people invading India, which is what the Aryan invasion theory claims to find revealed in the *Rig Veda*, is horribly like a mirror image of what the British had done themselves at the time of the first formulation of the theory. Bryant notes that the situation is exacerbated by several early extreme statements of the theory which remain in print in India, while recent refinements, such as the work of Michael Witzel, remain largely unknown in India. The counter-view, the 'indigenous Aryan' thesis, is upheld by a small group of enthusiastic Westerners, most notably Konrad Elst and David Frawley.

The latter's *Myth of the Aryan Invasion* sold out in 18 days on its first publication in India. But these writers, like the Hindu fundamentalists whose
cause they espouse, are vehemently anti-Muslim, and the two positions seem
generally tied together: the Aryan invasion has been refuted; and the Muslim invasion of several hundred years ago should be reversed. Long-ago
events have an overpowering effect today, as will be considered at length in
the final chapter of this book.

The Upanishads

The Upanishads, the latest parts of the Veda, are also called 'the end of the
Vedas' (Vedanta). However, the word Vedanta is in this book reserved, as is
now usual, for the philosophical systems built up as ways of explaining the
Upanishads. The Upanishads are generally seen as the culmination and fulfilment of the Veda, and lead on to the *Bhagavad Gita* and the philosophies
of the Vedanta. The Upanishads replace the many esoteric analogies that
underpinned the sympathetic magic of the sacrifice texts of the Veda by a
single equation: 'That [brahman] is You [the individual self]'. The individual self (*atman*) is the universal self (brahman): this is the highest truth;
everything else is ultimately unreal. This remains the dominant philosophy
of Hinduism.

The Upanishads are referred to in the *Bhagavad Gita* as the 'yoga of knowledge'; their teachings are summarized around AD 450 in a text called the
Brahma Sutra, sometimes attributed to Vyasa, and commented on by Sankara
around 700, followed by the various other Vedanta philosophers, all brahmans.
The brahmans kept the Veda to themselves as long as they could. In 1656 the
ill-fated Dara Shukoh, who shared the admiration for Hindu culture of his
great-grandfather, the Emperor Akbar, had extensive portions of the
Upanishads translated into Persian, believing them to be the secret scriptures
referred to by the Koran. The Frenchman Anquetil-Duperron brought them
back from India in 1762, and in 1801–2 Duperron published the *Oupnekhat*
in two volumes, with a Latin translation. Schopenhauer read this translation
in 1814 at the age of 26, and continued to prefer it to the more accurate
translations of Ram Mohan Roy. The Upanishads form the core of the teachings of many gurus today, and are for many people the main justification for
the high status of the Veda.

Ram Mohan Roy (1772–1833), a Bengali brahman, founded the Brahmo
Samaj. He translated the Upanishads into English and Bengali, and presented
them as a rational humanism akin to Unitarianism, on the basis of which
Hinduism could be shown to be suitable for the modern world. The society's
ceremonies resembled Protestant church services. In Max Müller's enthusiastic words, Ram Mohan was 'the first who came from East to West, the first to

join hands and to complete that worldwide circle through which henceforth, like an electric current, Oriental thought could run to the West and Western thought return to the East'.[6] But in so doing he transformed his Vedic source into a trickle of Protestantism. Ram Mohan Roy is an early proponent of what has been called Neo-Hinduism. According to Paul Hacker, the 'typical Neo-Hindu has . . . lost his confidence in his native religion'.[7] The Neo-Hindu seeks a national revival through modernization of Hinduism, bypassing popular Hinduism and reformulating classical Hinduism, and as such is of only marginal concern to the opposition I am positing between modernity and Hinduism in its full extent.[8]

The *Bhagavad Gita* (*c.*200 BC)

Contained within the *Mahabharata*, the *Bhagavad Gita*, 'Song of the Lord Krishna', is the instruction given to the great bowman Arjuna by his kinsman and charioteer Krishna. Just as the great battle is about to begin, Arjuna feels unable to fight his cousins and teachers on the opposing side. Krishna teaches him that it is his caste duty to fight, and that in any case the self is eternal, and therefore no lasting damage will be done to the enemy. He teaches Arjuna the yoga of knowledge (the teachings of the Upanishads) and two new yogas.

His first new yoga is that of action, which is especially suited to a warrior, in that it is the discipline of doing one's duty without any regard for the consequences. The retreat from action that asceticism entails is now unnecessary: this new yoga of action has the same result of freedom from rebirth. His second new yoga builds on the yoga of action and raises it to a higher level: actions can be devoted to God out of love of God. Love of God brings freedom from rebirth. Krishna reveals himself to be the god Vishnu, who comes to earth to remove unrighteousness (*A-dharma*) whenever it appears.

Along with the Upanishad*s* and the *Brahma Sutra* the *Bhagavad Gita* is commented on by the various philosophers of the Vedanta. Until modern times it remains an essentially Vaishnava text. Many parallel and similar texts exist, but the *Bhagavad Gita* is the oldest, and in modern times has become the most read text amongst Hindus and all interested in Hinduism. The best-known Hindu of modern times, Mahatma Gandhi, declared his love for the *Bhagavad Gita,* and found inspiration there for his teaching of non-harming, notwithstanding the fact that Krishna's teaching was precisely that killing does not matter since the body is eternal. The atomic scientist Oppenheimer quoted from Arjuna's vision of the cosmic form of Krishna – 'Brighter than a thousand suns' – when he witnessed the explosion of the first atom bomb.

The *Mahabharata* (400 BC–AD 400) and the *Ramayana* (200 BC–AD 200)

Both the *Mahabharata*, 'the great epic of India', and the *Ramayana*, 'the wanderings of Rama', describe the great deeds of warriors but are heavily influenced by the world-view of the brahmans. The forests are full of Vedic sages, Rishis, conducting their Vedic sacrifices; the royal heroes protect these sacrifices from the demons who seek to stop them; and in both epics are themselves banished to the forest for long periods, living a life removed from the proper sphere of kings.

The *Mahabharata*'s great battle, that kills off most of the population, marks the beginning of the current world age, the Kali Yuga, the last and worst of the four ages. The *Mahabharata*'s often grim reality contrasts with the fairy story of the other epic, where Prince Charming (for that is the meaning of the name Rama) recaptures his wife Sita from a 10-headed demon with the aid of monkeys and bears. Valmiki's *Ramayana* is largely conceived and written as a single work of art; the *Mahabharata*, probably the work of many, is attributed to the sage Vyasa, who collated the Veda, sired one of the heroes of the *Mahabharata*, and went on to write the many Puranas. The universal scope of the *Mahabharata* is expressed in the traditional saying, 'What is not in the *Mahabharata* does not exist.'

Both epics have been at the heart of Hinduism virtually from the time of their composition onwards. Both have been the primary material for storytelling, both have provided material for and inspired innumerable literary texts and folk tales. The more manageable *Ramayana* was several times rewritten by vernacular poets, as for instance the fourteenth-century Tamil *Ramayana* by Kamban. A hundred years later the Rama of Tulsidas's *Ramcaritmanas* flourished in the Muslim-dominated north, not least because he was the most straightforward and least complex of Hindu deities, and thus a better parallel to Allah. But now the new iconography of Rama as active warrior has helped drive the right-wing anti-Muslim movement of contemporary India. Strong traditions of folk performance of the two epics persist. Both epics have had enormous success in television serialization in India, following decades of popularity in film.

The Laws of Manu (*c*.200 BC)

Manu was the First Man, the progenitor of mankind; the Puranas describe particular Manus for each of the successive periods of cosmic time. To the Manu of our era is attributed the best known of the many lawbooks of Hinduism, the Laws of Manu. This remains the authoritative account of *varna-*

ashrama-dharma, the *dharma* of the caste system (*varna*) and the stages of life (*ashrama*). The text owes its success in comparison to other similar texts to the fact that it deals with politics (*artha-shastra*) in addition to providing exhaustive coverage of religious and civil law.

Manu sets out in detail the duties of the four castes (*varna*s) that arose from the sacrifice of the cosmic man (Purusha), and explains the proliferation of sub-castes (*jati*s) as the result of mixed marriages between the *varna*s. He also elaborates the theory of four life-stages: student, married householder, forest dweller, and wandering ascetic. The last two are renunciant, and overlap: the final stage of wandering is hardly suitable for extreme old age, and is the incorporation of the practices of Jains and Buddhists into the orthodox scheme of things. Release from the round of births and deaths (*samsara*) is achieved in an ordered process that avoids the radical denial of caste and Veda at the core of Buddhism and Jainism. The householder of the three highest castes studies and venerates the Veda, the gods, his own ancestors – the whole hierarchy of living forms, but should ideally end up as the wandering ascetic who has left behind the sacrificial fire.

From the earliest commentator on Manu, Bharuchi (*c.* AD 600–700), until the scholars who worked for the maharajas of Tanjore (Madras State) in the nineteenth century, the work of reducing the law books to a practical and coherent shape went on without interruption, and in every quarter of India. Manu and other law books are still referred to in Indian legal rulings today. The use of ancient codes of law over such a long period and in varied kingdoms and cultures is explained by the fact that these laws were extremely flexible in application, and meant what the jurists of the day wanted them to mean. There were variant readings and interpretations of almost every verse; there were schools and sub-schools of interpretation. As early as the ninth century it was decided that some rules did not apply to the present world age, the age of Kali. The phrase, 'not leading to heaven' was applied to those rules which met with determined opposition–though *dharma*, righteous, they were no longer applicable.

The *Bhagavata Purana* and other Puranas (AD 500–1700)

The Puranas are sacred repositories of story, legend, and other religious information. Usually celebrating one principal deity, whether Vishnu, Shiva, or the goddess, they are each as it were a Bible for the worshippers of that deity. There are eighteen principal Puranas, plus others, but much the most important is the *Bhagavata Purana*, which gives the final canonical statement of the life of Krishna in a text deliberately antiquated, even Vedicized, dating from around 800.

It is the Puranas that give the sacred geography of India, the geography which Macaulay cited scornfully as seas of milk and treacle when he dismissed all Indian literature as not being worth a shelf of European books, and ended the British policy of funding traditional learning in India. Translations of the Puranas were important sources for H. P. Blavatsky's Theosophical Society, whose claims for the value of Eastern religion were influential in both India and Europe. The *Bhagavata Purana* inspired several schools of Krishna theology, of which the best known today is the Hare Krishna movement, the International Society for Krishna Consciousness. Its founder, Prabhupada, translated and commented on the whole of the *Bhagavata Purana*. The television version of the *Mahabharata* incorporated the *Bhagavata Purana*'s version of the early life of Krishna; and there are several video versions of Puranas. Much of popular Hinduism is sometimes put under the heading of Puranic Hinduism, since these texts codify practice, often incorporating folk practices outside the Vedic tradition. Some of the Puranas' mythical histories reflect historical events. The presentations and interpretations of Puranic mythology made by Heinrich Zimmer and Wendy Doniger have been influential in the West.

All the foregoing texts were the special preserve of brahmans. Nevertheless, from a historical perspective, outside influences are clearly visible. The Veda generated opposition: Buddhism and Jainism mocked its proclaimed sanctity and opposed the caste system. Much of the foregoing literature shows traces of having originated among the Kshatriyas, the warrior caste. The *Bhagavad Gita* dismisses the Veda as flowery words. Its own teachings are the direct speech of God, and it also gives in Arjuna's words a first-hand account of a personal vision of the cosmic glory of God. The *Bhagavata Purana*, being written in an archaic would-be Vedic style, again makes implicit claims to replace the Veda. For the Hare Krishna movement both texts are indeed part of the Veda; they are Vedic.

Yoga practices are described in some of the Upanishads and in the *Bhagavad Gita*, but the first independent text on yoga is Patanjali's *Yoga Sutra* written around AD 200, though this is clearly a compilation of earlier texts, and shows some Buddhist influence. This 'eightfold yoga', later called 'royal yoga', sets out the essential features of yoga, but a more physical yoga, based on an elaborate physiology, developed under the name of *hatha* yoga. Gorakhnatha's Hundred Verses (*c*. 1300) are perhaps the oldest text of this school. But many branches of Hinduism have meditational practices which may be described as yoga. Many modern gurus have developed what they claim are their own systems of yoga.

From around the fifth century we have the first traces of a movement, discerned by modern scholars and given the name Tantra, that swept across Hinduism, Buddhism and Jainism, and gained an ever-increasing hold on Hinduism, and which has persisted up to the present day. To begin with it seems to have been composed of two separate strands: a magical ritualism that was entirely non-Vedic (Tantrism) and an equally non-Vedic worship of the feminine (Shaktism). It owed nothing to the Vedas, but was written in Sanskrit; it opposed caste, but functioned secretly within the caste system. All three strands of Hinduism, Vaishnavism, Shaivism, and Shaktism, came to have their own Tantric texts, and their own cosmologies and rituals; each core divinity had associated with it an esoteric doctrine that came directly from its own mouth, and provided a complete theological account of the world. The Veda were completely bypassed. A noteworthy feature of some Tantric texts is the claim that they represent an easy path, especially suitable for the present Kali age, and these are therefore pre-eminently modern texts. At the same time Tantra had special appeal in the sexual liberation of the 1960s in the West, an appeal that continues up to the present.

Most orthodox Hindus and Western scholars ignored the Tantric traditions until the last quarter of the twentieth century. A fascinating sequence of changing attitudes could be plotted from the declaration of Horace Hayman Wilson, the first Oxford Professor of Sanskrit, in 1840 that tantras 'are authorities for all that is most abominable in the present state of Hinduism' to the affirmation made by Philip Rawson in 1971 that 'Tantra has a particular wisdom of its own. This sets it far apart from all other religious and psychological systems . . . [it] is a cult of ecstasy, focused on a vision of cosmic sexuality.'[9]

The Songs of the Saints

Entirely outside the Sanskrit tradition are the myriad songs of low-caste and outcaste saints, traces of which are preserved in regional languages from around 800. The largest group, from North India around the fifteenth and sixteenth centuries, are the Sants (holy men), influenced by Islam, singing of God as nameless and without qualities. Notable are Ravidas (fifteenth century) the leather-worker, Kabir (1398–1448) the weaver, and Guru Nanak (1469–1539), founder of Sikhism, a clerk. A story about Nanak shows well the intermediate position such figures occupied: when he died, his body turned to vapour and two piles of flowers appeared in its place, one for Hindus and the other for Muslims. These saints were critical of caste, and both Hindu and Muslim religious practices: 'The Hindu says Ram is the beloved, the Muslim says Allah is the Compassionate One. Then they kill each other.'

Voices of women

The poems and songs of several women saints from the Middle Ages have been preserved, but women's voices are now being published and constituted into texts to an ever-increasing degree. Mirabai (1498–1546) was a Rajasthani princess, who in the common pattern of Hindu women saints married but left her husband for God, in her case Krishna. Among her own caste she remains in bad odour for defying the rules, but her songs have always been popular with underprivileged Krishna devotees in North India.[10] Her defiance of social norms and her assertion of personal liberty come over clearly in the popular 1979 film *Meera*.

A. K. Ramanujan, describing women's private ceremonies within weddings, when bawdy and scatological songs are sung, says, 'They remind one of the double plots of Shakespearean or Sanskrit plays, with a diglossia articulating different worlds of the solemn and the comic, verse and prose, the cosmic and the familial. The second alternate world speaks of what the first cannot – incest, the secret wishes of good men and chaste women, the doubts and imperfections of idealized heroes.'[11] At the same time, the role of women in transmitting formal as well as informal tradition should be remembered. It is very often the grandmother who is the family storyteller, and in general women take religion more seriously than men, excepting male religious specialists. A sign of radical change to come is the claim of Madhu Kishwar, influential editor of the journal *Manushi* ('Woman'), that Manu 'would fully endorse my writing a *Madhusmriti* [i.e. the Lawbook of Madhu Kishwar], no matter how much I differ with him. He would probably rejoice in the fact that many people of today prefer *Madhusmriti* to *Manusmriti* because Manu, like all other *smritikars* [writers of lawbooks], emphasised that codes of morality are not fixed by some divine authority, but must evolve with respect to the changing requirements of generations and communities.'[12]

Women's songs present their own perspectives on the story of Rama and Sita. In the *Ramayana*, Rama puts Sita to the test twice because she was kidnapped by the demon Ravana and spent many weeks in his custody; the second time, the earth swallows her up. The goddess of the furrow returns to her native place. Broken-hearted at losing her, Rama has a golden statue of her made, referred to simply as 'a golden Sita', to accompany him in the performance of sacrifices. One song of Telugu brahman women tells how the golden image of Sita to be placed beside Rama in the sacrifice must be bathed by Rama's sister, but she refuses to perform the bathing because she was not consulted when Sita was abandoned.[13]

Another song tells how Shurpanakha, Ravana's sister, jealous of Rama's happiness in Ayodhya after killing her brother, seeks vengeance with a woman's cunning. Taking the form of a female hermit, she asks Sita to paint a picture of Ravana. Sita cannot, since she has never looked at his face, only at his feet. Asked then to draw his feet, Sita draws his big toe. Shurpanakha takes this drawing, puts in the rest of Ravana, and asks Brahma to bring it to life so that she can see her dead brother again. Brahma does this, and Shurpanakha takes the picture back to Sita. Ravana's image starts trying to drag Sita back to

Lanka. All the women in the palace try to help Sita get rid of the painting. Fire does not burn it. They throw it in a well, but it comes back up. At last Sita subdues the image by uttering Rama's name. When Rama comes, she hides the picture under the bed. Rama wants to make love, but Sita is distracted. Finding the picture, Rama thinks she is in love with the dead Ravana and banishes her. The women of the palace tell him what happened, but he won't listen, and tells Lakshmana to take her to the forest and kill her.[14] The women's protest culminates with the wives of Rama's three brothers singing that they are all one family and they all love Ravana together, 'so kill us all together', female solidarity making Rama yet more angry.

The voice of anti-Hindu outcastes, the Dalits

Corresponding to the growing sense of unity among many Hindus is the realization of outcastes, one in five of all Indians, that Hinduism has nothing to offer them, and their growing literature of protest attacks Hinduism. Gandhi called outcastes Harijans, 'the children of God', but they now call themselves Dalits ('the downtrodden', 'broken men') and have a vision of a classless and casteless society, where the 330 million gods of traditional Hinduism, 'which have kept the human minds and bodies imprisoned will be burned up in the flames of equality'.[15]

Part II

Hinduism for Others

Chapter Four

Islam and Hinduism

This and the following two chapters present various external views of Hinduism. Here I consider aspects of Islam's relationship with Hinduism, principally when Islamic power was at its height in India, and when modernity was taking shape in Europe. Of particular relevance to the argument of this book is the attitude of Islam to polytheism and the representation of deities in images and temples; some instances of this attitude, along with the closely related topic of kingship, will be dealt with in the present chapter.

The meeting of Hinduism and Islam is of crucial importance in the history of India. The recent history of modern Hinduism is overwhelmingly affected by partition and subsequent conflict with Pakistan; the preceeding eight centuries are richly coloured by Hindu–Muslim relations. In modern times Hindus came to play a large part in the subordinate administration of British India, while Muslims stood apart, though praised for their martial ability by the British. Once it became clear that independence was inevitable, there was increasing rivalry between Hindu and Muslim elites. Gandhi played an important role in reducing Hindu–Muslim conflict, and by his policy of non-violent action allowed the British Raj to end without violence between Britain and India. But Hindu and Muslim interests proved irreconcilable. Partition between Pakistan and India was hurried through by the British. 'The English have flung away their Raj like a bundle of old straw and we have been chopped in pieces like butcher's meat', was the comment of one Muslim peasant.[1] Intercommunal murder took a million lives as Hindu/Sikh and Muslim crossed from one side to the other of the new border. Both countries, India and Pakistan, were deeply scarred by this traumatic event. India became a secular state, thanks to Nehru (prime minister 1947–64), with its Muslim population halved (according to the 1991 census, this was 82.41 per cent Hindu and 11.67 per cent Muslim).

The subsequent political history of India is one of conflict with Pakistan and a gradual crumbling of the founding ideal of the secular state which Nehru had cherished and brought to fruition against all the odds. While refusing to recognize a state religion, Nehru gave a favoured role to minority religions, being especially concerned to make welcome those Muslims who had elected to remain in India rather than withdraw to Pakistan. A dynastic form of democratic leadership evolved, with Nehru's daughter Indira Gandhi (1917–84) becoming prime minister,[2] followed by her son, Rajiv Gandhi (1944–91). Rajiv's widow Sonia, Italian by origin, is currently head of the Congress Party. At partition, Kashmir had a Hindu ruler and a mainly Islamic population. Pakistan attempted to seize control but secured only half the state. The border remains in dispute, and tension is constant. Both sides possess nuclear weapons and threaten their use. The position of Muslims within India is difficult.

In several of their doctrines Islam and Hinduism are at completely opposite poles. Islam is monotheist, while Hinduism is polytheist – though not rigidly so since since both Vaishnavism and Shaivism have versions which are monotheistic – and also monist. In India Islam, in Sufi mysticism and worship of shrines of saints, came close to Hinduism, but there were always those who wanted to return to the original purity of the Koran. As we have seen, Hinduism lacks that clarity of a single-minded origin. Again, the ideal of the single brotherhood of Islam is the complete opposite of the hierarchy of the caste system, although Muslim converts retained caste affiliation and Hindu *bhakti* movements rejoiced in equality. A great difference is openness to the external world. Although Hinduism absorbed alien thought, it did not do so openly, remaining closed in on itself and self-centred, while the missionary zeal of Islam did not prevent considerable intellectual dialogue, especially when Islamic civilization was at its height. Indeed, Islam began in close contact with Judaism and Christianity, and in contact with Greek and Roman thought. From the start it was free from ethnic limitations. Muhammad said, 'Seek knowledge, though as far as China.' That Bernier was employed by the governor of Delhi to translate Descartes and Gassendi into Persian is an excellent example of Islamic interest in foreign ideas.

Arab traders had long been living on the west coast of India when in the eleventh century wave after wave of vigorous bands of Muslims – Afghans, Turks, Mughals/Mongols – raided then took over northern India, and eventually southern India. Following the initial forced conversions, low-caste Hindus, especially in Kashmir and eastern Bengal, continued to convert to Islam, as did those individuals who wished to approach the seat of power. The spiritual centre of Islam was outside India, in Mecca; and India was to the east of several Muslim kingdoms or empires: Afghanistan, Persia, and Turkey. Muslims from those lands continued to come to India to make their fortune – or, in the case of Shias and Sufis, for refuge – as long as Muslim rule continued.

Islamic encounter with Hinduism: Al-Biruni

Legends of Indian magicians featured in the Arabic genre of books dealing with the wonders of the world. But rational and careful accounts were early provided by Arab travellers and geographers, and Muslim encyclopedists collected data. A detailed account of Hinduism is given by the outstanding intellectual Al-Biruni in the eleventh century. Islam had reached Sind (now Gujarat) in western India at the same time as it entered the Iberian peninsula (711–12), but this Arab conquest in India spread no further, and there was no other Islamic conquest until the raids of the Turk Sultan Mahmud (d. 1030) of Ghazni in Afghanistan. In Mahmud's court and travelling with him was Al-Biruni, among whose many works is a penetrating account of India: 'Not for over eight hundred years would any other writer examine India with such thoroughness and understanding.'[3] Al-Biruni was not translated into English until 1888; it was only a few decades previously that European understanding of Hinduism caught up with what Al-Biruni knew in the early eleventh century.

Accompanying Mahmud's almost yearly raids into India, he witnessed how he 'utterly ruined the prosperity of the country': 'The Hindus became like the atoms of dust scattered in all directions and like a tale of old in the mouths of people. Their scattered remains cherish, of course, the most inveterate aversion toward all Muslims.' Mahmud kept his base in Ghazni, but maintained control of Sind and the Punjab. The most famous of the temples he destroyed was the Shiva temple at Somanath. Subsequent Muslim chroniclers made Somanath an Indian equivalent of Mecca, so that it stood for the conquest of all India, and Mahmud became 'the archetype of the perfect Muslim hero, a model for imitation by succeeding generations of Muslims'.[4]

Valued in the Islamic world for his knowledge of astrology, Al-Biruni was nevertheless a forerunner of modernity. Intellectually voracious, he studied Sanskrit as well as Greek. He shows first-hand knowledge of Hindu texts; his Arabic translation of the primary text of yoga, Patanjali's *Yoga Sutra*, has survived. He was able to contrast Greek and Indian ideas. The Hindus had no men such as Socrates who were willing to die for the truth, and thus 'the scientific theorems of the Hindus are in a state of utter confusion . . . always mixed up with the silly superstitions of the crowd'.[5] Hindu texts were corrupt because of careless copyists. (We should note that the perceived superiority of oral tradition underlay this carelessness.)

Al-Biruni's manifest intelligence and concern for accurate scholarship give his judgements great weight. Here is his summary of Hindu–Muslim relations:

they totally differ from us in religion, as we believe in nothing in which they believe, and vice versa. On the whole, there is very little disputing about theological topics among themselves; at the utmost, they fight with words, but they will never stake their soul or body or their property on religious controversy. On the contrary, all their fanaticism is directed against those who do not belong to them – against all foreigners. They call them *mleccha*, i.e., impure, and forbid having any connection with them, be it by intermarriage or any other kind of relationship, or by sitting, eating, and drinking with them, because thereby, they think, they would be polluted. They consider as impure anything which touches the fire and the water of a foreigner; and no household can exist without these two elements. Besides, they never desire that a thing which once has been polluted should be purified and thus recovered, as, under ordinary circumstances, if anybody or anything has become unclean, he or it would strive to regain the state of purity. They are not allowed to receive anybody who does not belong to them, even if he wished it, or was inclined to their religion. This, too, renders any connection with them quite impossible, and constitutes the widest gulf between us and them.[6]

Al-Biruni prefaces his translation of Patanjali by referring to his own love of knowledge and his desire to impart it to others, 'For niggardliness with regard to sciences is one of the worst crimes and sins. What is written black on white cannot but constitute a new learning whose knowledge should lead to the attainment of some good and to the avoidance of harm.'[7] The commentary that Al-Biruni translates along with the core text (*sutra*) has not been identified, but he himself seems to change it into the form of question and answer, familiar to him in Arabic texts, making the work more dramatic and readable.

Babur (reigned 1526–30)

Modernity began to form in Europe at the same time as accounts were received from travellers such as Bernier of the rich and powerful kingdom of the Mughals. After 1600, the year of the East India Company's charter, Europeans came more and more frequently to the Mughal court. The founder of the Mughal empire was Babur, descended from the Turk Tamerlane the Great and the Mongol Genghis Khan. Dispelled from his father's empire in Samarkhand, he took control of northern India, on the eastern boundaries of the well-established Islamic empires of Afghanistan and Persia. Babur's conquest of the Delhi sultanate through his brilliant use of mobile light canon had made him worthy of his illustrious forebears and the first of a new line of great emperors. His contact with India was slight:

> Babar had won the throne of Delhi in 1526, but he was a stranger to India and continued to feel so . . . He missed the friendly society he was used to, the delights of conversation, the amenities and refinements of life which had spread

from Baghdad and Iran . . . He died within four years of his coming to India, and much of his time was spent in fighting and laying out a splendid capital at Agra, for which he obtained the services of a famous architect from Constantinople.[8]

In his autobiography, Babur briefly comments on the people he ruled over:

Most of the inhabitants of Hindustan are pagans; they call a pagan a Hindu. Most Hindus believe in the transmigration of souls. All artisans, wage-earners, and officials are Hindus . . . every artisan there follows the trade that has come down to him from forefather to forefather . . . Hindustan . . . has unnumbered and endless workmen of every kind. There is a fixed caste [*jam'i*] for every sort of work and for every thing, which has done that work or that thing from father to son till now.[9]

Babur's autobiography, the *Babur Nama*, written in his native Turkish dialect, 'one of the most attractive and instructive books ever written by a ruler',[10] unfortunately breaks off on 2 April 1528, resuming again in 18 September 1528. Specific dates might seem unnecessary in such a wide-ranging study as I here have in hand, but on 29 March Babur had arrived in Ayodhya, and 'stayed a few days in order to settle the affairs of Ayodhya'.[11] The same year Babur's mosque was built there; inside was a Persian inscription which read:

By the command of the Emperor Babur, whose justice is an edifice reaching up to the very height of the heavens, the good-hearted Mir Baqi built this alighting-place of angels. May this goodness last for ever. The year of building it was . . . 1528.[12]

So it was presumably during the days immediately following the breaking off of the autobiography that Babur ordered the building of the mosque. In the nineteenth century, British administrators reported local traditions that Babur built the mosque on the site of Rama's birthplace temple. Annette Beveridge, the translator of the *Babur Nama*, suggests that Babur 'would be impressed by the dignity and sanctity of the ancient Hindu shrine it (at least in part) displaced' and being, as a good Muslim, intolerant of another religion, 'would regard the substitution of a temple by a mosque as dutiful and worthy'.[13]

Nearby is the tomb of the Muslim saint Khwajah Fazl Abbas who, according to local tradition, persuaded Babur to destroy the temple. Both this tomb and the mosque contained pillars which had come from a Hindu temple. Such are the facts and legends that lie behind the destruction of the Babri mosque by Hindu fundamentalists in 1992, and the thousands of deaths caused in the subsequent rioting in Bombay and elsewhere. Had those pages of Babur's book not been lost, the facts – whatever they might be – would have been known for centuries and there would have no tissue of uncertainties to erupt with such disastrous consequences.

The Sufi scholar Carl Ernst seeks to counter the automatic assumption of Muslim iconoclasm, and takes Babur as his example. One day in 1528 near Gwalior, Babur suffered much discomfort from opium sickness, and when he saw in the pleasant Urwah valley some 'idol-statues, large and small . . . quite naked without covering for the privities' he 'ordered them destroyed'. The heads of these Jain statues were cut off. The next day he visited Gwalior's fort and made a tour of its temples, with sculptured images on their plinths and idols carved in the rock in the lower cells. After enjoying the sight of these buildings, he was given an outdoor feast. Ernst asks, 'What part of Babur's behaviour was Islamic? . . . Why did he destroy idols on one day and enjoy them the next?' His good mood on the second day 'may have had something to do with either his recovery from hangover or the embassy of submission he received that morning from a major Rajput ruler'. Or he may have thought it impolite to destroy part of a monument a subordinate was in charge of. 'In any case it is clear that it is highly problematic to predict political behaviour (such as destruction of temples) from the nominal religious identity that may be ascribed to an individual or a group, without reference to personal, political, and historical factors.'[14]

As it happens, this diary entry is just after the text of the *Babur Nama* resumes after the above-mentioned gap. The Babri mosque would have been under construction at the time. On Ernst's logic, if Babur had had a hangover and no nice barbecue, he might well have ordered the destruction of the birthplace temple of Rama, assuming such a temple existed, which is by no means certain.

Akbar (reigned 1556–1605)

The greatest Mughal sovereign was Babur's grandson, Akbar. He extended the empire in all directions by conquest and, though illiterate, was an excellent administrator. His victories included the defeat of the Rajput chiefs, who were the champions of Hinduism in North India. Chittorgarh, key fortress in Rajasthan, fell three times into the hands of the Muslims and was as many times the theatre of the fantastic and bloody rite of self-immolation by fire (*jauhar*). The proud warrior caste held it the worst of dishonours to let their wives fall into the hands of their conquerors, and before finding death in battle, the only end worthy of a Rajput warrior in defeat, they lit a pyre on to which their wives threw themselves. When Akbar entered the conquered Chittorgarh in February 1568 the fort was nothing but an immense crematorium.

Akbar made other Rajput chiefs generals in his army, and married their daughters. His son and successor, Jahangir, was half-Mughal and half-Rajput. To Nehru and the Indian nationalists of the twentieth century, Akbar was a shining example of the religious toleration necessary for independent India: 'As a warrior he conquered large parts of India, but his eyes were set on another and more enduring conquest, the conquest of the minds and hearts of the people.'[15] He took a lively interest in religion, and conversed with Hindu yogis and European Jesuits as well as Muslim fakirs. He abolished the tax on non-Muslims. The revenue system was thoroughly revised and centralized. His own central role was expressed in Abu 'l-Fazl's definition of a king as 'a light emanating from God, a ray from the world-illuminating sun'. In 1582 Akbar announced the Din-i-ilahi ('the Divine Faith'), a syncretic statement that owed much to the Sufi tradition of Islam as well as to Hinduism and Zoroastrianism. Emphasizing the union of the soul with the divine, it insisted on such ethical precepts as almsgiving, chastity, vegetarianism, and kindness to all. By the following year, rejecting public prayer, he began to worship the sun four times a day, with rituals of his own invention, including for instance recitation of 1,001 Sanskrit names for the sun as part of the midday ceremony. He may have come to believe in the transmigration of the soul.[16] Marriages of Rajput women with Mughals led to the Rajput bardic tradition equating Akbar with the Hindu god Rama.[17] At the end of his reign his mint at Ayodhya even issued coins featuring Rama and Sita![18]

Although he could not read, Akbar had a great love of books, and was read to every day. He arranged for many texts to be illustrated. His first such project was the illustration of the *Hamza Nama* in fourteen volumes, each of a hundred paintings. Set in hand when he was 20, it took 15 years to complete. This 'romance of the adventures of Hamza, the Prophet's uncle' was a strange choice for Akbar to have illustrated 'on such a vast scale, as its theme of the slaughter of infidels is foreign to his tolerant nature'.[19] At all events, Akbar went on to have a number of Hindu texts in Sanskrit and Hindi translated into Persian, including the *Mahabharata, Ramayana, Harivamsa,* the Vedantic epic called the *Yogavasistha,* and even the fourth Veda, the *Atharva Veda.* Copies of such works were distributed to his courtiers, for Akbar wanted to break down barriers. The manuscripts of the Hindu epics were on the grandest scale, with an average of 150 full-page paintings each.

Abu 'l-Fazl, chronicler of Akbar's reign, necessarily refers to the emperor's love of painting, and quotes him as saying,

> There are many that hate painting; but such men I dislike. It appears to me as if a painter had quite special means of recognizing God; for a painter in sketching anything that has life, and in devising its limbs, one after the other, must come to feel that he cannot bestow individuality upon his work, and thus is forced to think of God, the giver of life, and will thus increase in knowledge.[20]

This is somewhat disingenuous, for it is in the delineation of individual identity that Mughal painting is so spectacularly successful.

One of his most splendid commissions was the classical 'Quintet' of the twelfth-century Persian poet Nizami. The last part of this text, the *Iskandar Nama*, is the Persian version of the deeds of Alexander the Great. Notable is the final illustration of the book, a two-page spread showing an image of the Buddha. In a second visit to India, Iskandar comes to Kandahar:

> He finds a temple where many maidens venerate an enormous golden image of the Buddha that has two glittering jewels for eyes. He orders the image to be reduced to its component gold and jewels. A beautiful damsel comes forward and begs him to hear the story of the image. In former times when the dome of the temple had half fallen in, two birds had appeared carrying in their beaks jewels, which they had deposited there. To prevent strife over the ownership of these, the people had made an image of gold and set in it the jewels, which were evidently a gift from heaven. Hearing this, Iskandar spares the image.'[21]

Early the same year (1595) the Mughals had taken Kandahar from the Safavids of Persia without bloodshed. The image is more Hindu than Buddhist in character, as might be expected from Akbar's painters drawing on their own experience.[22]

Nehru noted that Jesuits presented Akbar with a printed Bible and perhaps one or two other printed books and plaintively asks, 'Why did he not get curious about printing?'[23] In other words: 'Why did he not seize at least this instance of modernity?' But Akbar could not read or write, and the form of printing that would have appealed to him was full-colour photographic reproduction. Indeed, with his repeated production of heavily illustrated manuscripts that is virtually what he achieved. Barthes remarked on modernity's taste for 'the reality effect', attested to by 'the realistic novel, the private diary, documentary literature, the news item, the historical museum, the exhibition of ancient objects, and, above all, the massive development of photography, whose sole pertinent feature (in relation to drawing) is precisely to signify that the event represented has really taken place'.[24] This concern with reality, with the exact representation of what really happened is a key feature of Mughal painting, complementing Mughal autobiography and biography.

Jahangir (reigned 1605–1627)

Akbar's eldest son was 36 when he succeeded to the throne. He took the name Jahangir, the 'world seizer', but was more interested in acquiring works of art than in conquest. He was keen to record his own reign and had his painters record significant events – not only assemblies and festivities, but also interesting birds, animals and flowers that he had seen. As a prince he had refused administrative tasks, and though a just and intelligent ruler he was a heavy drinker, and his brilliant wife, Nur Jahan, was in control of the empire from 1611 to 1627, her name even appearing on coins.[25]

Jahangir had no wish to tie his artists to the illustration of texts or to dilute their talent by demanding multiple copies – his concern was the achievement of masterpieces. For almost 900 years Muslim rulers were represented either realistically in some activity or simply sitting on the throne, motionless and timeless, the visual expression of the phrase 'May Allah make his reign ever-lasting.' Jahangir, however, got his artists to go beyond this two-dimensional iconography. A remarkable painting exists which shows King James I before the Emperor Jahangir; the painting in fact shows the meeting of civilizations (Mughal, Turkish, English). The English envoy Sir Thomas Roe, attempting to win unfettered trading rights in Surat (in present-day Gujarat) presented portraits of his king to the emperor. The emperor's atelier had no problem in making exact copies of any painting; and Vicitr's painting shows King James in the presence of the emperor, who is seated on a huge hourglass, his profiled head set in a giant aureole of the sun and crescent moon combined, present-ing a book to a Sufi saint, perhaps Shaikh Husain Chishti, who stands above the Ottoman sultan, King James, and a Hindu. James alone looks away from the emperor – perhaps because it is an exact copy of a portrait that Roe brought; but also because James had not in fact had the honour of seeing the emperor. The picture is known as *Jahangir Preferring a Sufi Sheikh to Kings*. The final and lowest figure is that of a Hindu, the artist himself; Hindus were consid-ered of the lowest religion by Jahangir. Nonetheless, the aureole that shows his golden glory is a Hindu touch, while the hourglass is European, suggest-ing a Baroque awareness of the finality of the passing of time. There is also the graphic realism, the exact representation of real people, of a brilliant photo-graphic clarity in full colour. This contrasts with the hazy inexactitude of back-ground in Hindu painting, concerned to show the emotion, the underlying psychological essence, and oblivious to anything outside its own spiritual – in the widest possible sense – frame of reference. Here the symbolism is carefully spelled out. The emperor himself transcends earthly time by sitting on the hourglass. On the base of the hourglass, overriding its symbolism, angels write the message that his fame will last 1,000 years. 'His court painters were the first to cope in Muslim painting with the issue of moral choice and to reveal a deliberate consciousness of time and the limits it set on mortal man.'[26]

As his reign progressed, Jahangir's addiction to alcohol and opium took its toll. While Nur Jahan became all-powerful, the emperor's painters exagger-ated his status. Although he never met Shah 'Abbas of Persia, he has his paint-ers show him receiving and embracing him; although he could never subdue his enemy Malik Ambar, he is shown shooting an arrow at his severed head. In the latter picture he stands on top of the globe of the world, and several other portraits show a parallel mastery of the world by putting it under his feet. In Abu 'l Hasan's Durbar scene of Jahangir (*c*.1615), not only does the globe function as his footstool, but it is provided with a keyhole, with the key hanging from the emperor's waist.

Jahangir was the outstanding Mughal collector. One of his most cherished possessions was a set of three miniatures illustrating Sa'di's *Bustan* ('The Orchard'). This had been copied for the sultan of Bukhara between 1540 and 1550. With bold confidence Jahangir had his Hindu painter Bishndas repaint the faces of all the figures in one of these paintings, presumably with those of people known to him. It is the illustration of Sa'di's tale in which priests at the famous Somanath temple, the one demolished by Sultan Mahmud of Ghazni in 1024, are revealed to trick worshippers by attaching a hidden string to an arm of the image, which then miraculously moves. The original painter Shaikh-Zada set this in a Muslim fantasy of a temple, tiled and carpeted in the best Islamic taste.

> At Somanath I saw an ivory idol. It was set with jewels . . . and nothing more beautiful could have been devised. Caravans from every country brought travelers to its side; the eloquent from every clime made supplication before its lifeless figure.[27]

Sa'di's narrator is astonished at such admiration for an immobile figure, but is told that it can raise its hand to God. On being shown this regular miracle, he kisses its hand. Posing as a believer, he is made a guardian of the temple. He discovers the high priest behind a screen pulling the rope that raises the hand. Caught out, the priest runs away, but the narrator throws him down a well, and flees the land.

Much here is improbable, quite apart from the fact that the main icon at Somanath was really a linga. The image would not raise its hand to God, since it is itself God. Kissing the hand of the image would be an appalling blasphemy, necessitating the elaborate and expensive reconsecration of the image. A non-Hindu would never be allowed near the image, nor be made a temple guardian. Most importantly, the moving of the arm – though not impossible – was scarcely necessary. So fervent is Hindu belief in the immanence of divinity within the consecrated image, images are frequently said to move an arm or otherwise display occasional signs of life, and my guess is that the story sprang from accounts of such movement, in fact from the intensity of Hindu belief in images.

Shah Jahan (reigned 1627–1658)

Under Shah Jahan, Akbar's favourite grandson, the Mughal empire reached the height of its prosperity. The rich commercial provinces of Gujarat and Bengal were successfully absorbed. Shah Jahan's exuberant building programme was the final statement of Mughal power. The emphatic power of Akbar's buildings in virile red sandstone and influenced by indigenous forms was replaced by the luxury of pure white marble and Persian style. The illustrations of the official history of his reign, the *Padshah Nama*, coldly formal, are nevertheless the most technically accomplished of Mughal paintings.[28]

By birth Shah Jahan was only a quarter Muslim, but significantly, unlike Jahangir and Akbar, he did not marry Hindu women, and while he was not a bigot, he was certainly a more orthodox Muslim than either of them. In 1631 his favourite wife, Mumtaz, died giving birth to their fourteenth child. He mourned for two years, and planned her tomb. Ignoring the lessons of his grandfather, he turned to the Koran for solace, and in 1632 he ordered the destruction of all recently built Hindu temples throughout the empire. Mumtaz's tomb, the Taj Mahal, 20 years in the building, was to become the most famous tomb in the world.

Dara Shukoh

After his wife's death Shah Jahan was increasingly influenced by his eldest daughter Jahanara and his eldest son Dara Shukoh, both of whom were intellectually liberal and religiously tolerant. Dara emerges as a public figure only about 1630. 'Always the favorite of the emperor, he was spared the physical exertions, military experience, decision making, and absences from court that would have been the proper preparation for a ruler.'[29] Several paintings show him with Muslim and Hindu holy men.[30] His deep interest in religion led to the composition of highly important texts. In his *Majma 'al-Bahrain* ('The Mingling of Two Oceans'), completed in 1655, he claimed that 'there were not many differences, except verbal, in the ways in which Hindu monistic philosophers and Muslim Sufis sought and comprehended truth'. He found parallels between *maya*, the illusion that creates the world, and love in Sufi thought, between *pralaya*, the universal destruction at the end of each cosmic age, and Islamic resurrection, and so on.[31] The Persian translation of the *Bhagavad Gita* is attributed to him; and he assembled a team of pandits to help him translate the Upanishads into Persian, whence in due course those texts first became known in Europe. These activities offended Islamic orthodoxy. Mirza Muhammad Kazim, the contemporary historian of his brother's reign, describes him with considerable distaste:

> Dara Shukoh in his later days did not restrain himself to the freethinking and heretical notions which he had adopted under the name of Sufism, but showed an inclination for the religion and institutions of the Hindus. He was constantly in the society of brahmans, Yogis, and Sannyasis, and he used to regard these worthless teachers of delusions as learned and true masters of wisdom. He con-

sidered their books, which they call *Veda*, as being the Word of God and revealed from Heaven, and he called them ancient and excellent books. He was
under such delusion about this *Veda* that he collected *brahmans* and *Sannyasis*
from all parts of the country, and paying them great respect and attention, he
employed them in translating the *Veda* [i.e. the Upanishads]. He spent all his
time in this unholy work, and devoted all his attention to the contents of these
wretched books . . . Through these perverted opinions he had given up the
prayers, fasting, and other obligations imposed by the law . . . It became manifest that if Dara Shukoh obtained the throne and established his power, the
foundations of the faith would be in danger and the precepts of Islam would be
changed for the rant of infidelity . . .[32]

Aurangzib (reigned 1658–1707)

Aurangzib, the last great Mughal, undid the work of Akbar, for though he
extended the empire he fatally weakened it within. Taking the title Alamgir
('Conqueror of the World'), his implacable orthodoxy led him to use the
empire's resources in extending Islamic dominion over almost the whole of
India. His interest in art was confined to calligraphy, and there exist several
copies of the Koran from his pen.

He imprisoned his father and murdered his brothers and cousins. The reason given for murdering his elder brother Dara was that Dara was a heretic. In
1675 the emperor had the ninth Sikh guru, Tegh Bahadur, tortured and be-
headed for refusing to become a Muslim. In 1679 he brought back the hated
poll tax on non-Muslims that Akbar had abolished. In 1688 he demolished all
the temples in Mathura, holy city of Krishna. In 1697 he ordered the destruction of the Jagannath temple and its images. In Ayodhya, holy city of Rama's
birth and rule, the last old temples were destroyed and mosques built on their
sites.

Bernier on Aurangzib

On his arrival in India in 1659 the French physician Bernier was caught up in
Dara Shukoh's tragic flight, but went on to be employed by the governor of
Delhi, for whom he translated Descartes and Gassendi into Persian. Bernier's
'travels' are presented in the form of letters, but each letter is in fact a carefully
planned formal treatise on particular topics addressed to an important and
influential person. Thus Bernier's account of the Mughal state, in fact a fully
fledged theory of Oriental despotism, was addressed to Colbert, the great
architect of France's prosperity under Louis XIV. Influential throughout Europe were Bernier's remarks on Aurangzib as absolute monarch, over and
above the dramatic account he gave of that emperor's doings. These remarks
were made in the context of Louis XIV's decisive movement towards absolut-

ism, and Bernier can be seen as presenting Aurangzib as an allegory of the very nature of the state.[33]

Bernier stresses that the Great Mughal, the emperor, is a foreigner in India. India is a hostile country , with hundreds of Hindus to every Mughal, or even to every Muslim. Amidst powerful enemies in India and liable to attack from Persia and other foreign countries, he is forced to maintain a huge army at all times.

> The King being proprietor of all the lands in the empire, there can exist neither Dukedoms nor Marquisates; nor can any family be found possessed of wealth arising from a domain, and living upon its own patrimony . . . The Omrahs [Lords of the Mughal court], therefore, mostly consist of adventurers from different nations who entice one another to the court; and are generally persons of low descent, some having been originally slaves, and the majority being destitute of education. The Mughal raises them to dignities, or degrades them to obscurity, according to his own pleasure and caprice.[34]

In fact the emperor maintains a meritocracy, though he himself is the only arbiter of merit!

> The country is ruined by the necessity of defraying the enormous charges required to maintain the splendour of a numerous court, and to pay a large army maintained for the purpose of keeping the people in subjection. . . .
> The misery of this ill-fated country is increased by the practice which prevails too much at all times, but especially on the breaking out of an important war, of selling the different governments for immense sums in hard cash. Hence it naturally becomes the principal object of the individual thus appointed Governor, to obtain repayment of the purchase-money, which he borrowed as he could at a ruinous rate of interest . . . Thus do ruin and desolation overspread the land.
> The provincial governors, as before observed, are so many petty tyrants, possessing a boundless authority; and as there is no one to whom the oppressed subject may appeal, he cannot hope for redress, let his injuries be ever so grievous or ever so frequently repeated.[35]

Bernier and everyone who followed his view of despotism, including most notably Marx, are today faulted for giving an inadequate account of landholding in Mughal India. But Bernier's analysis of the evil of a single employer, inevitably becoming arbitrary, is a dreadful warning of the dangers of totalitarianism. The Mughal system of salaried nobility was highly rational, and even modern in conception.

Shivaji (1627–1680)

Bernier briefly mentions as 'a bold adventurer' the Hindu Shivaji, and describes his sacking of Surat in 1664. 'He rushed into the place sword in hand, and remained nearly three days, torturing the population to compel a discovery of their concealed riches. Burning what he could not take away, Shivaji returned without the least opposition, laden with gold and silver to the amount of several millions; with pearls, silken stuffs, fine cloths, and a variety of other costly merchandise.'[36] Surat was then the place of embarkation of pilgrims to Mecca; known as Bab al-Makkah, or the Gate of Mecca, it was almost a sacred place for the Muslims of India. More to the point, it was the main city for foreign imports, where many merchants had their bases, and all the European trading companies were established. Its population was more than 100,000.

Aurangzib had expanded Mughal power to the south, but roused Hindu resistance there. The hardy Marathas from the mountainous western Ghats found a leader of uncompromising boldness, bravery and indeed genius. Despite Aurangzib's persistent efforts to control him, Shivaji brought into being a Hindu Raj that ended by being for a while the chief rival to Britain for control of all India.

> After his death, however, the Marathas' militarism became increasingly predatory, and though they carried their presence and fame over immense distances, it was more often as a scourge than an inspiration. Individual leaders of ability were to appear in the succession states of their first empire, but it was only by their failure to achieve central power that the dream that they could have used it for India's good was able to survive.[37]

Max Weber, in his study of the religions of India, notes that when Shivaji once went a year without doing battle his neighbouring kings thought he must be on his deathbed – Hindu texts saw every king as inherently ruler of the world and therefore bound to do down his neighbours by force or fraud.[38] Shivaji has now become an icon of Hindu fundamentalism. A fervent Hindu, he had an elaborate and costly coronation. A dictionary of Sanskrit terms, the *Rajavyavaharakosha*, was prepared in order to replace the Urdu and Persian which had been the court languages of India for centuries. His guru Ramdas, devotee of Rama the holder of the bow, was himself an effective administrator, setting up, it is claimed, no less than 1,100 monasteries (*maths*). Yet Shivaji 'was no bigot and allowed equal freedom to all faiths. He was served as zealously by the Muslims as by the Hindus . . . He built a mosque opposite his palace at Raigarh for the use of his Muslim subjects.'[39] He treated the Muslim saint Baba Yakut of Kelsi as another guru. His confidential secretary and his naval commanders were Muslims.

A common theme for the great Mughal painters, and reflecting a general interest among open-minded Muslims, was that of the Hindu holy man, or yogi. Al-Biruni translated Patanjali, and noted the close connection between Hindu spirituality and that of the Sufis. Akbar had many meetings with Hindu holy men, as did Dara; and Jahangir was greatly taken with the Shaivite ascetic Jadrup, mentioning a desire for his company several times in his memoirs. Hindu holy men frequently feature in Mughal paintings. All was far from being smooth sailing, however, between kings and ascetics. Jahangir, prior to meeting Jadrup, mentions hearing, during a visit to Malwa, of a yogi whose spittle was honoured by his devotees. The emperor at once ordered the yogi's shrine to be demolished, the idol destroyed, and the yogi driven away. Even Jadrup was later cruelly beaten by Hakim Beg, Nur Jahan's brother-in-law. Bernier mentions a famous naked yogi who was killed by Aurangzib for his refusal to wear clothes. Nevertheless, uneasy lies the head that wears the crown, and holy men have always been sought out by rulers in India as possible remedies to the uncertainty of fortune.

This arbitary attitude to yogis rather parallels the attitude to Hindu temples, which were liable to be destroyed when noticed at the wrong moment. Such a parallel, however, though effectively in accord with Ernst's assessment of Babur mentioned above, must be set against an important paper on temple desecration by Richard Eaton. It is of course vital to get a proper understanding of this most vexed and contentious issue, over which many have died in rioting in India in the last decade. Eaton, having mentioned Hindu kings' desecration of the temples of other Hindu kings, distinguishes two forms of temple desecration by Muslims. First, 'in the annexation of newly conquered territories held by enemy kings whose domains lay in the path of moving military frontiers'.[40] Secondly, 'when Hindu patrons of prominent temples committed acts of treason or disloyalty to the Indo-Muslim states they served'. Eaton draws the important conclusion that, if temple desecration had been driven by a 'theology of iconoclasm', 'such a theology would have committed Muslims in India to destroying all temples everywhere, including ordinary village temples, as opposed to the strategically selective operation that seems actually to have taken place'. Eaton's key thesis is that major Hindu temples (he specifies 'monumental royal temple complexes of the early medieval period') were 'politically active'. Thus looting and destroying them was a political rather than a religious matter: 'when they [Indo-Muslim rulers] destroyed a royal temple or converted it into a mosque . . . [they] were building on a political logic that they knew placed supreme political significance on such temples'. It is important to note that Eaton adds that the same political significance 'rendered temples just as deserving of peacetime protection as it rendered them vulnerable in times of conflict'.[41]

Nevertheless, the debate cannot simply be switched from theology to politics. While for Islam God is everywhere, for the Hindu the divine also has a local name and a local face. The temple and the king partake of divinity, and in a Hindu state politics cannot be separated from religion.

Conclusion

This chapter has touched on some key issues, on Al-Baruni's view of Hindus and on the Mughal emperors who represent the high point of Islamic culture in India and their attitude to Hinduism. By looking at the Babri mosque at Ayodhya and the destruction of temples, it has prepared the ground for discussion of Hindu fundamentalism with which this book concludes. It has raised also the issue of accuracy in the delineation of reality that will be further considered in the chapters on goddesses, gods, and the self. More generally, it has given some indication of the historical relationship of Hinduism and Islam in India, and the shifting patterns of tolerance and intolerance.

Chapter Five

The European Discovery of Hinduism

A full account of the European discovery of Hinduism remains to be written.[1] In this chapter, I concentrate on a handful of major figures, while the chapter that follows deals more generally with the topic of Orientalism. Here, after an introduction to Europe's encounter with India, we look at a broad spectrum of approaches, seeking help from images where possible. After Abraham Roger's *Open Door to Hidden Paganism*, an exceptionally unbiased account of Hinduism in South India by a Dutch minister, we return to Bernier and his surprising failure to comprehend Hindu theology. Then the most famous of Orientalists, Sir William Jones, and his association with the embodiment of British power in India, Warren Hastings, are considered. Leaving aside the long roll-call of Jones's successors, we then look at the writings on Hinduism by two key definers of modernity, Marx and Weber, where the process of discovery goes into reverse. As a coda to the consideration of Weber, the chapter concludes with the anthropologist, Louis Dumont, whose discovery of the underlying structure of caste culminated in a differentiation of the individual East and West into 'hierarchical man' and 'equal man'.

After centuries of exporting spices and textiles to ancient Rome, with gold as India's principal import, India disappeared from European view during the European dark ages, except for fables of its wealth. In due course, improved navigation led Europeans themselves to seek to buy spices from their sources in South-East Asia and India. Spices made preserved meat much more palatable, and nutmeg was believed to be a remedy against the dreaded plague. Spices became the most valuable of all objects, and their trade enormously lucrative. India had long been a major player in world trade, in cotton, and also in specialized high-grade iron and steel, and European traders began to buy Indian textiles directly. The great land mass of Asia was the world centre of both raw materials and manufactured goods. Italian merchants led the way, but commercial considerations held back dissemination of up-to-date information, and printing, that harbinger of modernity, held back development of geographical knowledge by disseminating the ancient geography of Ptolemy and prolonging its ancient errors.[2]

At first the Portuguese dominated the European end of this eastern trade, making Goa the base for their seaborne empire in 1510. Dellon, a French doctor, gives a horrific account of the work of the Catholic Inquisition in Goa in the seventeenth century. The archives of the Holy Office show the persistence of Hinduism among the Christian converts of Goa, with almost 2,000 trials of the crime of *gentilidade* (Hindu practices) between 1560 and 1623.[3]

When Vasco da Gama arrived in Calicut on the west coast of India in 1498, he took a Hindu temple to be a Christian church and knelt before a shrine he thought was that of the Virgin Mary. The Portuguese and other Europeans persisted in believing the religion of the Hindus was an early form of Christianity for the most part suppressed by Islam. But in the seventeenth and eighteenth centuries, the period when modernity was taking shape, the European view came to be that Hinduism, known as the religion of the Gentoos, that is to say, gentiles or heathens, had been hidden and was being discovered. The myriad surface events, the temples, the festivals, the gods, were there for those who chose to look; but the higher gods were hidden in shrines accessible only to the twice-born, and the brahmans kept their scriptures secret as long as they could. Even so, Hinduism was most hidden by other factors – by its lack of interest in communicating with the outside, by its vast extent, by its lack of unity, by its diffuseness, by its lack of a specific name. One of the best early accounts of Hinduism by a European, the Dutchman Abraham Roger, was called *The Open Door of Hidden Paganism* (1651).[4] Yet 150 years later, in 1807, the governor of Madras, Bentinck, observed, 'The Europeans know little or nothing about the customs and manners of the Hindus . . . We understand very imperfectly their language. They perhaps know more of ours . . . We do not, we cannot associate with the natives . . . all our wants and businesses which could create a greater intercourse with the natives is done for us, and we are, in fact, strangers in the land.'[5] The discovery was slow in coming, Hinduism remained hidden.

Portuguese observers of Vijayanagara, the last Hindu empire

Portuguese writers gave vivid accounts of Hinduism's last great metropolis, Vijayanagara, which flourished in south India from 1336 to 1567. While Muslim sovereignty was secure in the north of India, Vijayanagara, 'City of Victory', was the centre of a Hindu empire in South India. Its river and hills were associated with episodes from the *Ramayana* epic. It was the Kishkindha of the epic, the abode of the epic's monkey chiefs, where Rama met Hanuman and Sugriva, and where the campaign to conquer Sri Lanka and regain Rama's kidnapped wife, Sita, was planned. The cult of Rama was of particular significance for the Vijayanagara rulers. The city had no less than five Rama temples.[6] Nilakanta Shastri described it as 'that great empire which, by resisting the onslaughts of Islam, championed the cause of Hindu civilization and culture in the South for close upon three hundred years and thus preserved the ancient tradition of the country in its polity, its learning and its arts'.[7] But Muslims as well as Europeans were welcomed in this wealthy and cultured metropolis; and 'those who bore the brunt of Vijayanagara military power were most often Hindu rulers, not Muslims'.[8] Muslim soldiers and artisans were allowed mosques, tombs, and cemeteries within the city. It was the desertion of two Muslim commanders from the royal army that led to the sacking of the city in 1583 and the empire's collapse. Islamic military and administrative forms, of demonstrated efficacy – and in our terms instances of modern efficiency – were adopted in Vijayanagara.[9]

Portuguese writers described the pomp and ceremony of the empire's monarchs, especially the autumn festival which commemorated Rama's setting forth to defeat Ravana. Alone with the image of the deity on a mighty stone platform, the king received the offerings of the assembled nobles, and gave gifts in return, and the army was reconsecrated, with the sacrifice of thousands of animals to the goddess, dancing and singing of thousands of women from the whole realm, and firework displays.

> The focus of these diverse and magnificent entertainments was always the King as glorious and conquering warrior, as the possessor of vast riches lavishly displayed by him and his women (queens and their maids of honour) and distributed to his followers. The King was fructifier and agent of prosperity of the world.[10]

The king dominated the festival, and in one description of the festival the brahmans appear to have been publicly reviled.[11]

The Open Door of Hidden Paganism

After the collapse of the Vijayanagara empire little of India remained outside Muslim control. The Islamic kingdoms of Bijapur and Golconda extended southward, and Dutch and English merchants established fortresses on the east coast. In the Dutch town of Pulicut on the eastern coast, the Dutch clergyman Abraham Roger (d. 1649) ministered to the Dutch and their Indian wives in Dutch, Tamil, and Portuguese. With the help of a brahman from Goa, Roger wrote *The Open Door of Hidden Paganism*. In the judgement of Partha Mitter, this book was 'the most important contribution to Western knowledge of Hinduism, until the arrival of Sir William Jones on the scene'.[12]

Before we consider his text, the illustrations have their own tale to tell. The title page sets the title amid eight vignettes. At the top is a Hindu temple, with statues of Ganesha and Vishnu in front of it. This is flanked by pictures of asceticism, as described briefly in the text: an ascetic hangs by his feet above a fire while a naked man marches past with his head hidden in a cage; to the right a man is suspended by hooks in his back from a mobile beam. On one side is a picture of a corpse burning; beneath this is the image of a god on horseback, being carried on a platform with musicians proceeding. At the bottom a temple car is hauled along, a woman about to throw herself beneath its wheels. In La Grue's French translation of 1670 the pictorial details on the original title page were enlarged and printed separately in the book, but the frontispiece itself is uncompromisingly antagonistic, the book's title being displayed aloft by a horned devil with dragon wings and bird-feet, while the downturned torch he holds drops coals that light the funeral pyre beneath, on to which jumps a bare-breasted widow, arms outstretched in Baroque style. A throng of Hindus in European dress applaud and blow horns.

Aided by his brahman informant Roger was able to calmly set out details of Hindu beliefs and practices which were usually dismissed out of hand as horrible superstitions, as in the French title page just mentioned. After a brief account of caste, the first half of the book deals with the practices of brahmans, and the second part with the gods and ascetic practices. Sati, which invariably attracted the notice of Europeans, was an inevitable topic for Roger. Indeed, shortly before he left Pulicut he reported that 60 wives of a Kshatriya were burned with their husband.[13] He notes general caste differences in sati. Kshatriyas allowed wives to commit sati apart from their husbands, who might die while campaigning in other parts of the country. Brahmans and Vaishnavas insisted on them burning with their husband on the pyre. Roger describes the practice of digging a pit for the pyre, and making a mound with the excavated soil so that the widow could leap on the burning pyre. He does expostulate – 'Oh inhuman cruelty!' – at the brahman practice of not allowing this leap, and instead making the widow lie down beside her husband and heaping wood on top of her.[14]

Typical of Roger's unbiased accuracy is his account of the origin of linga worship – Shiva worshipped in the form of a convex-topped stone column representing the erect phallus, the primary object of worship of all Shaivas – which was to horrify the Victorians:

The report then that I had from the very mouth of the brahman Padmamabha is as follows. At a certain time there arrived a great ascetic [Bhrigu] to visit Ishvara [Shiva]. Now at this very time Ishvara was very joyous with his wife Parvati, so that the great ascetic came at a time that was not at all opportune, but nevertheless he wished to enter. The porter did not wish him to enter, and told him that it was not the right time because Ishvara was disporting with Parvati, so that it was necessary for the ascetic to wait a long time, against his will, but at last he lost patience and became infuriated, and said in his anger, that Ishvara should become like the action in which he was engaged. Ishvara heard that and said to him, why do you speak in this way? Then the great ascetic replied, praying, and said, I said it out of anger, forgive me. Now it is necessary that you also grant me this, that those who serve the form of the linga (which is the male member in the woman's member), that that will profit them more than if they served your figure with hands and feet; and . . . Ishvara is served and adored by all the country in his temple under such a form. But when procession is made through the towns with the idol of Ishvara . . . he is not carried in the form of the lingam, but in the figure of a man. The reason is, as the brahman bears witness, that men have more pleasure and content in viewing a human figure than in viewing the lingam, in which figure he is in his temple.[15]

Roger's precise and systematic account stands out when compared to those of others. The account the Englishman Lord gave of Hinduism in 1630 is typical in its inability to escape from a biblical frame of reference. The Italian independent traveller, Della Valle (1586–1652), gives a wonderfully vivid account of his time in India, including a meeting with a queen who is busy superintending irrigation works. He talks at length with an intending sati of surprisingly low caste, and writes three sonnets in praise of her. But he has no sympathy for Hinduism, and takes the opportunity when unobserved to spit on the deity in one shrine.

Another Dutch minister, Philipp Baldaeus (1632–72), who spent 10 years on both the west and east coasts of South India, relied principally on Roger for his knowledge of Hinduism, but makes his own comment on the character of brahmans: 'the brahmans are for the most part men of great morality, sober, clean, industrious, civil, obliging, and very moderate both in eating and drinking; they use no strong liquors, wash or bathe twice a day, eat nothing that has had or may have life, yet are much addicted (like all the rest of the Indians) to [sexual] pleasure'.[16] (But of course sexual characteristics and behaviour are more apparent and striking in other cultures, one's own being unremarked or repressed.) The frontispiece of Baldaeus's book presents the India that Europe preferred and understood: a Muslim, helmeted and holding up a drawn sword, seated on a great elephant at whose feet Indians hold open caskets of jewels and display other miscellaneous goods to traders from all parts of the world. Counteracting Baldaeus's unsympathetic text are the 10 full-page engravings of the incarnations of Vishnu clearly based on Indian paintings. These authentic representations contrast markedly with other illustrations in his book, in which a European artist has tried to render Shiva and Vishnu, all the more monstrous in being displayed in churchlike surroundings.

Turning now once again to Bernier's letters from India, we find that his own perspective is linked to that of the Muslims he lived among. The most striking engraving in Bernier's book is a two-page spread of the splendour of the court of the Great Mughal at Agra. Close to the centre of the Mughal court, Bernier was in an exceptionally privileged position, even if his status was low and he didn't always get enough to eat. The section of Bernier's book devoted to the Hindus, dated 1667, begins with the description of the behaviour he witnessed during the eclipse of the sun the year before, and then moves on to a general account of their 'superstitions, strange customs, and doctrines'. Two pages are devoted to the festival of the Jagannath temple at Puri, half a page on *devadasis*, nine pages on sati, seven pages on yogis, concluding with a dozen pages on the sacred literature of the brahmans. These proportions and the order of topics exemplify the usual levels of interest aroused in foreigners by Hinduism.

Bernier reports that ascetics practised 'painful austerities in the confident hope that they will be *Rajas* in their renascent state; or, if they do not become *Rajas*, that they shall be placed in a condition of life capable of more exquisite enjoyment than is experienced by those sovereign princes'. Some have the reputation of being really united to God. Living in seclusion, they eat if food is brought to them, and if food is not brought to them, people think that they can live without food 'by the favour of God'. It is claimed, 'and one of the favoured saints himself assured me, that their souls are often rapt in an ecstasy of several hours' duration; that their external senses lose their functions; that the *Yogis* are blessed with a sight of God, who appears as a light ineffably white and vivid, and that they experience transports of holy joy, and a contempt of temporal concerns which defy every power of description'. Bernier notes that 'not one of the individuals who are in the habit of visiting the *Yogis* doubts the reality of these vaunted ecstasies' and drily concludes, 'It is possible that the imagination, distempered by continued fasts and uninterrupted solitude, may be brought into these illusions.'[17] These matters are kept secret, says Bernier, and it is only because his employer had a pandit in his pay who did not dare conceal anything from his patron that Bernier was able to find out as much as he did.

In contrast to this secrecy of the brahmans, Bernier reports that Dara Shukoh's mysticism, which he speaks of as a 'great sect', had 'latterly made great noise in Hindustan'[18] – that is to say amongst Muslims. No sooner had Bernier arrived in India and set out for the capital than he was caught up in Dara's pitiful retreat from Ahmedabad, but his personal contact with that great prince did not make Bernier's interpretation of his views any more sympathetic. Nevertheless, Bernier provides an account of Hindu views that had appealed to Dara and resonated with Sufi doctrines. The doctrine here is authentically Hindu, namely that

God, or that supreme being whom they call . . . immovable, unchangeable, has not only produced life from his own substance, but also generally everything material or corporeal in the universe, and that this production is not formed simply after the manner of efficient causes, but as a spider which produces a web from its own navel, and withdraws it at pleasure. The Creation then, say these visionary doctors, is nothing more than an extraction or extension of the individual substance of *God*, of those filaments which He draws from his own bowels; and, in like manner, destruction is merely the recalling of that divine substance and filaments into Himself; so that the last day of the world, which they call *mahapralaya* [the Great Dissolution] . . . and in which they believe every being will be annihilated, will be the general recalling of those filaments which God had before drawn forth from Himself.

There is, therefore, say they, nothing real or substantial in that which we think we see, hear or smell, taste or touch; the whole of this world is, as it were, an illusory dream, inasmuch as all that variety which appears to our outward senses is but one only and the same thing, which is God Himself; in the same manner as all those different numbers, of ten, twenty, a hundred, a thousand, etc., are but the frequent repetition of the same unit.

But ask them some reason for this idea; beg them to explain how this extraction and reception of substance occurs, or to account for that apparent variety; or how it is that God not being corporeal but *vyapaka* [pervasive], as they allow, and incorruptible, He can be thus divided into so many portions of body and soul, they will answer you only with some fine similes: – That *God* is as an immense ocean in which many vessels of water are in continual motion; let these vessels go where they will, they always remain in the same ocean, in the same water; and if they should break, the water they contain would then be united to the whole, to that ocean of which they were but parts.

Or they will tell you that it is with *God* as with the light, which is the same everywhere, but causes the objects on which it falls to assume a hundred different appearances, according to the various colours or forms of the glasses through which it passes.

They will never attempt to satisfy you, I say, but with such comparisons as these, which bear no proportion with *God*, and which serve only to blind an ignorant people. In vain will you look for any solid answer. If one should reply that these vessels might float in a water similar to their own, but not in the same; and that the light all over the world is indeed similar, but not the same, and so on to other strong objections which may be made to their theory, they have recourse continually to the same similes, to fine words, or, in the case of the Sufis , to the beautiful poems of their *Goul-tchen-raz* [*Gulshan-i-Raz*, 'Mystic Rose Garden' by Muhammad Shabistari, composed in 1317].[19]

It is deeply significant that Bernier, the leading proponent of the atomism of Gassendi, after three years' regular discussion with a learned Hindu, found himself incapable of understanding a viewpoint in itself logical and coherent. The key Hindu cosmological view, though it has many variations, is that the subtle develops into the gross, the infinitely subtle at the beginning of things into the infinitely gross at the end of things. In the monistic view the Divine One emits the world as a solidification and coarsening of its divine nature. The phenomenal world around us stems from God, but is so greatly removed from the original divine as to be relatively unreal. Bernier correctly summarizes it but fails to comprehend it.

The pandit had worked on Dara Shukoh's Upanishad translation project and was claimed by Bernier to be 'one of the most celebrated pandits in all India'. When weary of explaining to his patron the recent discoveries of Harvey on the circulation of blood and discoursing on the philosophies of Gassendi and Descartes, 'we had generally recourse to our pandit who, in his turn, was called upon to reason in his own manner, and to communicate his fables'. Here indeed were optimum conditions for finding out about the Hinduism of learned brahmans. But Bernier goes on: 'these [fables] he related with all imaginable gravity without ever smiling; but at length we became disgusted both with his tales and his childish arguments'. It is astonishing that Bernier does not name this pandit with whom he spent so much time – his 'constant companion over a period of three years'.[20] His dismissiveness shows the profound intellectual gulf between them.

Hastings and Jones: Orientalism and colonial power

Passing over the decline and fall of the Mughal empire after Aurangzib, we move east to Calcutta, whence British power eventually spread over all India after the battle of Plassey in 1757. Here ruled governors and then governors general under the authority of the East India Company, but with London two or three months' voyage away masterful men such as Clive and Hastings could behave like kings. Hastings – who not only saved, by his military and political genius, the British possessions in India when British interests elsewhere in the world were collapsing, but inspired company officials with his own love of India – was to be impeached for behaving like an Oriental despot. Hastings collected Indian paintings and manuscripts, and learned Persian, the official language of India; he also established a college of Oriental learning and gave full backing to Orientalists. According to one scholar, he felt that 'To rule effectively, one must love India; to love India, one must communicate with her people; and to communicate with her people, one must learn her languages.'[21]

Macaulay summed up the situation:

> The Pundits of Bengal had always looked with great jealousy on the attempts of foreigners to pry into those mysteries which were locked up in the sacred dialect. The Brahminical religion had been persecuted by the Mahommedans. What the Hindoos knew of the spirit of the Portuguese Government might warrant

them in apprehending persecution from Christians. That apprehension, the wisdom and moderation of Hastings removed. He was the first foreign ruler who succeeded in gaining the confidence of the hereditary priests of India, and who induced them to lay open to English scholars the secrets of the old Brahminical theology and jurisprudence.[22]

Dara Shukoh had won the confidence of brahmans, but then he never came to power. Hastings persuaded the directors of the East India Company, men always concerned to curb expenditure, to pay for the publication of the translation of the *Bhagavad Gita* by 'Sanskrit-mad' Charles Wilkins in 1785. Wilkins, in his introduction, had his intended audience in mind, and no doubt shared its prejudices when he claimed that the *Bhagavad Gita* was opposed to the worship of images: its author's design was 'to bring about the downfall of polytheism; or, at least, to induce men to believe *God* present in every image before which they bent, and the object of all their ceremonies and sacrifices'. Today, he said, the most learned brahmans likewise believed in one God, but

> so far comply with the prejudices of the vulgar, as outwardly to perform all the ceremonies inculcated by the Véds, such as sacrifices, ablutions, &c. They do this, probably, more for the support of their own consequence, which could only arise from the great ignorance of the people, than in compliance with the dictates of *Krishna*: indeed, this ignorance, and these ceremonies, are as much the bread of the *brahmans*, as the superstition of the vulgar is the support of the priesthood in many other countries.

In fact, far from opposition to the worship of images, Krishna makes one of the earliest references to such worship by recommending offerings of water and flowers. The standard Hindu term for worship of a divine being or image is *puja*, probably from the Tamil word for flower, and the overwhelming theophany beheld by Arjuna is the ultimate sanction of image worship. The imputation of self-interest to the brahmans is unfair, for Wilkins fails to understand the multiple levels of truth in Hinduism. From the highest point of view, that of the Upanishads and subsequent developments of their thought, Brahman is the ultimate reality; but no less true, for brahmans as well as for non-brahmans, is the divinity of Krishna and all the other gods, though lesser divinities will provide lesser benefits.

Hastings in his preface stresses the 'generosity of sentiment' diffused by such studies, declaring that the writings of the Hindus 'will survive when the British dominion in India shall have long ceased to exist'. He gives greatest space in his preface to the most characteristic feature of Hindu mysticism, an account more sympathetic than Bernier's, noting that the 'spiritual discipline' of the brahmans resembles that of some Catholic religious orders: 'It is required of those who practise this exercise, not only that they divest their minds of all sensual desire, but that their attention be abstracted from every external

object, and absorbed, with every sense, in the prescribed subject of their meditation.' He cites Krishna's closing words to Arjuna in the *Bhagavad Gita*:

> 'Hath what I have been speaking, O Arjuna, been heard *with thy mind fixed to*
> *one point?*' . . . To those who have never been accustomed to this separation of
> the mind from the notices of the senses, it may not be easy to conceive by what
> means such a power is to be attained; since even the most studious men of our
> hemisphere will find it difficult so to restrain their attention but that it will
> wander to some object of present sense or recollection; and even the buzzing of
> a fly will sometimes have the power to disturb it. But if we are told that there
> have been men who were successively, for ages past, in the daily habit of ab-
> stracted contemplation, begun in the earliest period of youth, and continued in
> many to the maturity of age, each adding some portion of knowledge to the
> store accumulated by his predecessors; it is not assuming too much to conclude,
> that, as the mind ever gathers strength, like the body, by exercise, so in such an
> exercise it may in each have acquired the faculty to which they aspired, and that
> their collective studies may have led them to the discovery of new tracks and
> combinations of sentiment, totally different from the doctrines with which the
> learned of other nations are acquainted . . .

He adds that these 'new tracks and combinations of sentiment' are unintelli-
gible in so far as we lack the appropriate terminology to describe them.

Hastings quoted the *Bhagavad Gita* in his letters to his wife, finding it a
source of inspiration. In his private notebook he asked himself 'Is the incarnation of Christ more intelligible than . . . those of Vishnu?' The current European superiority owed nothing to Christianity, but was due to 'a free
government, cold climate and printing and navigation.'[23] In other words, if
we except the cold climate, modernity. From the time of the Enlightenment,
climate was believed to be an important factor in the formation of culture.

The most famous of the British Orientalists whom Hastings encouraged,
was Sir William Jones, known as 'Oriental Jones', whose statue stands in St
Paul's Cathedral in London. Jones is perhaps most often cited nowadays for
his elegant statement of the relation of Sanskrit to the other Indo-European
languages, and their descent from a common ancestor, though he was not the
first to suggest this. A brilliant linguist, he was totally confident that Hindus
were a 'people with a fertile and inventive genius', who 'in some early age . . .
were splendid in arts and arms, happy in government; wise in legislation, and
eminent in various knowledge'. The first president of the Asiatic Society of
Bengal, he translated into English the Laws of Manu and Kalidasa's play
Shakuntala.

Jones's statue, erected in his memory by the East India Company, is clad in
a Roman toga, bare-footed, and leans on a mighty tome which is his translation of Manu, the Law Book of the brahmans. Jones was a judge in the Supreme Court of Calcutta from 1783 until his death 11 years later, and in that

period saw as his main duty the codification of Indian laws. It was essential that English judges should not have to rely solely on brahmans' interpretation of legal texts. Moreover, Jones was eager to make Indians' 'slavery lighter by giving them their own laws', and he worked long and hard with some of the greatest Indian pandits (traditional scholars). His translation of the Laws of Manu was published in the year of his death, and the statue shows the importance of his project.

As Thomas Trautman has pointed out, the pedestal of Jones's statue is a remarkable expression of Hindu mythology in a Christian church, inasmuch as it features a disc whereon a semi-reclining female clad in a sari, one breast exposed, supports a square relief of the churning of the ocean, while her right arm encloses four-headed Brahma, though he might have been misread by the sculptor as a three-headed god. The top edge of the disc shows the zodiac with the words 'Courma Avatar' ('the Tortoise incarnation [of Vishnu]') above.[24] Trautman credits here the influence of Jones's admirer Thomas Maurice, who saw the Hindu account of the churning of the ocean as corroboration of the biblical record of the universal flood. The rainbow, explains Trautman, is both one of the good things produced by the churning of the ocean, and the rainbow that in the Bible manifests to Noah God's promise that he will never again destroy the earth in a deluge; the 'three-headed' god is the Hindu trinity as 'testimony to the truth of the Christian doctrine of the Trinity'.

Two male figures remove the drape from this complex scene. One – young, winged and upright – is the Genius of Jones, the face clearly his, holding a torch aloft, illuminating the world; the other is a philosopher or academic, old and bent, with a lamp held close to the disc. One of Jones's papers was on the Indian origin of the zodiac. The statue shows how the modernizing West sees itself in the model of ancient Rome, a Rome whose predecessor was India.

Jones's researches spread far beyond his professional concern with law. He described what seemed to him the greatness of Hindu civilization, and he persuaded all Europe of that greatness. Speaking 'the language of the Gods, as the brahmans call it, with great fluency', Jones's Sanskrit interests were by no means restricted to legal texts. His translation of Kalidasa's play *Shakuntala* had far greater impact than his translation of Manu. Manu was already familiar to learned Europeans thanks to the translation of a Persian paraphrase by Halhed in 1776, but nothing was known of Sanskrit drama. Abraham Roger had given a translation of an important Sanskrit collection of verses by Bhartrihari – the first Sanskrit translation to be printed, but that had had no impact. Jones had immediately been struck by the play's Shakespearean qualities: 'I am deep into the second act of a Sanscrit play, near 2,000 years old, and so much like Shakespeare, that I should have thought our great dramatick poet had studied Kalidasa.' Shakuntala was to take Europe by storm. As Mary Wollstonecraft said in her review, 'the poetic delineation of Indian manners and the artless touches of nature . . . come home to the human bosom in every climate'.[25] Educated Indians rejoiced in the European approval of their literature.

Kalidasa's play shows a king led by his deer hunt into the ashrama of a notable ascetic, whose ward he makes love to in what Hindu theory calls a fairy marriage. The mutual attraction of the seasoned monarch and the innocent girl is delicately but emphatically described. (The 'artless touches of nature' noticed by Wollstonecraft are especially apparent in the opening scenes where the king meets the young females in the ashrama, the girls' pretty confusion before the male lead being echoed in many Indian films.) Called away, the king – thanks to another ascetic's curse – forgets the girl. She loses the ring the king had given her. When she comes to court with her son, the product of their brief union, the king repudiates her, until the ring, found in the fish that had swallowed it, jogs his memory, and Shakuntala joins the king's harem. Her son, Bharata, as we know from the *Mahabharata*, goes on to rule all India, and Bharata is indeed India's Indian name.

In this presentation of Hastings and Jones, no mention has been made of Edward Said and his redefinition of Orientalism. Said will be considered in the next chapter, but let us note in passing that Jones's motivation – as indeed, to a large extent, was that of Hastings – was love of knowledge.

There is now an abrupt turnabout in our story. Indophobia replaces Indomania. The enthusiasm of the Orientalists gives way to the incomprehension of Utilitarians and Baptists. Two men demand our particular attention: James Mill (1773–1836), a major exponent of utilitarianism, wrote the *History of British India* (1817), and Thomas Macaulay (1800–59), whose judgement on Warren Hastings was noted above, and who is the Victorian literary figure, considered by some to be Britain's greatest historian. His writings on India were not extensive, but even today his views reverberate in India, where his name is infamous.

Ironically, Macaulay was to conclude the unfinished legal work of Jones, while being completely opposed to all Jones stood for. Mill recommended Macaulay for the post of legal member of the governor general's council, to frame a body of codified law for the whole of British India. Inspired by the legal and constitutional proposals of Jeremy Bentham, the founder of utilitarianism, Mill declared in 1834, 'India will be the first country on earth to boast a system of law and judicature as near perfection as the circumstances of the people would admit.'[26] This view was wildly optimistic, as is perhaps so often the case in the hasty application of pure reason to human affairs. The relevance, however, of both Mill and Macaulay at this juncture of our study is that they both mounted a ferocious attack on Hinduism. Macaulay's brilliance as a stylist gave his few words the greatest weight. His *Minute on Education*, in favour of English rather than indigenous languages as the medium of instruction for India's new schools and universities, declared that a single shelf of European books was infinitely more valuable than all the books of India; Hinduism, with its mythical geography of seas of milk and treacle, was, for him, a joke.

Mill's attack on Hinduism is sustained for hundreds of pages. In brief, 'the natives of [India] are distinguished by a greater deficiency in the important article of practical good sense, than any people, above the rank of savages, of whom we have any record'.[27] We shall have occasion in subsequent chapters to return to these two, but for now it is necessary only to note that from 1840 Mill's *History* was provided with a continuation and annotation by the Sanskritist H. H. Wilson. In his footnotes Wilson defended Jones and Hindu civilization against Mill's attacks: 'With very imperfect knowledge, with materials exceedingly defective, with an implicit faith in all testimony hostile to Hindu pretensions, he has elaborated a portrait of the Hindus which has no resemblance whatever to the original and which outrages humanity.'[28] More generally, Mill's view of despotism as the natural condition and model of government in the East was to influence Marx's notion of the so-called Asiatic mode of production.

Marx

Both Marx and Weber were concerned with the explanation of capitalism, and considered India only for instructive contrast. Marx, helped by Engels, wrote a series of articles for American newspapers on India; Engels was sufficiently interested in India to start learning Persian. They accepted the British stereotypes of India, having few other sources available to them. Marx dismissed Indian towns as merely military camps, and stressed the static nature of the Indian village:

> these idyllic village communities . . . had always been the solid foundation of oriental despotism . . . they had restrained the human mind within the smallest possible compass, making it the unresisting tool of superstition, enslaving it beneath traditional rules, depriving it of all grandeur and historical energies . . .[29]

Ahmad points out that this closely resembles Marx's verdict on the idiocy of the rural life of the European peasant.[30] Marx continues:

> We must not forget that this undignified, stagnatory and vegetative life, that this passive sort of existence, evoked on the other part, in contradistinction, wild, aimless unbounded forces of destruction, and rendered murder itself a religious rite in Hindustan.[31] . . . It thus brought about a brutalizing worship of nature, exhibiting its degradation in the fact that man, the sovereign of nature, fell down on his knees in adoration of Hanuman, the monkey, and Shabala, the cow.[32]

It may be noted that Marx referred to Hanuman the monkey god and Shabala the divine cow in his very first publication, simply as a regular topic of the Indian press.[33] Thirty-three years later, he welcomed the Mutiny, a war of liberation and freedom that would properly succeed when undertaken, not by the indigenous landlords, but by the proletariat. The proletariat would soon be produced. The coming of the railways would transform India, that India where 'man the sovereign of nature' under Hinduism bowed down to animals.

In his first dispatch on India to the USA, Marx declared that he did not share 'the opinion of those who believe in a golden age of Hindustan'.[34] And he certainly had a low opinion of contemporary Hinduism. For Marx, Hinduism was a religion of worthless extremes, summed up as 'the religion of the Lingam and of the Juggernaut; the religion of the Monk and of the Bayadère'. Various manifestations of the juggernaut have been examined above in chapter 2; worship of the linga, said Macaulay in the British parliament in 1842, was 'not merely idolatry, but idolatry in its most pernicious form'. As for the human side of the equation, there was little good to be said about the monk in India and less about the infamous dancing-girls. As Pinch says, 'the colonial willingness to see evil and corruption in the figure of the Indian monk was remarkable for its longevity and imaginative creativity';[35] and so-called sacred prostitution complemented the stark and naked veneration of sexuality manifested in the linga in the dark centre of the temple.

Marx adopted the Evangelical distaste and incomprehension of Macaulay and others in respect of temple dancers, but the British public were more open-minded, enjoying the Indian dancers who made their way to London.[36] The great importance of Marx in the formation of modernity necessitates consideration of what he said about Hinduism, even though, as with Bernier, we find only incomprehension and distaste.

Weber

Whereas Marx had almost nothing to say about Hinduism, Weber devoted a book-length essay to Hinduism and Buddhism. This was one of a series of essays on what he called 'economic ethics'.[37] By this term he meant 'the practical impulses for action which are founded in the psychological and pragmatic contexts of religions'. To investigate these impulses he sought 'to peel off the directive elements in the life-conduct of those social strata which have most strongly influenced the practical ethic of their respective religions. These elements have stamped the most characteristic features upon practical ethics, the features that distinguish one ethic from others; and, at the same time, they have been important for the respective economic ethics.'[38] Weber's concern was to show how Indian religion had prevented capitalistic development, and thus to buttress his thesis of the uniqueness of the West.

His essay on Hinduism and Buddhism falls into three parts. He first gives an account of the Hindu social system, which is to say the caste system; his account is based on the latest information available to him, especially the censuses of 1901 and 1911. The second part deals with 'those social *strata* which have most strongly influenced the practical ethic of religion' in India: the brahmans in Hinduism, the monks in Buddhism and Jainism – the intellectuals, the cultured literati. This part deals both with the origins of the various religions, very briefly in respect of Buddhism and Jainism, and with their core, their essence, in so far as the literati in question are key factors throughout the history of all three religions. In the third part, which quickly gives the subsequent histories of Buddhism and Hinduism, the literati retain their key role even though we now hear much about the middle classes and the 'masses'. Not only are the masses 'uncultivated, plebeian', but the middle classes are illiterate. Both, in Weber's eyes, have a strong tendency to 'orgiasticism': excessive sensual indulgence for religious ends.

In his treatment of Hinduism Weber stresses the brahmans' key role in the perpetuation of tradition. There is little trace of fellow feeling between the German scholar and the not entirely dissimilar brahmans he writes about, who were in their own way no less dedicated to the life of the mind, but it has been suggested by Kantowsky that the orgiasticism so prominent in Weber's account of Hinduism is perhaps stressed by Weber because he was then himself for the first time experiencing sexual fulfilment. Kantowsky points out that *The Religion of India* was dedicated to Weber's mistress.[39] The first work in his series of studies on economic ethics, *Religion and the Spirit of Capitalism*, was dedicated to his wife; their marriage was unconsummated.

Weber's goal is to explain India's failure to develop industrial capitalism. He does find certain forms of rationality in India. He carefully notes the wide extent of trade in ancient India, the great stress placed on the desirability of gaining wealth in the classical literature, and the many rational aspects of Hinduism. Thus, he says, 'Technically, Indian asceticism was the most rationally developed in the world. There is hardly an ascetic method not practised with virtuosity in India and often rationalized into a theoretical technology.'[40]

Again the caste system itself, according to Weber, was based on a rational structure:

> *Karma* doctrine transformed the world into a strictly rational, ethically-determined cosmos; it represents the most consistent theodicy ever produced by history. The devout Hindu was accursed to remain in a structure which made sense only in this intellectual context; its consequences burdened his conduct. The *Communist Manifesto* concludes with the phrase 'they (the proletariat) have nothing to lose but their chains, they have a world to win.' The same holds for the pious Hindu of low castes. He too can 'win the world,' even the heavenly world; he can become a kshatriya, a brahman, he can gain Heaven and become a god – only not in this life, but in the life of the future after rebirth into the same world pattern.

Thus, it follows that

> It was impossible to shatter traditionalism, based on caste ritualism anchored in *karma* doctrine, by rationalizing the economy. In this eternal caste world, the very gods in truth, constituted a mere caste – to be sure, superior to the brahmans, but as we shall see later – inferior to the sorcerers who through asceticism were provided with magical power. Anyone who wished to emancipate himself from this world and the inescapable cycle of recurrent births and deaths had to leave it altogether – to set out for that unreal realm to which Hindu 'salvation' leads.[41]

The caste system was supported by what Weber thought were the two key doctrines of Hinduism:

> No Hindu denies two basic principles: the *samsara* belief in the transmigration of souls and the related *karma* doctrine of compensation. These alone are the truly 'dogmatic' doctrines of all Hinduism, and in their very interrelatedness they represent the unique Hindu theodicy of the existing social, that is to say caste system.[42]

Weber concludes his study of Hinduism by remarking that, on top of the constraints of the caste system, there developed the worship of gurus: 'It is quite evident that no society dominated by such inner powers could have brought forth what we here understand by the spirit of capitalism.'[43] In addition to the ties of caste and the domination by gurus, there was the dogma of the unalterability of the world order, the devaluation of the world by contemplative mysticism. Either religious paths were orgiastic and anti-rational, or they were rational in method but irrational in goal. 'Instead of a drive toward the rational economic accumulation of property and the utilization of capital, Hinduism created irrational accumulation opportunities for magicians and spiritual counsellors, and prebends [revenues] for mystagogues and ritualistically or soteriologically oriented intellectual strata.'[44] But this conclusion follows inevitably from Weber's decision to concentrate on the literate strata, on brahmans and monks, who alone left us the textual information on which Weber's study is built.

   Weber's concluding statement is backed, ludicrously, by a story about a dead vulture. It is by this that 'The special Indian form of the accumulation of great wealth is best illustrated'! To quote directly from Weber's source, 'The founder of the Vaidika family of Kotalipahar was invited from Kanoj by a Hindu prince who ruled over the district of Bakergunge in the thirteenth century, was led to celebrate at an immense cost a religious ceremony for avoiding an evil that was foreboded by the fall of a dead vulture on the roof of his palace. The lucky priest secured for himself, by way of remuneration for his

services, a valuable zemindari [hereditary estate] which is now in the possession of his descendants.'[45] Weber ends this by referring to more normal ways
of earning money, a list taken from the *Panchatantra*, the book of animal
stories![46]

Such are Weber's final words on Hinduism. A paragraph referring to the
emergence of modern reform movements and growing nationalism follows,
with the remark that these are necessarily alien to the basic Indian character,
and have nothing to do with the historical Hinduism that Weber has been
describing. The essay concludes with 15 pages on the general character of
Asiatic religion. Weber finds aspects of Hinduism to be highly rational, but
working from sources created by religious specialists, whether brahmans or
Buddhist monks, his findings are inevitably skewed.

These two thinkers, Marx and Weber, have done nothing to assist Western understanding of Hinduism. Marx of course unwittingly founded a
messianic religion that profoundly reshaped the world, including parts of
India. Kerala had the first democratically elected Marxist government in the
world, and both Kerala and Bengal continue to have Marxist state governments. In respect of intellectual history and the formulation of modernity,
the views of Marx and Weber on India have been profoundly significant, but
what they say about India is wrong. Marx's view of the Asiatic mode of
production and Oriental despotism is based on inadequate sources. Weber
was likewise limited by his sources, but still more by his Eurocentrism. Marx
saw Hinduism, like all religion, as the reflection of social and economic
realities; Weber saw the social and economic condition of India as the result
of Hinduism.

Weber's views on India, and the Eurocentric views of the world that he did
much to shape, have been subject to exhilarating critique by thinkers such as
Hodgson,[47] Goody,[48] and, most emphatically, the economist Frank, who forcefully argues that India played a leading role in world trade up to the eighteenth century, and that all arguments about the special nature of Europe are
based on wilful ignorance of the rest of the world:

> the notions of 'development,' 'modernization,' 'capitalism,' and even 'depend-
> ence,' or call it what you will . . . are procrustean and empty categories; because
> the original sin of Marx, Weber, and their followers was to look for the 'origin,'
> 'cause,' 'nature,' 'mechanism,' indeed the 'essence' of it all essentially in Euro-
> pean exceptionalism instead of in the real world economy/system. All of these
> allegedly essential exceptionalisms, whatever their name, were derived from the
> same Eurocentric perspective that . . . has absolutely no foundation in historical
> reality–that is in 'universal' history, 'as it really was.' They were all derived only
> from European/Western ethnocentrism, which was propagated around the world
> – West and East, North and South – as part and parcel of Western colonialism
> and cultural imperialism.[49]

Louis Dumont (1911–1998)

Weber's study of India has received little attention from students of religion; its rationale was limited to buttressing his attempt to prove the uniqueness of Western capitalism. A project no less ambitious than that of Weber is Louis Dumont's sociological study of the East and West: his study of caste, entitled *Homo Hierarchicus* ('Hierarchical Man'), which has been enormously influential, and his study of the individual in the West, *Homo Aequalis* ('Equal Man'). For Dumont, it is the idea of the individual that constitutes the fundamental sociological problem. He took as his starting point a footnote in Weber's *The Protestant Ethic and the Rise of Capitalism*: 'The expression "individualism" includes the most heterogeneous things imaginable . . . a thorough analysis of these concepts in historical terms would . . . be highly valuable to science.'[50]

Dumont tells us that there are two mutually opposed configurations of the individual: that of traditional societies and that of modern society. In traditional society, the stress is placed on the society as a whole. The ideal is above all a matter of order, of hierarchy: 'each particular man in his place must contribute to the global order; and justice consists in ensuring that the proportions between social functions are adapted to the whole'. But in modern society each man incarnates the whole of mankind. 'Ontologically, society no longer exists, it is no more than an irreducible datum, which must in no way thwart the demands of liberty and equality.' However, Dumont makes the essential qualification that this modern view of the individual is a description of values. 'With respect to what happens in fact in this [i.e. modern] society, observation often refers us to the first type of society.'[51]

Dumont found Tocqueville's contrast between aristocratic and democratic nations the best introduction to the universe of hierarchical man as found in India, quoting him as follows:

> Aristocracy had made a chain of all the members of the community, from the peasant to the king: democracy breaks that chain and severs every link of it . . . They owe nothing to any man, they expect nothing from any man; they acquire the habit of always considering themselves as standing alone, and they are apt to imagine that their whole destiny is in their own hands. Thus not only does democracy make every man forget his ancestors, but it hides his descendants, and separates his contemporaries from him; it throws him back for ever upon himself alone, and threatens in the end to confine him entirely within the solitude of his own heart.[52]

For Dumont, the caste system, which has received so many explanations, springs from the opposition between pure and impure, an opposition that is only fully apparent at the top and bottom, with the pure brahmans and the permanently impure outcastes, who are impure because their work is impure:

they work with animal skins, or remove human excrement. It is this ideological divide that gives rise to the multitude of different castes. The pure and the impure must be kept separate, and this separation is the structure that underlies all the divisions that form the hierarchy of caste. Almost every caste is above some castes and below others. The opposition between pure and impure is the ultimate explanation of this hierarchy. Dumont's discovery of 'the necessary and hierarchical coexistence of the two opposites' 'is of extreme importance, since it transports us at once to a purely structural universe'.[53]

A verse of Manu (II. 27) clearly shows the nature of impurity: 'The pollution of semen and of the womb [i.e. birth] is effaced for the twice-born by the sacraments of pregnancy, birth, tonsure and initiation.' It can be seen that impurity corresponds to the organic aspect of man. Religion generally speaks in the name of universal order; but in this case, though unaware in this form of what it is doing, by proscribing impurity it in fact sets up an opposition between religious and social man on the one hand, and nature on the other.[54]

Dumont makes abundantly clear that the impurities of personal life are not at all independent of caste pollution – the two are interdependent. In addition to the central opposition between pure and impure, Dumont stresses two other sets of opposition. He makes great play of the opposition between brahman and king, and between householder and renouncer.

Weber claimed that transmigration – along with the related doctrine that successive existences are the consequences of the actions of the self – constitutes a dogmatic belief of Hinduism. Dumont takes a different view in his essay on world renunciation. Rather than being a product of brahmanic intellectualism it is 'a product of the situation and the thought of the sannyasi'. 'Transmigration is the idea that the renouncer turned towards liberation, has of the world he has left behind. Rather than a pessimistic view, transmigration appears as a bold design lending to the men-in-the-world some reality taken from that which the renouncer has found for himself.'[55]

Dumont shows that Hinduism draws a series of distinctions which are not those to which we are accustomed, and that this series flows logically from an initial choice: 'that the society must submit and entirely conform to the absolute order, that consequently the temporal, and hence the human, will be subordinate, and that, while there is no room here for the individual, whoever wants to become one may leave society proper'.[56] On the way to this conclusion, he makes an amazingly sweeping claim:

> Is it really too adventurous to say that the agent of development in Indian religion and speculation, the 'creator of values', has been the renouncer? The brahman, as a scholar, has mainly preserved, aggregated, and combined; he may well have created and developed special branches of knowledge. Not only the founding of sects and their maintenance, but the major ideas, the 'inventions' are due to the renouncer, whose unique position gave him a sort of monopoly for putting everything in question.[57]

A fine-sounding theory, but where are the facts? No historical substantiation is provided. With regard to kingship, Dumont argues that brahman superiority to the Kshatriya caste meant the secularization of kingship:

> the very word hierarchy, and its history, should recall that the gradation of status is rooted in religion: the first rank normally goes, not to power, but to religion, simply because for those societies religion represents what Hegel has called the Universal, i.e. absolute truth, in other words because hierarchy integrates the society in relation to its ultimate values . . . In most of the societies in which kingship is found, it is a magico-religious as well as a political function. [In India, however] the king depends on the priests for the religious functions, he cannot be his own sacrificer, instead he 'puts in front' of himself a priest, the *purohita*, and *then* he loses the hierarchical preeminence in favour of the priests, retaining for himself power only.[58]

But the history of Hindu India shows rather that dynamic outsiders set up dynasties and bring in brahmans to legitimize their rule. They choose the brahmans who will validate them. External accounts of the last Hindu empire, in Vijayanagara, make plain that the king played a commanding role in the ritual life of the kingdom.

Much of Dumont's argument is extreme, and cannot be supported by historical evidence. In particular his view of kingship and the originality special to the renouncer cannot be supported. But as a way of making sense of a lot of Hinduism, above all caste, his work is of unparalleled importance. His stress on the significance for anthropologists of the classical tradition of Hinduism as set out by brahmans in their Sanskrit texts, is perhaps the last major affirmation of old-style Orientalism in the context of India.

This chapter has reviewed the attempts of individual Europeans to objectively understand Hinduism. Roger, Bernier, Jones, Hastings, Marx, Weber, Dumont have been the principal figures considered. The latter three, along with Bernier, were concerned with a general understanding of the world, within which they situated Hinduism. In the next chapter I will consider those Westerners who, like Jones, devoted themselves to the understanding of Hinduism.

Chapter Six

Hinduism and Orientalism

'The horror, the horror.' These words taken by the director Francis Ford Coppola from Joseph Conrad's *Heart of Darkness* (1899) sum up, in the film *Apocalypse Now* (1979), both the American war against Vietnam and Oriental religion. In Coppola's film the US soldiers in Cambodia, confronted by the ruins of Angkor, exclaim at their strangeness, at the giant heads of the Bodhisattva-Shivas entwined with the roots of the all-swallowing jungle. Amid the ruins, the boat rounds a bend in the river to discover a motley array of native soldiers, accompanied by a profusion of hanging corpses. The lost colonel Kurtz – like Conrad's Kurtz – has gone mad and is killing wildly deep in the jungle. He, then, is horrifying to those who are searching for him. But Kurtz has a little shelf of books in his womb-like centre of the temple complex, where a statue of the Buddha sits beside him, a shelf that bears the *Golden Bough* and Jessie Weston's *The Quest for the Holy Grail*. The mad colonel, once an 'outstanding officer' is not only waging a private war, but is also a solitary student of Religious Studies. He has been overwhelmed by what he sees as the obscenity, the horror of America's war machine, but is driven to rival it, his chamber containing what seems to be a large wall panel of Kali. The venturing hero of the film slays this wicked colonel with the sacrificial axe from a buffalo sacrifice just about to take place. The film in its released version ends with the wicked American bombers raining destruction on the mad colonel. There is a bizarre diversion here of the American bombing from its perceived exterior foe to Kurtz, its inner self. Perhaps the most startling contrast between the film and Conrad's novel is between the massive fire power of the Americans and the impotence of the French gunboat blindly shelling the jungle shoreline – but the Americans were no less impotent in the end. In Coppola's film we have modernity gone mad, no less mad than the film's version of Eastern religion!

A year before Coppola's film was released a book was published that has proved to be an extraordinarily successful counterblast to the imperialism and colonialism implicit in modernity – Edward Said's *Orientalism*. Once the study of 'Oriental' or Near Eastern and Asian languages and literatures, Orientalism is now taken to mean the Western domination and exploitation of the East, the West viewing the East as alien, as 'the other'; all study of Hinduism in the West is taken to be an instance of Orientalism in the new sense. It was the literary critic Said, a Palestinian Christian, who brought about this revolution. His first book a study of Joseph Conrad, in *Orientalism* Said introduced and popularized the ideas of Foucault. Although partly inspired by Raymond Schwab's *La Renaissance orientale* (1950) which makes India the centrepiece of an expected cultural rebirth of Europe through the study of the Orient, Sanskrit performing the role of Greek in the first Renaissance, Said is principally concerned with the Arab world and its treatment by the West. European novels remain his primary area of expertise, and not for a moment does he take on board Schwab's thesis that the East has influenced the West. Said makes use of Foucault's notion of discourse, of a manner of thinking that is adopted willy-nilly by a generation or more of writers, while at the same time having as his preferred procedure the literary analysis of individual works of literature. The two methods sit ill together: 'Said denounces with Foucauldian vitriol what he loves with Auerbachian passion.'[1] Nevertheless, following Foucault, Said suggests that the effect of Orientalist discourse is 'to formulate the Orient, to give it shape, identity, definition with full recognition of its place in memory, its importance to imperial strategy, and its "natural" role as an appendage to Europe'.[2]

A significant and malign manoeuvre on Said's part is to extend the term Orientalist from students of Oriental languages to all those who deal with the Orient, whether or not they use texts in the original languages. His final option for the meaning of Orientalism of course turns it on its head; as taken up by the sociologist Bryan Turner, Orientalism is taken to mean ignorance of the Orient: 'From the seventeenth century onwards, orientalism had constituted a profound sense of otherness with respect to alien cultures.'[3] This perverse sleight of hand magics away into thin air the editions, translations and dictionaries of the true and original Orientalists who devoted their lives to understanding the meaning of instances of Oriental culture and civilization. In the words of Gyan Prakash, 'The towering . . . images of men like William ('Oriental') Jones have cracked and come tumbling down.'[4]

So well established is Said that a young scholar, Joan-Pau Rubies, recently wrote that '"Orientalism" has traditionally been defined as a western imperialist attitude in which the colonized subjects are perceived according to purely western ideological concerns.'[5] Said's brilliant success has swept away all that preceded it, and his redefinition of Orientalism has become 'traditional'. The choice of the term Orientalism is unfortunate on several counts. In the first place, why limit it to the West? As Rubies remarks, 'If we define orientalism as a manipulative historical gaze based on a crude separation between us and *other*, and which denies the representation of this *other* any intrinsic voice, then there was very little in the Muslim discourse about Hindu India which was less orientalist than what contemporary Europeans perceived and wrote.'[6] Then again, within Hinduism, brahmans might be said to have an Orientalist attitude to the lower castes. Original Orientalism was precisely the attempt to understand the Oriental other. This attempt was not completely successful, but it was all the attempt at understanding there was. Orientalism can be faulted for undue concentration on classical texts, but this was only mirroring the crucial role of study of ancient Greek and Latin, the ancients, in the intellectual life of the West.

First and foremost a literary critic, turning again and again in his *Orientalism* to the modern European novel as his favourite medium and source, Said sweepingly dismisses Orientalists in the strict sense in exactly the same way as he says that the West dismisses the East, as inferior others. He has been dismissed, not altogether unfairly, as 'a literary critic rummaging through history to find scraps of evidence to support his personal and political purposes'[7] by David Kopf, author of a pioneering historical study of British Orientalism in India.[8]

Said's work is continued with reference to India by the anthropologist turned historian-Sanskritist, Ronald Inden, in his *Imagining India* (1992), a book whose success has been no less than that of Said's. Indeed, its intellectual basis is perhaps stronger than that of *Orientalism*; Inden's thesis is that Orientalists have deprived Indians of 'agency' 'by imagining an India kept eternally ancient by various Essences attributed to it, most notably that of caste'. Inden contends that Indologists present the texts they study as 'distorted portrayals of reality', as 'manifestations of an "alien" mentality'.[9]

Early in the book he gives as an example of this some remarks on Vedic ritual by Louis Renou (1896–1966), the great French Sanskritist. These remarks are taken from Renou's masterly survey of the main problems in the study of Indian religion, as he saw them in 1951. Renou says in the quoted passage that Vedic ritual is overburdened with system, that there was 'an advancing scholasticism'. Two paragraphs later in Renou's text, the following sentences are quoted by Inden: 'Ritual has a strong attraction for the Indian mind, which tends to see everything in terms of the formulae and methods of procedure, even when such adjuncts no longer seem really necessary for its religious experience.' Inden believes that this is to transform 'the thoughts and actions of ancient Indians into a distortion of reality'. Renou might have shown that the Vedic priests 'were part of a coherent and rational whole' based on different presuppositions than his own; but, like many Indologists, he holds that there is a single external reality to which Western science has privileged access. Implicit in the texts of Renou and other Indologists is the 'metaphor of the Other as a dreamer, as a . . . mad man'. Like Freud on dreams, Indologists attribute condensation and displacement to the Indian mind. For Renou, says Inden, 'the priestly mind takes up rituals which are not meant to be enacted while the priestly hand performs rituals that have no religious rationale'; 'Renou, we have seen, attributed the same dreaming irrationality to the Indian mind that Hegel did'.[10]

Inden's polemic leads him away from Renou. When Renou speaks of the Indian mind, he means the Indian mind as expressed in Vedic texts, a continuous and highly specific tradition to which certain general characteristics might fairly be attributed. He goes on to say that there is a tendency in the ritual texts to build up complex structures from simpler elements, that they are sometimes intellectual exercises: 'we must not regard them as consisting entirely of accounts of actual religious practice'.[11] Renou's account of Vedism is, to my mind, sympathetic and luminous. As he says, 'Of religious feeling and community life in the Vedic period we can know virtually nothing.'[12] But he gives us a description of a present-day performance of a Vedic sacrifice, ending with the following comment on ancient times: 'In those distant days India had a feeling for liturgy comparable to that of the Roman Church.'[13] We might also note Renou's remark that 'the prose-style of the *Shatapatha* [the largest of the sacrificial texts] is a model of skilful articulation, and in its severe purity reminds us of Plato'.[14] In another essay on Vedic studies Renou notes that 'Indian scholars have come relatively late to these studies. It may be that an excess of attachment (very respectable in itself) to the tradition has prevented them from considering the Veda with eyes sufficiently objective, with the same "indifference" with which a naturalist studies a plant.'[15]

Not only did Renou devote his life to the objective study of Sanskrit and the Veda, more than most Sanskritists he took the large view, giving an accurate account of the whole scope of classical Indian civilization in the two volumes of *L'Inde classique* which he edited with Jean Filliozat, writing much of it himself. To say that Renou attributed 'dreaming irrationality' to the Indian mind is false. As his pupil Malamoud wrote in the introduction to a posthumous collection of Renou's essays, *L'Inde fondamentale*, Renou described an India that was rigorous and cheerful, animated by a powerful ardour for speculation, directed to the intrepid analysis of language rather than to rumination on the ineffable.[16]

Renou had no conceivable imperial designs on India. Nor did Georg Bühler (1837–98), the Sanskritist's Sanskritist of the second half of the nineteenth century, who worked for the Raj's Bombay presidency. This Austrian scholar had the reputation of having read everything extant in Sanskrit, and he conceived and edited the *Encyclopedia of Indo-Aryan Research*, contributed to by Indologists from all over the world. Renou and Bühler are prime examples of the mastery sought by all scholars, the lordship of understanding that is as complete as possible. British Orientalists had the same ambitions, of understanding through first-hand knowledge. Mill and Hegel, on the other hand,

claimed universal dominion for their ideas without any first-hand knowledge
of India or Indian languages – this is the difference between scholars and
philosophers.

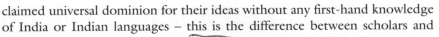

   At the same time, it is certainly true that the understanding of many
Sanskritists was limited to their particular texts, and that some had little or no
sympathy for modern India. Thus for Richard Garbe, who visited India in
1885–6, the worship of the common Hindu was a worthless fetishism, and he
confessed to the anger of a Hebrew prophet, wanting to whip the Hindus,
especially the priests, from the stinking lairs that were their temples.[17] But it
behoves us to remember how far away India was from the West before the
advent of the aeroplane. Both Garbe and Paul Deussen, the German Vedanta
scholar, gave a careful account of the ships in which they voyaged to India.
Very little was known about how Hindus lived and thought. There is nothing
to be gained by reduplicating Garbe's moral indignation and heaping it back
on him, for he lived on a different planet; and he had a very good understanding of Samkhya and other Sanskrit texts.
   Said's reversal of the meaning of the word Orientalism has been so successful because there was a need for a word for Western misunderstanding and
mistreatment of the East, but his choice was unfortunate. No one has offered
any evidence that Indological Orientalist learning, in the strict old sense of
linguistic and textual study, served imperial ends. Those concerned with conquest and exploitation, with practical affairs, had no time and little sympathy
for such studies.[18] Warren Hastings was the exception here, but he had a great
love of all things Indian. It was he who set Orientalism – in its old and original
meaning – in train in India. He found Hinduism scarcely less attractive than
Christianity.[19] He spoke of himself as well as others when he told the man he
was sending to explore Tibet that there were 'thousands of men in England'
who would listen to the story of an expedition 'in search of knowledge', with
'ten times' the interest they would take in 'victories that slaughtered thousands of the national enemies'.[20] Nor does colonial discourse theory make
allowance for the kind of love of learning that led Anquetil-Duperron to enlist
as a soldier so that he could get to India and study Old Persian and Sanskrit.[21]
Indeed, Said speaks of 'the madness of Anquetil-Duperron's life'.[22]
   Not only does Inden accuse Renou, without a shred of justification, of
attributing 'the same dreaming irrationality to the Indian mind that Hegel
did', he also makes the astonishing claim that the writings of James Mill (*The
History of British India*) and Hegel were hegemonic texts for Indology.[23] As
Trautman says, 'neither Mill nor Hegel learned an Indian language or set foot
in India' and 'they used their secondhand knowledge to fashion arguments
against the authority of the Orientalists and the enthusiasm for India with
which it was associated'.[24] Numerous writers today claim that Mill was studied at Haileybury, the East India Company's college in England, but a rare
published account of life there makes no mention of the *History of British*

India. John Beames, an Indian civil servant whose love of learning led him to write a comparative grammar of Indo-Aryan languages, describes his time at Haileybury, learning languages but nothing whatever about life in India, not even what Mill has to say:

> it was considered 'bad form' to talk about India or to allude to the fact that we were all going there soon. Even the study of Oriental languages, which was the chief feature of the place, and in fact the reason for its existence, was carried on as though we had no personal interest in the countries in which those languages were spoken, and no attempt was made to practise talking them or to acquire any practical familiarity with them. If at any time one wanted to know what sort of place India was, or what one's future life or work there was to be like, it was impossible to find anyone who could give the requisite information.[25]

The indifference to India on the part of Beames and his fellow students seems to be innocent of any knowledge of the *History* of James Mill.

Oriental despotism

Coppola transposes the horror from the African jungle, with its cannibals and fences topped with skulls, to the jungle of Cambodia, where the giant heads of the divine kings of Angkor loom out of the vegetation. Angkor, 'the City', from the Sanskrit *nagara* ('city'), was on the eastern edge of the huge spread of Sanskritic culture. Sanskrit was 'the paramount linguistic medium by which ruling elites expressed their power from Purusapura [Peshawar] in Gandhara in the northwest of the subcontinent to as far east as Panduranga in Annam [South Vietnam] and Prambanam in central Java'.[26] In describing the formation of what he calls the Sanskrit Cosmopolis, Sheldon Pollock refers to the 'efforts of small groups of traders, adventurers, religious professionals. There is no evidence that large-scale state initiatives were ever at issue, or that anything remotely resembling "colonization" took place.'[27]

Yet, however Sanskritic religious culture spread to South-East Asia, the huge temple-palaces in Cambodia are a patent manifestation of royalty's will to power. An important early instance of Said's version of Orientalism is the European notion of Oriental despotism, a category that allows the West to dismiss Eastern political concerns as inherently inferior. The notion goes back to Aristotle: 'Asians are more servile by nature . . . hence they endure despotic rule without protest.'[28] Bernier is here a key figure, for his account of the despotism of the Mughals was taken up by Montesquieu and Marx, to name only two. In fact, as Murr suggests, Bernier's account of India under Aurangzib and his predecessors reflects his fear that the absolutism of Louis XIV might degenerate into tyranny. He studiously resists using the term despot, and presents Aurangzib as by no means a barbarian, but as a great king worthy of comparison with European kings.[29] The Mughal emperors differed from European kings in that the most powerful son rather than the first-born became the successor; in parallel with this lack of regularly rewarded primogeniture there was no landed aristocracy as independent counterweight to the sovereign since the sovereign owned – it was supposed – all the land. Nobles were salaried and liable to dismissal if their performance was not satisfactory. Oriental despotism becomes a key concept in pro-imperialist interpretations of ancient Indian politics and society.

Anquetil-Duperron was the first European to argue against the notion that there was no private ownership of land in India, though his motive was primarily antipathy to the British. It is interesting to note a lack of such anti-British animus in the most important Enlightenment work on colonialism, Raynal's *Philosophical and Political History of the Two Indies* (first published 1760), no less a contributory factor to the French Revolution than Rousseau, but now scarcely known. For Raynal England was one among four powers in contemporary South India, no more out of place than the Marathas, Tipu Sultan, and the Nizam of Hyderbad.[30] All four powers were conquering outside their own territories. But the notion of Oriental despotism is an instance where Said's critique is fully justified. So too the notion of the unchanging Indian village, dealt with by Inden. But, in these and many other cases, the mistaken interpretation on the part of Orientalists arises from ignorance, from lack of sources of information.

Orientalism and empire

Today the British empire is widely seen as a blot on the history of the world. Assessment of British rule in India is difficult. Post-colonialism has produced a vast amount of literary criticism predicated on the cruelty and injustice of the Raj; Vinay Lal declares that getting to grips with the products of this industry leaves no time for old-fashioned history – even 'the quest for objectivity' in assessing the British empire is 'morally dubious'. A measured judgement relevant in the present context is that of Nirad C. Chaudhuri, even if Lal dismisses him as 'an indefatigable Anglophile'.[31] Describing the 1920s, Chaudhuri's empathy with Englishness – though he disliked the few Englishmen he met while under the Raj – does come out in his not unfavourable summary of early British imperialism as 'a mixture of humanitarianism, Evangelism, Utilitarianism, and Liberalism'. But Chaudhuri continues: 'That old imperialism had been replaced by the end of the nineteenth century by a wholly shoddy theory, which was nothing better than boastful verbiage. By 1920, even that had been discredited, and the Empire in India survived only as a practical reality supported by vested interests.'[32] Tapan Raychaudhuri, in his important assessment of British rule in India, remarks that 'in post-independence India, serious thinkers and historians who see anything good in the imperial record can probably be counted on the fingers of one hand';[33] nor is he one of their number.

There can be no doubt that the British, with a few exceptions, had no sympathy for Indian culture or religion, least of all for Hindus and Hinduism. But that is all the more reason to give due allowance to the exceptions. Kejariwal shows commendable boldness in blaming Indian nationalism for not giving credit to the early British Orientalists: 'Indian historians were more than eager to accept the glory of India's past as revealed by British historians, but the historians themselves were rejected as biased and motivated.'[34]

The British empire should not be considered in isolation from other empires. Not only is the British Raj to be set beside the Turkish, Persian, Roman, and other empires, we must also note Chaudhuri's assertion of Hindu imperialism:

> I had better confess that all Hindus are traditionally imperialists, and they condemned imperialism only in so far as British imperialism made them subjects to an empire instead of its masters. This is due to the fact that the strongest political passion of the ancient Hindus was directed towards conquest and domination. All Sanskrit literature and all the historical inscriptions are full of glorification of both. This aspiration to conquer and dominate was suppressed during Muslim and British rule, but today, even if not given practical expression, it conditions the attitude of the present Hindu ruling class towards the neighbours of India.[35]

Har Bilas Sarda's *Hindu Superiority* (1906) invents an account of Hindu colonization of the world.[36] R. C. Majumdar's history of India, widely used in schools and colleges in India, sees the spread of Hinduism and Buddhism in South-East Asia as the result of colonization by the Indian master race. Pollock claims that the source of such thinking is European.[37] True, but the goal of the traditional Hindu king was universal empire. Pollock concedes that domination did not enter India with European colonialism, and that 'gross asymmetries of power . . . appear to have characterized India in particular times and places over the last three millennia and have formed the background against which ideological power, intellectual and spiritual resistance, and many forms of physical and psychological violence crystallized'.[38] Indeed, he seems to put the blame partly on Sanskrit: 'Sanskrit was the principal discursive instrument of domination in premodern India and . . . it has been continuously reappropriated in modern India by many of the most reactionary and communalist sectors of the population.'[39] Inden's *Imagining India* seeks to refute the 'Orientalist' account (in Said's sense) of India which, Inden says, deprives Hindus of agency by defining Hinduism in terms of essence, caste and spirituality. Yet his refutation of the supposed colonialism and imperialism of his predecessors in the field of Indology proceeds by setting against them the medieval imperialism of Hinduism – universal empire was always the theoretical goal of Hindu kings.

Orientalism and racial theories

Various views on the origin and types of mankind were current in seventeenth-century Europe, including the theory of pre-Adamite man, but 'racial theory has as its official birthdate 24 April 1664',[40] when Bernier published in the *Journal des Scavans* a new division of the earth according to the different races that occupy it. He did not sign his paper because of intense theological opposition to the theory of pre-Adamite man published by his friend La Peyrère nine years earlier. Bernier's conception was biological and based on heredity. He distinguishes four or five 'species'; we need only note that he considered Europeans and a good part of Asia (including the states of the Great Mughal, the kingdom of Golconda, and that of Bijapur) to be of the same race. He made no other mention of India. Amongst the peoples with whom he is well acquainted, Bernier makes no hierarchical distinction.

The worst and most dangerous aspect of the British empire was its racism. As Peter van der Veer notes, 'Racial difference between the British and the colonized and among the colonized themselves became the explanation and legitimation of colonial rule.'[41] The British thought that they proved their superiority to Indians by conquering and holding India with a remarkably small number of men. They achieved this by convincing themselves of their invincibility and persuading many Indians that they were inferior to the British in respect of their ability to rule and wage war, though buying out the enemy was sometimes more effective than bravery. The matchless self-confidence of the British produced the inverse effect on those who beheld it. The British rulers kidded themselves and kidded the Indians, but it might well be argued that the confidence trick took its inspiration from India, from the caste system. It was brahmans who did the trick first, claiming to be the mouth of God, gods among men, the twice-born. The British civil servants took over for themselves the very term 'twice-born'. Brahmans did not eat with non-brahmans; the British rulers would not eat, drink or mix with Indians. The brahmans were essentially different from the other castes, for all castes were essentially different from each other. Well and good; the British rulers would be essentially different from the Indians, just as they were from their own lower classes back in England.

The British caste maintained its mindset all the better by having nothing to do with Hinduism. Their rejigging of the Hindu legal system and their censuses sharpened up notions of caste, but, by having as little as possible to do with Hinduism, they hid from themselves the caste nature of the imagined essential inner power that enabled them to rule successfully. In some sense it was their ignorance of Hinduism that enabled the British to rule for so long. When Nietzsche's friend Paul Deussen, travelling by train in India in 1893, rejoiced in friendly relations with Hindus, the cold and unfriendly Englishman in the same compartment remarked, 'We have to rule these people.'[42]

Many of the statistics of British imperial presence in India are striking, as for instance that 'In one district of Lower Bengal, 20 Britons lived among 2.5 million natives. As late as 1939, about 28 million Punjabis – people not renowned for their docility – were governed by 60 British civil servants.' However, the size of the army – '65,000 white soldiers in an area populated by 300 million people that now includes not only India but Pakistan, Bangladesh, and Burma'[43] – was not inconsiderable, given modern weapons and transport. For the civil and military officer cadres English public schools produced 'a courage caste with its ambitions turned from gain or learning towards an ideal of rule'.[44] The British civil servant, incredible as it seems now, believed that he was infallible and invulnerable in dealing with Indians. The army was there in the background, but many Indians had never seen British soldiers. As Walter Lawrence put it in the 1920s, British power in India was based on 'mutual make-believe': 'They, the millions, made us believe we had a divine mission. We made them believe that they were right.'[45] It rested on mutual collusion, on illusion.

But this dominance came to be explained by race. Herbert Risley (1851–1911), commissioner for the 1901 census of India, tried to show that caste had its origins in the interactions of the Aryan and Dravidian races: the caste system had its basis in community of race rather than community of function. He takes as starting point in his *People of India* (1915) a carved panel from the Buddhist stupa at Sanchi (100 BC–AD 100) which shows a monkey offering honey to the Buddha.[46] Tutelary spirits, *yakshas*, look on. The Buddha was not shown in person in this early phase of Buddhist art – his presence is signified by the empty dais beneath a sala tree. Risley bizarrely misreads this compassionate representation of spiritual community as an 'expression of the race sentiment of the Aryans towards the Dravidians', showing us 'the higher race on friendly terms with the lower, but keenly conscious of the essential difference of type and taking no active part in the ceremony at which they appear as sympathetic but patronizing spectators'.[47] Through ignorance of the basic conventions of Buddhist art, Risley sees only a primitive ritual devoid of point carried out by a subhuman no better than a monkey. He sees the demi-god *yakshas* as Aryans, and the monkey as a Dravidian!

In trying to understand caste as race, imperial officials were not setting India aside as a separate ethnographic park, as the other that is the unavoidable trope of colonial discourse analysis. Such racial analysis was to be applied everywhere. As Susan Bayly has pointed out, their work for them was pathbreaking science.[48] It was neither old-style Orientalism nor new Orientalism. It was for them an application and instance of universal reason, even though today it seems false and absurd.

David Cannadine argues that the British empire was not really concerned with the creation of 'otherness': society on the imperial periphery was the same or even superior to society in the imperial metropolis; 'for the British, their overseas realms were at least as much about sameness as they were about difference'.[49] British colonialism exacerbated caste, made it a system, but British interest in caste was by no means merely knowledge as power over its object, for it arose from a sense of similarity, of fellow feeling. For many Britons, says Cannadine, 'the social arrangements in South Asia seemed easily recognizable and comfortingly familiar'.[50] The rigid hierarchy of the British in British India has often been remarked on. 'British India was as much infected by caste as Indian India.'[51]

Cannadine's revisionism, salutary as it is, must not prevent us from examining the role of racial theory in understanding Western and Eastern confrontation. The supposition of racial characteristics and stereotypes, beyond the natural tendency of all peoples to believe themselves and their ways the best, has one supremely bad quality. This is ranking, forming a hierarchy, asserting superiority and inferiority. Without going into the question of what is race and what is caste, the clearest model of such ranking of peoples is the caste system, where birth determines value and status. It is striking how the notion of caste comes to permeate English discourse in the nineteenth century, to the point that Marx, for example, worries about his daughters losing caste through not being able to return hospitality.[52] Doubtless the notion of caste resonated with aspects of the class system in Britain, but the implacable and powerful presence of caste in India, it may be argued, had a profound effect on the British. This effect was much greater once Muslim power had been crushed, and the British had ever more consequential dealings with Hindus, whose quite different patterns of hospitality became increasingly significant. It is surely likely that British exclusivity mirrored the pre-existing caste exclusivity of the brahmans. Cannadine finds similarity between British and Indian society, but the radical change from Georgian to Victorian society marches in parallel with the British discovery of caste. The separation of human levels in the Victorian country house, for instance, where 'it was considered undesirable for children, servants and parents to see, smell or hear each other except at certain recognized times and places'[53] parallels the newly discovered social distinctions of the caste system in India.

A term used tirelessly since the appearance of *Orientalism* is 'the Other'. Its origins go back to Hegel, and Lacan made much of it. In the context of the Orient, it has been grossly overworked. John MacKenzie makes the important point that in the eighteenth and early nineteenth centuries Britain's principal 'other' was France; and in the century and a half that followed, France, Russia, Germany and the Soviet Union.[54] Risley's misinterpretation of the monkey in the Sanchi sculpture referred to above is perhaps less obnoxious when we remember the story that, during the Napoleonic Wars, Hartlepool fishermen hanged a shipwrecked monkey because they took it to be a Frenchman. The rudimentary logic of self and other has today led to an exaggerated idea of the importance of the East for nineteenth-century Europe. Bayly points out that 'Indological debates were almost always occidental debates as well; Orientalism was as much a representation of the Contested Self as it was of the Other.' Many of the offensive characterizations of Hindus by Englishmen 'are indistinguishable from what contemporaries were saying about those addicted to the Demon Drink, the working class, the Irish, Roman Catholics in general, or indeed about women'.[55]

Orientalism and the female

It is fascinating to note how the contemporary decline of philology, of the study of foreign literatures in their original languages, has been accompanied by the use of philological terms such as grammar, syntax and poetics in sociological discourse. Vinay Lal declares that 'the trope of effeminacy, the first element of an Orientalist grammar of India, had a particular place in colonial discourse'. Lal refers to Robert Orme's essay on 'The Effeminacy of the Inhabitants of Hindustan' (1782), summed up in the confident assertion that 'very few of the inhabitants' of India were 'endowed with the nervous strength, or athletic size, of the robustest nations of Europe'.[56] Most frequently cited on this subject are Macaulay's words:

> The physical organisation of the Bengalee is feeble even to effeminacy. He lives in a constant vapour bath. His pursuits are sedentary, his limbs delicate, his movements languid. During many ages he has been trampled upon by men of bolder and more hardy breeds. Courage, independence, veracity, are qualities to which his constitution and his situation are equally unfavourable.[57]

Few bother with the context, his characterization of Warren Hastings's implacable foe, the Maharajah Nand Kumar, whose composure and serenity in death Macaulay honours. Nand Kumar 'prepared himself to die with that quiet fortitude with which the Bengalee, so effeminately timid in personal conflict, often encounters calamities for which there is no remedy'. Of the Bengali in general Macaulay adds, 'Nor does he lack a certain kind of courage which is often wanting to his masters. To inevitable evils he is sometimes found to oppose a passive fortitude, such as the Stoics attributed to their ideal sage.'

    This is not slight praise from a devoted classicist. But otherwise Macaulay was merely expressing with his incomparable trenchancy the general view of European travellers. For instance, Bernier's compatriot, the jewel merchant Tavernier, noting that for one Muslim there are five or six Hindus, finds it astonishing 'to see how this enormous multitude of men has allowed itself to be subjected by so small a number, and has readily submitted to the yoke of the Musalman Princes', but 'the Idolaters were effeminate people unable to make much resistance'. Tavernier finds further explanation for their defeat in their superstition, which 'has introduced so strange a diversity of opinions and customs that they never agree with one another'. He also notes that the second caste is that of warriors and soldiers: 'These are the only idolaters who are brave, and distinguish themselves in the profession of arms.'[58]

In so far as there was caste specialization, it is perhaps only reasonable that there should have been specialization in bravery. Anne McClintock claims that 'imperialism cannot be understood without a theory of gender power . . . gender dynamics were, from the outset, fundamental to the securing and maintenance of the imperial enterprise'.[59] This is to say that imperialism necessitates feminizing the subjugated, that being colonized makes men effeminate. Kanhayalal Gauba's 1930 study of native princes refers to Bismarck's distinction of male and female European nations. For Bismarck, the Germans and various other peoples including the English and the Turks were essentially male; all Slavonic and Celtic peoples were 'female races'. Female races were charming but inefficient. Bismarck's view is relevant here in that it shows that the sweeping attribution of femininity to males is not necessarily tied in with prejudices of conquest and colonization. Gauba, not resenting the Raj, credited British India with the 'virility of youth', and saw in the India ruled by princes 'all the attractiveness of fine clothes, fine living, love and the extravagance associated with the elegant and sensuous female'.[60] If one were to accept Gauba's analysis one could well argue that the India of the princes, as he describes it, represents a higher level of civilization. Of course, all such talk is really about style and presentation rather than substance.

The British after the Mutiny and War of Independence revised their view of what they saw as the regional differences between Indians, and General Roberts promulgated a doctrine of martial races in which the general problem of the possible unmanning of conquered peoples took on for many Indians, especially Bengalis, a particularly insulting tone. The hypermasculine colonialist claimed to find Indians relatively effeminate. There are many complex issues here, including a degree of homoeroticism in the English public school and in the relationship between British officers and Indian troops, but my concern is to show that this attribution of effeminacy to Hinduism was absent from the work of Orientalists. By and large the British had remarkably little understanding of Hindus and Hinduism. What is at issue is the attitude of those Britons and Europeans who were deeply interested in India and Hinduism, Orientalists in the pre-Saidian sense.

In his chapter on Hinduism in *Imagining India*, Inden tries to show that the West's understanding of Hinduism opposed its own claimed masculine reason to the imputed feminine imagination of India. Inden begins by quoting Speare's likening of Hinduism to a sponge because it absorbs all that enters it. Implicit here, says Inden, is the idea that Hinduism is 'a female presence who is able, through her very amorphousness and absorptive powers, to baffle and perhaps even threaten Western rationality'. He then quotes Sir Charles Eliot – 'Hinduism has often and justly been compared to a jungle'.[61] Inden quotes several other sentences from Eliot expanding on this, ending, 'The average Hindu who cannot live permanently in the altitudes of pantheistic thought, regards his gods as great natural forces akin to mighty rivers which he also worships, irresistible and often beneficent but also capricious and destructive.' Inden immediately comments, 'There is thus little doubt here that this jungle with its soul, is, like Spear's sponge, also a female, one that can be managed by its male masters and known so long as they don't become entwined in its embraces'.[62] Neither Spear nor Eliot said a word about femininity, nor about managing the forest, though Eliot spoke of brahmans as 'not gardeners but forest officers'. Inden unfairly finds a colonial implication in the brahmans being seen in this way, but Eliot's point is that Hinduism cannot be controlled like a garden. Far from the jungle of Hinduism being seen as feminine, Eliot, in the passage cited by Inden, explicitly says that 'men and women of all classes . . . and all stages of civilization have contributed to it'.

A page later Inden again says that, for Western writers, 'If Hinduism has a positive essence, it consists of its feminine imaginativeness, its ability to absorb and include, to move from one extreme to the other, and to tolerate inconsistencies'.[63] Again, the femininity is entirely his own addition. It is also interesting that, in the final part of his book, an account of what he calls 'the imperial formation' in medieval India, Inden happily refers to the traditional idiom wherein the conquered peoples of the universal emperor, the king of kings, are referred to as his wives,[64] that is to say they are feminized, the very thing he is trying to accuse the Indologists of doing to Hinduism.

In Inden's next section on Hinduism, 'Psychic Origins', we get a long discussion of Mill's *History of British India*, followed by Hegel's India as the sleeper dreaming before he awakes:

> What were more or less disconnected examples of Hindu irrationality and superstition for Mill, the empiricist, were, for the German idealists, including Hegel, instances of the core metaphysics of that religion, of its double displacement of the ideal and material, the subjective and objective and of the predominance in it of creative imagination or fantasy over true thought or reason. That becomes the positive inner essence of the female India that a masculine Europe with its inner essence of reason was coming to dominate . . .We would not have those later British depictions of India as a feminine sponge or jungle animated by a feminine imagination had the Romantics and Hegel not done their work.[65]

'When we turn to the historical narratives of this religion, we behold a degenerative psychohistory masterminded by Hegel', says Inden. 'Instead of witnessing the triumph of man, reason, and spirit, however, we see the triumph of the effeminate, the sensuous and the parochial'.[66] But no one says this; certainly no one whom Inden cites. Hinduism is indeed a sponge, a forest, precisely because, like Topsy, it just growed. There was no overall authority, no Inquisition, no Synod to rule and regulate what men thought; practice was regulated and behaviour was governed by caste councils. Social life was, relatively speaking, orderly and stable; intellectual life was a free for all. Inden refers, without any further reference, to the 'schizophrenic religion of Shiva and Vishnu',[67] implying that that attribution of schizophrenia was the view of some or all Indologists. It need hardly be added that a résumé of the history of religion in Europe, careful to note all schisms and sects, would be no less confused and probably more schizophrenic than that of India.

Inden proceeds to expose the Orientalist as claiming a

> shift of essences, from a masculine Aryan mentality that had been tropicalized, to a feminine Dravidian or aboriginal mind that had been Aryanized . . . The change from depicting an Indian mind that was the same in its racial origin as that of the Self to one that was fundamentally different was significant . . . the imperial jungle officers that took charge after the Mutiny . . . came to imagine themselves as presiding over an India comprised of Dravidian plants that could only be managed.[68]

Then come the tribals. Inden says that it is on to the tribals that the Jungians – Inden's term for scholars interested in Indian mythology and art in themselves, rather than as instrumental in social scientific understanding – 'offload the savagery, animal sacrifice, and general fetishism and animism formerly attributed to the Dravidian'. Campbell conjures up this essence: 'For the calmly ruthless power of the jungle . . . has supplied the drone base of whatever song has ever been sung in India of man, his destiny and escape from destiny'.[69]

Inden performs his customary trick of equating jungle with woman:

> This defining essence consists of nothing more than the female side of the mind, that which threatens to overcome man's consciousness and reason. There has, to be sure, been a beneficent side to this femininity [Inden quotes Campbell again]: 'New civilizations, races, philosophies, and great mythologies have poured into India and have been not only assimilated but greatly developed, enriched, and [made?] sophisticated.' But the goddess, Kali, condensation of this jungle essence, is always there [quoting Campbell]: 'Yet, in the end (and in fact, even secretly throughout), the enduring power in that land has always been the same old dark goddess of the long red dark tongue who turns everything into her own everlasting, awesome, yet finally somewhat tedious, self'.[70]

Inden comments, 'Thus have the Jungians pushed the romantic idea of Hinduism as an ambivalent feminine entity to its extreme.'

The reader gets from Inden no indication that India contains a great variety of cultures, that there is a real difference in many ways between North India and the Dravidian language speakers of the south, and that the great forests of central India still contain millions of tribal peoples, who only in the last hundred years or so have given up large-scale human sacrifice. These are not figments of the Orientalist imagination but facts. As Felix Padel remarks in his sensitive study of the Konds of Orissa, 'tribal India is as different from mainstream India, as that is from Britain, or more so'.[71] The jungle-dwelling primitive has been an important factor in Hinduism: Shiva and Parvati often dress as tribals. Hinduism and its authors have throughout history delighted in running the gamut from the grandeur of metropolitan monarchs, to warriors, to forest-dwelling ascetics, to forest-dwelling tribals, all part of life's natural hierarchy, just like the caste system.

Inden accuses Campbell of conjuring up an essence, but Inden himself is performing a conjuring trick, conjuring up an ascription of femininity where it does not exist – the Orientalist is the other over which he seeks hegemony. But the goddess does play a vital, indeed an essential, role, in Hinduism. In his zeal to put words into the mouths of Orientalists, Inden overlooks the realities of Indian texts. The flesh-eating goddess deep in the jungle was a standard theme of Sanskrit and Tamil heroic texts. Inden several times refers to the Emperor Harsha. Bana, the great prose-poet of Harsha's reign, in his unfinished prose-poem *Kadambari* gives a well-known portrayal of a Durga shrine in the depths of the Vindhya forest, manned by a Dravidian priest. The poem begins with a tribal princess bringing a parrot as present from her father to the king. Her feet marked with leaf patterns in lac resemble Durga's feet, reddened by the buffalo's blood. The leader of the tribal hunters who captured the parrot has his shoulders scarred from making blood offerings to Durga, his body, like Durga's, marked with blood of buffalo. All this foreshadows the final remaining part of the original, when the prince, having met and fallen in love with the beautiful Kadambari, is ordered home by his father, and deep in the jungle comes across a shrine of Durga, described by Bana in great detail; no less detailed is the account of the Dravidian priest who attends this goddess. Quarrelsome, irritable, ill educated, he is a figure of fun. He is an exponent of all the New Age fads of the day. One eye has been destroyed by a fake ointment to make him all-seeing; to the other eye he applies collyrium three times a day; his singing sounds like the buzzing of flies. On and on goes the scornful account of impossible goals – alchemy, levitation, invisibility and more. The prince laughs aloud when he sees this strange figure, but is then polite to him, restrains his followers from tormenting him, and gives him money when he leaves. The elegant prince, tormented by love in separation, here views an almost complete panorama of southern Hinduism exemplified in the priest with the distant reserve reminiscent of a colonial administrator.

In fact Bana is playfully referring to what was certainly later a well-established theme in Indian literature, namely that of a king visiting a goddess of destruction in the jungle prior to going into battle (as in the *Gaudavaho* and the *Kalinkattupparani*). Goddesses were indeed to be found in jungles, not just in the Orientalist imagination. Bayly remarks on Inden's swingeing critique, 'Few authorities escape his blade. If at times he appears in the guise of the many armed goddess Kali strutting through the scholarly carnage sporting a necklace of academic skulls, his goal is still Regeneration.'[72] This *jeu d'esprit* by the most authoritative of British historians of India credits Inden with a power he does not in fact achieve, as well as likening him to a goddess he chooses to ignore. Furthermore, the analogy between Inden and Kali shows a power of imagination that Inden would not approve of, for imagination is the second object of Inden's witch-hunt, though it has unquestionably played a major part in Hinduism, just as it does in every culture.

Britain exploited India and exerted power over India in many ways, but Orientalist Indologists, inevitably contaminated to some extent by the prejudices of their age – how could they not be? – were not 'making a career of the East'. They sought mastery of a body of knowledge in a way somewhat parallel to that of a Sanskrit pandit. The procedures were different, but the goal of both was purely intellectual: Orientalists and traditional Indian scholars sought the power and glory of the intellect. The analysis offered by Said and Inden at first had a seductive thrill, an overturning of idols, the laying bare of the dialectic of self and other, and seemed to throw a powerful searchlight on the underside of the study of the East. But what this attempted and apparently successful deconstruction overlooks is what is in fact blindingly obvious. Orientalism in its original meaning was not oppression of the East, but the colonization of the Western mind by the East. It is the strength of Indian ideas and Indian texts that overpowers the Western scholar, and forces him to spend his life in willing servitude to them.

Thus concludes the second part of this study. In the next four chapters aspects of traditional Hinduism are considered, aspects chosen not only for their inherent importance, but also for the contrast they make to modernity.

Part III

Hinduism Contrasted with Modernity

Chapter Seven

'Woman Caste'(*aurat jati*) and the Gender of Modernity

Introduction

Mill claimed in his *History of British India* that a civilization should be judged by its treatment of women, and on that account Hinduism stood condemned.[1] This view was widely held in the West. For hundreds of years sati, widows burning to death on their husband's funeral pyre, was, along with the juggernaut, the primary fact of Hinduism for Europeans. In Western eyes, the Hindu woman today is perhaps the primary human exemplar of Hinduism and its divergence from modernity. It is the woman who has not adopted Western dress, who has to leave her family home and enter her husband's house for the rest of her life, or at least the rest of her husband's life, and who, if widowed, has to suffer humiliation and even degradation. At the same time, it is now widely understood in the West that the most remarkable feature of Hinduism, in comparison to other established religions, is the importance of goddesses within it. It is arguably in respect of women and goddesses that Hinduism displays its most marked difference from modernity.

And yet there is some common ground in this area between Hinduism and the modernity of the late nineteenth century, as it was the twentieth century that saw a radical change in attitudes to the feminine in the West. For the founding definers of modernity, Marx and Weber, woman was an inferior creature. What feminists now call biological essentialism dominated late nineteenth-century constructions of sexual difference. For the fin-de-siècle period, woman was a dangerous temptress whose magical powers in fact had some analogies with aspects of certain Hindu goddesses. Salome and Medusa became potent symbols of castration and phallic power subverted by the female. The phantasm of Freud's phallic mother expresses the symbolic temper of that time.[2] Today, after the revolutionary rethinking of gender carried out by the women's movement, briefly set out in chapter 1, a strong strand in feminism welcomes Hindu goddesses as a natural resource for all women to draw upon for role models and general inspiration. Thus what at first is an extreme contrast between Hinduism and modernity in respect of the female becomes, in some perspectives at least, a rapprochement. In this chapter I set out an overview of woman in Hinduism, beginning an evaluation that will continue into the following chapter on goddesses. We begin with woman both as a key to what is unique in Hinduism and as relevant to feminism, a major force for change in the world today.

Miss World

In 1996 the Miss World competition was held in India for the first time. An Indian entrepreneur with global interests arranged to parade the world's most beautiful women in Bangalore, India's most modern city. Ms K. N. Shashikala, president of the Women's Awakening Movement, had argued that wearing a bikini was an offence under Section 292 of the Indian Penal Code as it amounted to indecent exposure; the promoters therefore had to hold the bathing costume part of the competition elsewhere than on the sacred soil of Mother India, and this part of the competition was shunted off to the Seychelles. In Bangalore the backdrop of the contest's stage was based on Vijayanagara, the deserted city of the last Hindu empire of India, the archaeological glory of Bangalore's state. Sixteen elephants filed across this set, a reminder of the hundreds of elephants possessed by the last Hindu kings, and doubtless the number 16 signifying the quarters and intermediate points of the compass, and affirming the global nature of the event, watched as it was by an estimated two and a half billion people. Throughout the two and a half hours of television time, the global audience was regaled with a synthesis of Indian culture – except that Islamic motifs were removed.[3]

Prior to the event women protesters stormed the showroom of the Godrej company, official sponsors of the Miss World contest, and smeared it with engine oil and cow dung. The same day in the far south a man burnt himself to death at a bus stop in protest against the contest. Ms Shashikala threatened multiple human torches to stop the event. She and her supporters planned to mingle among the 20,000 spectators and ignite their own saris after swallowing cyanide to avoid the pain of being burned alive: 'We want to bring awareness among poor women and fight exploitation of women in all walks of life.' Other protesters carried around the city a 10-foot drawing of the contest organizer, film superstar Amitabh Bachchan, shown naked. The right wing also threatened action. Uma Bharati, BJP MP, addressed 300 protesters holding banners which said 'Stop Miss World Pageant – Save National Honour' and, referring to Amitabh Bachchan, 'Big B Means Bring Bad Culture to

Bharat'. Bharati, in her usual manner, vowed a bloodbath: 'We will give our lives, we will take away lives but we will prevent the Miss World contest.' Ten thousand policemen were brought into the city, and nearby schools and colleges were closed as a precaution, but the event took place without any further disturbances.

Feminist opponents of the contest protested against the equation of woman with her body, and the exploitation of women, while the Hindu right saw the contest as pushing Indian woman off her triple pedestal as mother, mother goddess and Mother India. *India Today* argued that the opposition was more general than these two extremes, that the silent majority of Indians felt that the very foundation of their culture, their Indianness, was at stake.

The Miss World competition was the point of focus for competing views of womanhood. One aspect not picked up in the press was its distant connection with one of the four aspects of Hinduism highlighted by Marx, namely the dancing-girl. This Oriental exotic, who titillated nineteenth-century Europe in several ballets and operas,[4] was at the same time exemplar of what the West found corruptly alien in Hinduism, for the female who danced in temples was a prostitute, contaminating religion with sexuality. In fact, although women had danced in temples all over India for hundreds of years, by the eighteenth century the Muslim dominated-north had only secular dance (*nautch*) performed by women. Only in the east of India, most notably in Puri, and in South India did the traditional role in worship of the temple dancer persist. Missionary pressure and then general Westernization of influential public opinion led to the banning of temple dancing at the beginning of the twentieth century. Eventually dancing was revived as fit for proper females in the 1940s, but only in the concert hall. But up to the eighteenth century Hindu temple art had rejoiced in the female form, as did Buddhist and Jain art: the earliest Buddhist sculpture rejoices in the voluptuous bodies of naked women. A far cry from 1996, when nearly naked women were not allowed to be viewed in public on the Indian mainland. In a similar example of modern Hindu prudery BJP MPs objected to the inclusion of a photograph of the famous nude Mohenjo Daro dancing-girl (*c.*2100–1700 BC) in the 1997 diary given out by the Delhi Tourism and Transportation Development Coroporation.[5]

Mother India

From the perspective of the West in the nineteenth century, the dancing-girl was only one of the blots on the Indian landscape. Worst of all was the unfortunate sati, the Hindu widow who immolated herself on her husband's funeral pyre. Bad too was the institution of child marriage, and bad was the general lot of women in India. An American, Katherine Mayo, gathered together every appalling instance of mistreated Indian females that she could find in her book ironically titled *Mother India* (1927).[6] Today, the condition of women remains the principal fault of India in the perception of the West, ahead of the caste system, general poverty, and interreligious strife.[7]

The Hindu female as she progresses through life might be described by a present-day Mayo in the following terms. Many are destroyed as foetuses: amniocentesis is cheap in India, and some parents prefer to avoid at the earliest possible stage the trouble and expense of providing a dowry for daughter. The rate of female infant mortality is notably higher than that of males. In the traditional brahmanic culture, man enjoys four life-stages, from student, to householder, to forest-dweller, to wandering ascetic, while woman has only two, girlhood and marriage. Despite laws prohibiting it and strong government propaganda, child marriage is not unknown. The dowry system, despite being illegal, flourishes. When the unwanted daughter marries, she goes for ever to the husband's home. However, should she not bring sufficient dowry, should some expected consumer item be missing, she is liable to be sent back, or even murdered, in what is claimed to be a kitchen accident. Since the woman, dressed in her flowing sari, squats on the ground beside her kerosene stove to cook, genuine accidents by burning are frequent; so too are proven cases of murder, entitled 'dowry deaths'.

The most prominent aspect of Hinduism in the mind of the West in the nineteenth century was the institution of sati, made illegal in British India in 1829. Here was the apotheosis, as it were, of the sad lot of Hindu womanhood, and of the unenlightened condition of Hinduism. The issue is topical, for the 1989 sati of an 18-year-old widow, Roop Kanwar, continues to resonate.

In addition to these newsworthy events, there are more intractable aspects of Hindu culture, such as the impure state attributed to menstruating women, and the inauspiciousness attributed to widows. India, land of the linga, would seem in many ways to be an extreme instance of patriarchy.

But let us now turn to the Indian view of Mother India. The 1957 film *Bharat Mata* ('Mother India'), one of the highest-grossing Indian movies of all time, has risen to the status of a national epic.[8] In it the heroine Radha, as an old woman, remembers her past. Overworked by their greedy landlord, she, her husband, and their three sons are already impoverished when the husband loses both his arms in an accident. He becomes a wandering beggar, and Radha is left to support her sons while fending off the advances of the landlord. When the buffalo that pulls the plough dies, she shoulders the plough. This invincible resolution is commemorated in the film poster, as she strains forward, the beam of the plough weighing her down. One son dies in a flood, one remains dutiful, the third becomes a rebel and kills the landlord. Radha shoots the bad son: 'In the end, the long-suffering Mother India can only put an end to her rebellious son's activities by killing him, . . . his blood fertilises the soil.'[9] At the close of her memories, she opens a new dam for the village.

The film is an affirmation of motherhood sublimated into the idea of the nation.

Salman Rushdie refers to this film in his novel, *The Moor's Last Sigh* (1995), and introduces into his story the film actress Nargis, who plays Mother India. Although the film is a portrayal of village India 'made by the most cynical urbanites in the world', says the narrator of the novel, 'its leading lady . . . became . . . the living mother goddess of us all'; in Rushdie's book Nargis says: 'In our picture we put stress on the positive side. Courage of the masses is there, and also dams.' In the novel, we have comment on the 'sexy lives' of movie people – 'to marry your own son, I swear, wowie' (in real life Nargis married the actor Sunil Dutt, who plays her bad son, Birju, in the film). Another character glosses, 'Sublimation . . . of mutual parent–child longings is deep-rooted in the national psyche.' The narrator sums up Radha, Mother India of the film, as 'the Indian peasant woman idealised as . . . stoical, redemptive, and conservatively wedded to the maintenance of the social status quo'; but he also notes that for the bad son she becomes 'that image of an aggressive . . . annihilating mother who haunts the fantasy life of Indian males'.[10]

It so happens that Nargis was a Muslim, and a former courtesan from Lucknow; the director, Mehboob Khan, was a Muslim socialist. The title Mother India, Bharat Mata in Indian languages, recalls the worship of India perceived as a goddess of that name. Bharat Mata first appears in Bankim Chattopadhyaya's novel *Anandamath* (1882), where she is addressed in the hymn *Vande Mataram*; she then became the empowering concept of the independence movement for Hindus. In Mehboob's film she takes human form, as befitted Nehru's secular India. The film critic Chidananda Das Gupta notes that Mehboob's mother figure is very much of the 1950s: in the films of the 1970s and 1980s the mother turns passive and is actively protected by her sons. 'The onus of action had passed on from the father to the mother and finally to the son.'[11] However, Bharata Mata was resuscitated as a political icon in the 1990s, as will be considered in chapter 12.

Shakti

Crucial to understanding the place of women in Hinduism, and indeed to understanding Hinduism, is awareness of the importance of goddesses. Goddesses are either the wives of gods or independent deities. In either case they are powerful. Independent goddesses are often bad-tempered, and may use their power maliciously. On the divine level power, in the sense of power to create, to act in the world, lies with the female rather than male. The name of this power, as of power in general, is *shakti*. In the Samkhya philosophy, nature is *prakriti*, the feminine force that produces and constitutes material reality. The other element of existence, for Samkhya, is consciousness, which has the significant name, *purusha*, 'Man'. The aim of the philosophy is expressed metaphorically as the man, who is consciousness, turning away from the entrancing sight of the female dancer, who is nature, and at last realizing his individual separateness. In the worship of the goddess Kali in Bengal, the relationship of *shakti* to consciousness is expressed by the image of Kali dancing or standing on the corpse-like Shiva, whose lack of movement shows the powerless state of consciousness. In Hindi, *shakti* means 'power, strength, force, electricity', a 'power' in the sense of a nation; the energy of a deity personified as his wife; and the female genitalia. *Shakti* is embodied in women rather than men. Men are sometimes said to have some *shakti*, but they lose it to women in the sexual act. Women's inner heat is said to be 10 times greater than men's: it is this force which enables them to give birth, to as it were cook the foetus in the same way as they cook the food that maintains the life of the family they have given birth to. The husband is born again in the son that originates from his wife's womb. Husband and children are all given life and physical sustenance by the wife.

Life stages of women

The distinctive place of women in Hindu culture is expressed by the common phrase, 'woman caste' (*aurat jati*). Descent in India is generally patrilinear, with the woman leaving her natal family to join her husband's family. Normally marriage is arranged, not only within the same caste, but often within specific regional lineages. Society is divided up into many castes and into the two 'castes' of male and female. For the orthodox, caste itself is a biological division of the same order as the biological division of the sexes.

A generalized account of the life stages of women will now be given. There are considerable differences between North and South India, not to speak of every region and every caste. What follows is truer of higher than of lower castes. It is important to note that the Western notion of an individual is – from the point of view of Hindu culture – an unreal abstraction. Real people only exist within families: they are daughters, sons, sisters, brothers; they are enmeshed in a network of necessary and inevitable relationships. The strength of those relationships is shown by the fact that within the family kinship terms are used as personal names in preference to given names.

Daughters

Hindus, then, are members of families rather than isolated individuals. But families are patrilinear. Descent is through the male line. A daughter, therefore, is only a visitor in her natal family. When she marries she will leave the paternal home and join her husband's family. When she has a son, and has thus contributed to the future continuance of the family, she will be a full-fledged member of that family. It necessarily follows that a daughter is not such a joyous event for the family as a son. On the other hand, as a visitor, who one day will leave for ever, she is the more precious, the love that is felt for her can be all the keener. There are also economic considerations. The son will support his parents in their old age. The daughter will be gone; and for her marriage a dowry is usually necessary. It is these economic constraints that lead to female infanticide and foeticide. Yet the parents have a duty to marry their daughters as well as they can. They will gain respect for marrying them well: their sons' marriage prospects will benefit from this, and thus the whole family will benefit.

The young child is a welcome member of the family, to be cared for and indulged in all possible ways. Infants are fed longer at the breast than in the West. The mother's milk transfers her life-force, her blood as it is thought to be, to the child. The food that the child receives continues the creation not only of its physical body, but also its moral and psychological character. A girl's ears and left nostril are pierced as early as the second year. To start with, clothing is minimal, but subsequently it clearly marks out the stages of female life. By the age of 10 a girl is wearing a long skirt and a blouse, though girls who are receiving secondary education will wear school uniform. With the approach of puberty, it is thought that a girl should not attract attention to herself. Girls working in the fields usually wear a half-sari, with their heads covered with one end of the cloth.[12]

Various life-stages are ritually marked out, as for instance the first taking of solid food, and the first steps. But whereas boys of the higher castes have an initiation ceremony to mark their coming of age, girls have no such ritual affirmation. For girls the physical change is more explicit. However, in South India especially, the flowering of maidenhood, the menarche, may be marked by family rejoicing. Often the girl will put on a red sari to mark the occasion. She will now experience the ritual seclusion of the menstrual period.

For higher castes, a menstruating woman is held to be impure. She does not cook, nor does she enter a temple during her period. With the second ritual bath on the fifth day a brahman woman is considered pure. The pure/impure distinction is not entirely physical, since after her second bath on the fifth day she is considered pure even if she is actually still menstruating. And if she has ceased menstruating prior to the fifth day, she is still impure until the second bath of the fifth day. The opposition between pure and impure exists in tandem with another pair of concepts: auspicious and inauspicious. Impurity consists in the raw power of physicality, purity in the refinement of culture. Impurity is the obtrusive presence of the facts of life: blood, the afterbirth, rotting flesh, faeces. These are transition states, the dangerous interstices of life, the hideous face of biology. But the menstruating woman is the potential bringer of new life, she is auspicious. The pre-menopausal widow, having no male partner, cannot give birth, and is on that account inauspicious, not to speak of her failure to keep her husband alive. The menstruating wife glories in her potentially fertile condition. The red tilak mark, and even more the line of red painted on the parting of her hair, directly relate to the auspicious redness of menstruation. The red powder placed on images worshipped by women is an indirect glorification of menstruation.

Wives

Traditionally a girl should be married on or before attaining puberty; from puberty she should live with her husband. The government strongly urges later marriage, the woman not before 21, the man not before 23 years of age. However, child marriage, although illegal, still occurs occasionally, for instance in castes of temple priests where the male is entitled to a share of the income of the temple when married, whatever his age.

The proper human, and divine, condition is that of marriage. Male and female combine to form a single entity. Marriage alters the natural and moral qualities of the couple:

> The external and internal bodily parts of the bride and groom, and the gross and subtle substances of which they are made, are operated on with a kind of energetic activity that is difficult for persons from Christian cultures to imagine. They are purified and protected by bathing and anointment, sprinkled with powerful fluids, and made to fast so that their bodies will be more susceptible to auspicious influences.[13]

Once in her new home, the new wife wears her brightest clothes along with the marriage necklace her husband has tied round her neck at marriage; she wears this until her husband's death. The bright clothes express her sexual flowering. It is at this time that it is most important for her to be veiled, especially in the presence of her father-in-law or her husband's elder brothers. All her sexuality, even its outer appearance, is preserved for the husband whose duty it is to impregnate her. In the marriage ceremony, after he has marked the parting of his wife's hair with vermilion powder, symbolically activating her uterine blood for the birth of a son, he pulls the end of her sari over her face. She is from now onwards, for the rest of her life, faithful to her husband (*pativrata*).

The biological oneness in duality of the married couple mirrors the unity of god and goddess. All the Hindu law books agree that the foremost duty of a wife is to obey her husband and to honour him as her god. The good wife is *pativrata*, devoted to her husband. Whether or not her husband is worthy of her is irrelevant. As long as she honours him, she is honourable, she is – though this is not usually explicit – goddess to his god. The *shakti* within her is divine.

She is a manifestation of *shakti*. The mother of a son with her husband living is highly auspicious, the quintessence of prosperity, fertility, and success. With her oiled hair, adorned with fresh flowers, her gold ornaments, her silk sari, her well-fed flesh gleaming with rubbed-in oil and perfume, adorned with henna drawings, the auspicious woman (*sumangali*) is triumphant life-force.

In the marriage ceremony the couple walk seven times round the sacred fire. A marriage song from North India spells out the bride's male relations at each circuit, beginning, 'Here she makes the first circle, her grandfather's granddaughter', and so on, until the final: 'Here she makes the seventh circle, and lo! the darling becomes alien to our family.' On the penultimate circle, she is 'her brother's sister': it is the brother who is closest male relation – and often closest male friend. In North India, where stress is placed on the bride's family giving her as a free gift to her husband, her natal family cannot receive any hospitality in her marital home, and therefore cannot visit her at all. This restriction does not apply to younger brothers.

Mothers

It is only by the birth of a son that a wife becomes a full member of the affinal family. Only with the son does she contribute to the continuation of the lineage. In traditional terms, she also saves her husband from falling into the hell of those who do not have a son, for the son will feed the spirit of his father after death.

The relationship between mother and son is especially close. Arranged marriage being the norm, affection and love between spouses build up slowly. The son, who transforms the status of the new wife, receives a correspondingly greater emotional charge from his mother. This in turn results in sons being all the more deeply emotionally connected with their mothers, and the more remote from their new wives. In this system, the male is the more ready to accept the existence of very powerful females, and of goddesses. Prolonged breast feeding – till 4, even 8, years of age – gives more conscious awareness and memory of receiving the mother's breast, and also of being eventually denied it. The latter case, it has been suggested, gives rise to the notion of angry and denying supernatural beings.

The milk-giving mother is exalted in the form of the cow, symbol of Hinduism for several centuries, famous in myth as Shabala, the divine cow derided by Marx. First thrown into stronger focus by being eaten by Muslim conquerors, the selfless giver of milk came to have a numinous glow for Hindus. Milk products are crucial for vegetarian Indians. No less than the cow, the mother is the core of Hinduism. In ritual the key marker of divinity and prosperity is the pot filled with liquid. Ritually sanctified by mantras, each container is a womb of life and goodness. The process of conception and giving birth is endlessly replicated in religion.

In due course the mother of a son becomes a mother-in-law, receiving into her house a daughter-in-law, who will now become the junior female adult, under her mother-in-law's command. The mother-in-law is now by definition an old woman, who should dress in muted colours. One merit of this system is that age brings dignity and moral power within the family. In North India, the mother often has control over the wife's sexual activity by disciplining behaviour she disapproves of and by being in charge of the sleeping quarters.[14]

Widow and sati

If a husband dies before his wife, she has failed in her duty to preserve her lord, either through actual neglect, or through her bad karma. The wife's ability to preserve her husband is asserted by the belief in Tamilnadu that if she removes her marriage disk (*thali*) from her neck while her husband is alive his death will result from her action.

On her husband's death the widow breaks her bangles, wears only white saris, and no longer puts the red marks on her forehead and hair parting. Her forehead is marked with the yellow of sandalwood paste. Her hair should be short or shaved off. She is no longer auspicious, and therefore does not attend wedding ceremonies. She is a living instance of the unfortunate fact that male–female complementarity is not a permanent state. The position of a widow who has a son is utterly different from one who does not. In the best case, she is the honoured and powerful mistress of the household, in command of her daughter-in-law. In the worst, she is helpless.

Widows may seek solace in religion, and take up their abode in holy places. Mathura, home of the young god Krishna, is well known for its hymn-halls, institutions endowed for the support of widows to sing hymns in praise of Krishna. The good accommodation provided by the original endowments has been sold off, and widows receive little more than some rice for their long hours of recitation.

Temple dancing-girls avoided widowhood by marrying the god of the temple. Newar girls in Nepal may marry a bel fruit in a mock marriage before puberty, which means that nominally they will never be widows, but as widows they do in fact experience considerable loss of status.[15] In a remarkable film, *Sati*, set in late nineteenth-century Bengal, a dumb girl whose horoscope says her husband will die young naturally has trouble finding a husband. Her elders marry her to a tree. The film ends with a storm, and she is found dead beside her uprooted 'husband'. The horoscope was correct, and she has become a genuine sati, dying with her husband.

'The widow is the emblem of the culture's failure to perfect the ordinary world of experience.'[16] Husband and wife form a joint entity. This culturally produced entity cannot exist without the husband. If the wife dies, she can be replaced. Only birth can bring new males into the patrilinear system. Unless she can marry a brother of her dead husband, the living widow is in cultural terms irreparably damaged. The cultural solution is a terrible one. By dying on her husband's funeral pyre, the joint entity that is the married couple remains pure and unsullied. By this triumphant demonstration of her devotion to her husband, she will join him in their next rebirth, and will be honoured for ever by her family and lineage. The notorious case of Roop Kanwar, mentioned above, who committed sati in Rajasthan in 1989, sparked off a revival of interest in sati, and led to the creation of more than 100 new sati temples. The literature on sati is extensive,[17] but general consideration of the Hindu woman is easily skewed by excessive attention to what is in fact a very rare event.

Women's spheres of action

Hindu women today play prominent roles in all political spheres,[18] and indeed all spheres of life, but their place has traditionally been in the home. The organization of the Indian house removes the women's quarters as far as possible from its public area. For orthodox high-caste families, seclusion of women is desirable. Certain Tamil temple priestly castes claim that their wives 'do not cross the threshold' – do not leave the house. Until 10 years ago there existed in Tamilnadu a complex of houses combined in a mud-brick fort, where lived a sub-caste whose wives never left the precincts. The home is the woman's realm. This is dramatically demonstrated in Shyam Benegal's film *Ankur* ('The Seedling'). A group of village men are drunkenly gambling. One gambles away his wife, as does Yudhishthira in the *Mahabharata*. The next morning the winner comes to collect his winnings. The wife, who is big and strong, comes to the door, listens to her husband's recital of events, then shouts, 'I'll teach you the real *Mahabharata*', roughly pulls her husband inside and slams the door in the face of the other men of the village.

In the joint family household, the husband and wife may not regularly sleep together, the wife being in the women's quarters and the husband with the men. Or, if the couple have their own bedroom, it may be shared with children. The parents' sexual activity may well not be hidden from these children. Although sleeping quarters may be indeterminate, this is not true of the kitchen, which is indeed the most important room in the house, and is kept physically clean and ritually pure. As the purest room it is the appropriate place for the family shrine, when there is not a separate shrine room. The wife is here parallel to the priest, serving the family as the priest serves the temple deity. Food cooked in the kitchen is offered to the gods as well as to the family.

Cooking for the gods and goddesses is an activity that requires specialized knowledge. An informed familiarity with the palates and predilections of the household deities is essential. This information is passed down from wives to daughters and daughters-in-law. Daily offerings invariably include sweetmeats and fruits, made to please the taste of the particular deity being served, while more elaborate meals are prepared for special occasions.[19]

A major religious activity within the home is the vows taken by women. These are direct contracts with deities made exclusively by women, who undertake some form of personal deprivation such as periodic fasting in return for the sought-after boon. Authority for these vows is given by folk rhymes and stories. A famous cinema example is *Jai Santoshi Ma* ('In Praise of Mother Santoshi'), where the heroine first vows to visit all the goddess Santoshi's shrines in order to win a husband, and then vows to eat chick peas every Friday to get him back after he goes missing. The housewife's ceaseless concern for her family is also demonstrated by the rice-flour patterns made daily at the threshold in order to domestically replicate the true order of the well-lived life.

In a society where marriages are arranged by parents and public expression of affection between husband and wife is curtailed, compensatory romance in the arts is perhaps to be expected. The classical arts of Hinduism aim at producing pure and distinct emotions in the audience of the artwork. A parallel codification is to be found in the most vigorous of Indian art forms, the cinema. Here passionate romantic love is the norm, with eroticism emphasized by elaborate dance sequences, the principal actors mouthing the words of playback singers, with vocabulary simple and passion-laden. Divisions of class, caste, and even religion are readily crossed in the world of film. The heroine frequently runs the gamut of actions from demurest girlishness to extreme anger and bravery, all accomplished with endless changes of wardrobe.

Courtesans have been prominent in Indian culture from the time of the Buddha, who lunched with a famous courtesan and was given a mango grove by her. The role of the courtesan in the classical tradition is brilliantly presented in Dandin's (seventh-century) *Ten Princes' Stories*. A famous ascetic is approached by the grumbling mother of a courtesan, who brings her daughter with her. The mother complains that her daughter ignores clients because of her foolish wish to be an ascetic herself. She lists the expensive education that has been invested in the girl: 'thorough training in dance, song, instrumental music, acting, painting, also judgement of foods, perfumes, flowers, not forgetting writing and graceful speech; a conversational acquaintance with grammar and logic; profound skill in money-making, sport, and betting'. The girl stays in the forest to be brought to her senses. The ascetic falls head over heels in love with her. They drive to the city park, and, presenting the infatuated ascetic to the assembled court, she wins the bet she made that she would seduce him.

There is a great gulf between the surviving instances of temple prostitution and the glorious sculptural representations of sexual activity at certain Hindu temples. In some parts of South India particular castes still dedicate daughters to the goddess Yellama and a life of prostitution. Prostitution is a major problem in India today. Trafficking in children and women from Nepal and Assam is unchecked, and HIV is widespread.

One of the most remarkable women of modern India was the bandit Phoolan Devi, who reportedly slaughtered 20 landowners to avenge her rape, won a pardon, and became an MP. A popular film, *Bandit Queen*, was made about her, despite her protests against the screening of the rapes she suffered.[20] She was murdered in Delhi in 2001.

There are several examples in the history of North India of ruling queens who die in battle defending their kingdoms. Known as 'warrior women', they are depicted on horseback brandishing swords above their heads, female counterparts of the Rajput ideal. The Nautanki form of popular drama adds fictional instances of this ideal, where princesses attract humble lovers and, when their fathers are about to punish such presumption, ride to their lover's rescue sword in hand. Hansen notes,

> On the Nautanki stage, the visual symbology of cross-dressing arguably possesses voyeuristic appeal, and like other character transformations based on physical disguise it plays to the theatregoer's fascination with illusion and deception. It disturbs gender boundaries and masks in confusion the essential difference between female and male, much to the delight of an audience socialized to rigid codes of gendered dress and gesture.

But, Hansen goes on to say, the warrior woman arrives when moral order needs to be restored: 'Like the great goddess, she manifests her creative energy to restore the world to righteousness.'[21]

In addition to *shakti*, the power present in all women, some women also exemplify special religious powers. Suffice it to note here the important tradition of medieval female saints, and the activity today of female god-women. The female saint, such as Karaikal Ammaiyar, Andal, Lalla, and Mirabai, typically starts with a husband but then devotes herself to her chosen deity. The famous names have written poems and songs that have preserved their fame.

The foregoing summary of academic understanding of the Hindu female may seem stilted and unsubtle to a Hindu. A parallel treatment of, say, the British in the India of the Raj (leaving aside their arrogant ignorance of the culture they lived next to) would note that they lived in a world largely deprived of children, their children being sent away to school in England at an age when some Hindu boys are still drinking from their mother's breast. Boys were sent to private schools where buggery was often prevalent. Emotional life was stilted and often perverse. The wicked and perverted police inspector Ronald Merrick in Paul Scott's *Raj Quartet* (1976), though not from an Indian army family, would be an archetypal figure. In dealing with large topics it is difficult to avoid stereotypes. The foregoing account of Hindu women scarcely hints at the complexity, the subtlety, the richness of Hindu family life.

Gender and modernity

It is fruitful to distinguish between early and late modernity, between the founding definitions of twentieth-century modernity and the crumbling modernity of the later part of the twentieth century. Nietzsche, manifesting the biological essentialism of the second half of the nineteenth century, claimed that a man who 'has depth of spirit . . . can only think of woman as Orientals do: he must conceive of her as a possession . . . predestined for service – he must take his stand in this matter upon the immense rationality of Asia'.[22] He compares woman to a cat: 'her genuine, carnivora-like, cunning flexibility, her tiger-like claws beneath the glove . . . the dangerous and beautiful cat, "woman"'.[23] This comparison is exemplified in much fin-de-siècle art, with the lion's or tiger's head representing a woman's vagina.[24] A parallel reading may be given of full-frontal representations of Durga astride her tiger. Such symbolism is not discussed and is presumably not overt for Hindus.[25]

In modernity such as it is today, where feminism plays an ever greater role, Hindu femininity is a prime instance of subjection to patriarchy, to the phallus. Veena Geetha, in a paper on Indian men's violence against women, remarks on how men claim public space by publicly urinating on busy streets, next to a girls' school for instance; and on how their hands stray to their crotches even on stage at public meetings:

> It is as if a man prescribes not only those territorial norms which define home and the world, but he prescribes them in such a way, that he is able to inscribe on to either, literally and ideologically, the mark of the phallus . . . In fact, male body language, if carefully studied, will indicate how a man often presents himself as a penis writ large.[26]

For feminists, Indian and Western, Hinduism is a prime example of phallic patriarchy. However, it is interesting to note the difficulty of escaping from the language of the phallus, inasmuch as Jacques Lacan, whose theories are a major source of modern feminist thinking on gender, makes much use of it, though for him it is a linguistic rather than a physical reality. In Lacan's view, the self has no essential qualities, being constructed rather than born; and thus gender is a construct rather than a genetic destiny. Even so, Roberto Speziale-Bagliacca argues that 'the phallus evoked by Lacan, which allegedly brings knowledge, in fact brings subjugation and desperation' because one's mother and one's 'feminine part . . . have become threatening because they have been driven out, lost for ever'.[27] Without going into the detail of the elaborate counter-mythologies of various schools of psychoanalysis, it is salutary to look at the straightforward acceptance of human sexuality in classical Hinduism, in particular as represented in Shaivism.

The linga and yoni

The linga is worshipped by Shaivas as the central pillar of the universe, but it is definitely a phallus. Childless women may sit upon it, to be impregnated by Shiva. Milk is dripped upon it, inverting the production of the milk of semen from this convex-topped pillar that is not unlike a nippleless breast. That the linga is phallic is often denied by Hindus today. Even an extremely well-informed textual scholar such as N. Ramachandra Bhatt, who has written an authoritative account of Shaivism, is reluctant to acknowledge the phallic aspect, holding it to be late and of minor importance. He finds the linga's origin to be the Vedic sacrificial post.[28] He thus ignores the overwhelming case for the linga as phallus presented by its earliest appearance at Gudimallam in physiologically realistic form (in the third century BC), representations of phallic worship in Buddhist art, and the many Kushana coins (in the first to second centuries AD) which show Shiva as ithyphallic. Bhatt thus manifests what is perhaps a Victorian attitude to sexuality, found in India from the nineteenth century.

But the linga sits in the yoni, in the vagina of the goddess. Formally – though utterly unlike in spirit – the positions of the linga and the yoni correspond to a drawing by Hans Bellmer (1902–75), of a girl or doll lying back, with a erect penis rampant from her vagina, the vagina 'inside out' like the finger of a glove according to Jean Clair.[29] The linga rises up out of the yoni rather than penetrating it. Nor does the representation of the yoni (*pindika yoni*) make any claim to exact realism, being a circular trough with a conduit leading off; indeed precisely the shape needed to deal with the *abhishekas*, the various liquids which are ritually poured over the linga in worship. In the installation of a linga, after the linga has been set upright the yoni is lowered down on to it, like a ring on a finger. It might well be that the trough was initially merely a drainage convenience and was only later perceived to be a representation of the yoni. Nevertheless, the sexual organs of both sexes receive theological acknowledgement and direct worship.

The basic parameters of women's lives within traditional Hinduism have been set out. The issues raised here will be taken further in the following chapter, where it will be seen that Hindu women cannot be understood without reference to goddesses.

Chapter Eight

Kali East and West

Introduction

To begin again with beginnings: the baby in the womb, the baby at the breast, the child at the breast, the child and the mother; the mother as all, the mother as universe, the universal mother. Here lie the origins of the goddess, and the origins of Brahman, when we look reductively. If we discuss Hindu religious experience in relation to human biology, we should logically begin with the neuter absolute of the Upanishads, Brahman, for this may be seen as a regression to the unitary experience of the womb, where there is no inner or outer, where all needs are automatically met. But it is the female that provides this environment. Although the goddess can be identified with Supreme Brahman, we shall leave the unitary plenitude that is the result of the identification of the Hindu self with Supreme Brahman until a later chapter, and concentrate on the religious connotations of the child as drinker of the mother's milk.

The circle of the all-giving breast circumscribes the infant's universe. Weaning is very gradual, and is complete only at a relatively late age. The importance of the mother's breast is mirrored by the cow's teat. According to Gandhi, the cow is even more meritorious than the human mother, since she gives her milk to the farmer without wanting anything in return. Milk products are particularly important for vegetarians, and the cow became the key symbol of Hinduism from the time of the Muslim invasions. Milk is shown to be a key constituent of the sacred universe when the gods and demons churn the milk ocean to produce the nectar of immortality in a process modelled on the production of butter.

In the local myth of the temple city of Chidambaram in South India, the infant son of the first worshipper of Shiva's dance of bliss is fed milk from the divine cow when he stays with his maternal aunt, Vasishtha's wife. Returning home he is fed only on roots and fruit, the standard ascetic fare. He cries so much at this deprivation that his parents pray to Shiva, who at once responds by bringing the milk ocean to earth, thus forming one of Chidambaram's several holy tanks.[1] In the standard mythical geography, the world is composed of concentric continents and oceans. The milk ocean is only one of these oceans, but the circular world, the central mountain-nipple, and the milk ocean suggest that the whole world is modelled on the mother's breast.

Breast-feeding continues longer in India than the West for several cultural reasons: because of the greater importance of the child,[2] because of the greater importance of milk, the prime form of sustenance, because of the formation of the child from the substance of the mother, perhaps also because of the contraceptive effects of longer breast-feeding. Because breast-feeding continues longer, the child is more aware of itself and its milk-giving mother as separate entities, and more aware of its mother at last withdrawing her beneficence. The child has a clear perception of its mother as all-giving, but also as all-denying.

The emotional bond between mother and son carries greater cultural weight than in the West. The bride enters her husband's family as a stranger; even her husband is a stranger to her. The birth of a son incorporates her into the lineage of the family; and her relationship with her son can be more intense than with her husband. It is common practice for the mother to fondle and kiss the penis of her baby son. Her husband, like her son, will have had an intense, even overwhelming, relationship with his mother in early childhood, a relationship that leaves him diffident with his wife. Thus the wife's relationship with the husband is emotionally weaker than in the West, and the mother's relationship with the son is emotionally more intense. Many writers have noted this; particularly valuable is the work of the psychoanalyst Sudhir Kakar;[3] but Freud's own discernment in respect of India has only recently been revealed. Mulk Raj Anand (b. 1905), the great novelist, has mentioned in an interview that after his first nervous breakdown he was told by Freud that he was suffering from the 'mother fixation syndrome': 'Like most Indians you love your mother more than your father and to you every woman is a mother image.'[4]

In one important respect, however, the son's relationship with the mother is muted. The son is the continuation not just of his father but of all the patrilinear kinship group, all of whose members have a stake in his future reproduction which will be its own continuation. The nurture and protection of this new individual is the concern of all the females of the family. In the words of Stanley Kurtz, 'Hindu mothering is multiple mothering.'[5] Exclusivity between mother and child would weaken the joint family. Around the shared hearth all the women act as mothers to all the children. Thus the strong bond between mother and child is at the same time a strong bond with multiple mothers. The family situation predisposes not only to a goddess, refraction of the mother's power, but also to multiple goddesses, refractions of multiple mothers.

Not all goddesses are nice. A distinction can immediately be made between beautiful, giving goddesses such as Lakshmi, and fierce, dangerous goddesses such as Kali, black and redolent of death. Here the common reductive explanation, as already noted, is that the long-given breast is withdrawn from the conscious child, who is thus forcefully confronted by the mother who denies the breast. In Kakar's view, excellently summed up by Jeffrey Kripal, 'this "maternal-feminine" complex, these years of blissful but conflicted merger with the mother . . . functions as the hegemonic narrative of Hindu culture'.[6]

Another direction taken by reductive explanation is to distinguish between married and unmarried goddesses. Married goddesses are mild and controlled; unmarried goddesses are wild, uncontrolled, dangerous – Kali is the supreme example here. All this is exact transposition of the belief that unmarried women are dangerous, superheated by their rampant, unsatisfied sexuality, while married women are, so to speak, damped down. Women's sexual heat is said to be 10 times greater than that of men. Metalworking castes worship their furnaces as manifestations of Kali.

If the foregoing seems to Western feminists primarily the invention of men, it must be pointed out that such views are equally often expressed by women. The perspective of women is also apparent in a plethora of minor spirits who affect women and are held to have been women: women who died as virgins, or in childbirth, or without ever having given birth are dangerous, vengeful forces. Wives who die on their husbands' funeral pyres are subsequently powerful forces for good within their families, especially in Rajasthan.[7]

I begin with such explanations to aid comprehension, but also so that we can pass beyond simplification to understand the cultural and psychological richness of the phenomenon of goddesses in India. Take Kali, for instance. Kali, as the most striking of Hindu goddesses, has aroused much interest in the West, first horror and then fascination. Even so, Rachel McDermott, talking on this theme in Calcutta, was amazed to discover that her educated Bengali audience entirely dissented from such a view of Kali. For them, Kali was nothing but an all-loving mother. Familiar from earliest childhood with her form, they felt no horror.[8] Her protruding tongue, necklace of cut-off heads dripping blood and girdle of lopped-off arms had no power left to shock. Kali in Bengal is just one instance of the infinitely complex interrelationship of goddesses with the Hindu culture that gave rise to them and in which they flourish. For many Hindus they are real entities; on the level of analysis in this book, they are as real as anything else in the cultural matrix – indeed, they are the matrix.

Devimahatmya

Images that seem to have been representations of goddesses have been found in the remains of the Indus Valley civilization (*c*.2000 BC). Some seals show what seem to be a goddess in a tree receiving animal sacrifice, and perhaps the offering of a human head. Goddesses played little part in the religion of Vedic times, as far as we can tell from the texts. The goddess Lakshmi is mentioned in a hymn appended to the *Rig Veda*, but the first text to give a clear account of Hindu goddesses is the *Devimahatmya* ('Hymn to the Glory of the Goddess') around the fifth century AD. The central episode describes the goddess Durga killing a buffalo demon. Stone images of a goddess killing a buffalo go back to 100 BC around Mathura in North India.

The *Devimahatmya* is in three sections. The first describes how Vishnu, asleep on the cosmic ocean, is about to be attacked by two demons produced from his own ear wax. Brahma, sitting precariously in the lotus that has sprung from Vishnu's navel, saves the day by praying for the goddess who is illusion and the sleep of yoga to leave Vishnu's body so that he can deal with the danger that threatens. She does leave after being praised as universal goddess, and Vishnu kills his opponents. Land amid the ocean is formed by their squashed bodies.[9] What is required of the goddess here, as in the case of a disease goddess, is her absence.

The second episode is the only one that concerns the buffalo demon, Mahisha. Mahisha through his asceticism is given the boon by Brahma that he can only be slain by a woman. Thus empowered, he drives the lesser gods out of Indra's heaven: they appeal to Shiva and Vishnu for assistance. The anger of the assembled gods coalesces to form a incandescent mass that then solidifies into a beautiful goddess, Durga. They each give her a replica of a key attribute or property of their own. Thus kitted out, she confronts the buffalo, who after some shape-changing is finally pinned down and killed.

The third episode is noticeably artificial: here the goddess, under the name Ambika, fights not one but two demons, and each demon has a general. This doubling up, I think, mirrors the fact that the episode is a restatement in some sense of the foregoing episode, in order to explain the origin of Kali and the seven mother goddesses. Kali issues forth from the frown of Ambika in battle as a yet more furious form, and another name of Kali, Chamunda, is explained as a combination of the names of the two demon generals, whose heads she cuts off as a human sacrifice. The mothers, the Matrikas, are shown to be emanations from seven male gods, and at the end of the battle disappear into Ambika's body. At the beginning of the episode Ambika comes forth from Parvati, Shiva's wife. Thus various forms of the goddess come forth from the goddess's body or merge into it. The unity of the goddess is thus graphically expressed.

Ambika here is a mid-point between the mild, married Parvati and the wild, uncontrollable Kali who issues from her frown. Each of the episodes may be seen as a consciously artistic working over of the root facts of goddess worship. The third episode explains the origins of several forms of the goddess, the first implicitly links up goddesses who possess and bring disease with the ultimate goddess. The middle episode proceeds most transparently. For thousands of years male buffalo have been sacrificed. Expendable because they do not provide milk and only a few are necessary for the reproduction of the herd, they are eaten in village feasts, their blood providing fertility for the soil. The central episode works this into the Hindu pantheon, with the goddess made a heroine saviour figure on a par with the great gods Vishnu and Shiva. She is unmarried, but she is made up of gods. As the combined radiance of the gods, the female power of Durga encompasses and surpasses the masculine power of the gods and overwhelms the masculine power of the demon.

Durga as the goddess associated with a lion or tiger has very ancient roots; the fin-de-siècle reading of the symbolic implications was referred to in the preceding chapter. She also has many modern manifestations. Mother India, Bharat Mata, is often shown as Durga, with her lion beside her superimposed upon the map of India. During the Indo-Pakistan war of 1971, Indira Gandhi was readily perceived as Durga. The notorious Phoolan Devi, the female bandit, had her own rapport with Durga. When Phoolan surrendered to the authorities, she stipulated that the platform on which she did this should have pictures both of Durga and of Mahatma Gandhi. Her gang thought of her as Durga. She and they worshipped Durga.[10]

Kali is only one of many goddesses in Hinduism. Lakshmi, goddess of prosperity, has textual authority centuries older than the *Devimahatmya*. The late Vedic hymn to her is often used in ritual. She is the goddess of ordinary life, of the household, and all mundane concerns. Rising gorgeously yellow from the white lotus, she symbolizes gold and all things yellow, white and good: milk, nectar, butter, beauty. The divine cow was produced beside her at the churning of the milk ocean. She herself is the giver of the soothing milk of prosperity. The public display of wealth, the public display of the wealth goddess, is part and parcel of the glorious state of the auspicious wife (*sumangali*) whose husband and son are living, her body oiled, in silk sari, fresh flowers in her hair, and gold ornaments – all this reflecting her moral worth.

But if a goddess like Lakshmi, who as good fortune fickly comes and goes, is on public display in popular calendar prints in workplace, home, and temple, there are more secret goddesses whose delivery of wealth is more certain the more complex their rituals. Such goddesses are set like the princesses of fairy stories within guarded palaces. These palaces, with their successive courtyards, may be painted in full, or set out only schematically in the sacred diagrams called yantras. All gateways are guarded, and successive ranks of attendant deities must also be negotiated by the devotee's mental devotion.

There are yantras for many deities, but especially for goddesses. The supreme yantra is the Shri Chakra, nine interlaced triangles the interstices of which form a series of enclosures with a single triangle in the centre, standing on its point, symbol of femininity, the pubic triangle. The inner enclosures are set within a double lotus, and implicit in the Shri Chakra is a representation of the vagina and womb: the ritual, which explicitly works back to the origin of the universe, may be seen as expressing a return to the womb. At the centre dwells Rajarajeshvari, supreme empress, who is enthroned on top of the male gods. Worship of the Shri Chakra is associated with the philosopher Shankara, and the pontiffs of his monastic order worship the Shri Chakra. In this theology, the goddess herself becomes Brahman, supreme consciousness and supreme reality. Even she is not devoid of fierceness, however, in that most of her attendants are fierce, expressing or symbolizing negative emotions.

Sita

Lakshmi herself, after the independent appearance in her early hymn, features in iconography and myth mainly as the spouse of Vishnu; and the female partners of that god's *avataras* are considered to be versions of Lakshmi. The two heroines of the two epics are both associated with Lakshmi, though their stories, characters and subsequent histories differ greatly. Sita wears divinity very lightly: like Rama she is principally an exemplar of the ideal human, and as the ideal wife her role has continued more or less unchanged up to the present.

At the close of the second canto of the *Ramayana*, the banished Rama and Sita visit the seer Atri. Atri's wife, Anasuya, is herself an illustrious ascetic, who ended a 10-year drought by making the Jahnavi river flow, and has practised intense asceticism for 10,000 years. Anasuya, her skin wrinkled and loose, trembling like a plantain tree in the wind, tells Sita that to a woman of noble nature her husband is the supreme deity, however bad he may be. Sita politely replies that she knows this. Her husband behaves to all women as he does to his mother. Her mother taught her how to behave. Her mother-in-law has taught her how to behave. And she refers to famous exemplars: Savitri is exalted in heaven because she showed obedience to her husband, so too Arundhati. Rohini is never separate from her husband the moon. Women firm in their vows to their husbands are exalted in the world of the gods. Delighted with these words, the old female ascetic makes use of the power her austerities have gained to give the young woman a heavenly garland, raiment, jewellery and an everlasting beauty cream. Applying that cream to her body, Sita will adorn her husband to the same degree that Shri adorns the eternal Vishnu. Anasuya then asks to hear a tale that she is fond of, the story of Sita's choosing (*svayamvara*) of Rama. Sita obliges, adding the story of her own birth from a furrow ploughed by her childless father. Anasuya embraces her and praises the sweetness of her speech, the clarity of each word and syllable.

Here is much of the Hindu wife encapsulated. Sita, the paradigm of womanhood herself, relies on advice from mother and mother-in-law and the example of earlier heroines such as Savitri, who saved her husband from the world of death; Sita, who despite banishment in the forest is elegantly dressed as befits a sexually active Shakti, and who is brought to perfection by beauty cream. It is Sita who is proclaimed up to the present day by most Hindus, men and women, as the model Hindu wife.

Draupadi

Although over time, after the original epics, both Sita and Draupadi develop reputations as cooks, Draupadi is otherwise very different from Sita. In her previous incarnation, as Nalayani, Draupadi is a good wife (*sati*) not least because she remains devoted to her foul-smelling and eventually leprous husband. When one of his fingers drops off into the rice bowl, she is unperturbed and eats the rice. Pleased by this action, the husband grants her a boon. She asks for him to take on a fivefold body and grant her sexual fulfilment. He accedes to this request, but after thousands of years tires of it. She begs him to continue, but, angered by her importunity he curses her to have five husbands in her next life to assuage her lust. She is greatly upset at this fate, and practises severe austerities, amid the five fires (four fires and the sun overhead), to seek Shiva's help – dulling the radiance of her beauty in the process. Shiva promises five husbands each the equal of Indra – these, of course, will be the five Pandavas she will marry as Draupadi. This after-the-fact explanation is realistic in relating the multiplicity of husbands to excess of desire, and idealistic in combining this with perfect obedience. Draupadi herself in the *Mahabharata*, born from a sacrificial fire, is forceful, urging her husbands to carry out her will. Like Sita, she is threatened with violation, but her epic is realistic, not a fairy story like Sita's. Draupadi is assaulted within the family, by her husbands' cousin, Sita by an outlandish stranger. While Sita (whose name means 'furrow') rose up from the earth her father was ploughing, Draupadi was born from the sacrificial fire into which her mother was making an offering. One of M. F. Husain's paintings of Draupadi shows her tumbling backwards, large dice crashing on top of her. This entirely fails to capture what is her most characteristic feature: her dignity and poise in the most undignified of situations, her determination to seek revenge, her worthy righteousness at all times. Nevertheless, the attempt to strip her in public after Yudhishthira has gambled her away, although she is saved by Krishna's divine power endlessly extending her sari, resonates with many women as an expression of women's vulnerability.[11]

Folk goddesses

In the *Mahabharata*, the bedtime arrangements neatly show the relative importance of mother and wife, Kunti sleeping beside the aligned heads of her sons, and Drapaudi, their wife, at their feet. But after her humiliation at the dice match some of the folk traditions of South India present a very different picture from the epic. In the epic Draupadi resembles Kali inasmuch as her hair is always unbound, having sworn to lack this restraint until she gains vengeance for her treatment in the dice match. In folk traditions, she takes on the form and character of Kali at night. Leaving her husbands sleeping, she roams the forest, devouring whatever living creatures she can find.

There is a huge variety of Hindu folk goddesses, goddesses known only in a few villages, or only in one region, or in the north or south, whose stories are not given in the Sanskrit tradition, but are still living presences on their own ground. Knowledge of them has until recently been restricted largely to their own locale. In the past this was partly due to a lack of interest in goddesses on the part of non-Hindus: thus, Bishop Woodhead's readable and still useful work entitled *Village Gods of South India* (1921) is almost entirely about goddesses, but will not confess as much in the title! One folk goddess of recent origin (1964) among a fishing community in Andhra Pradesh, Raman Amma, is believed to have come from New York! Her temple contains the model of an ocean tanker.[12] She is a cholera goddess who in her myth is worshipped by her seven brothers. Among the fishing caste she belongs to, married sisters become their brothers' trading partners, buying and selling their fish. Charles Nuckolls explains that her myth may be seen as an exploration of what life would be like if sisters were never alienated from their brothers.[13]

A very famous instance of a recent goddess is Santoshi Ma, an unknown who made the big time in a film (*Jai Santoshi Ma*, 1975), dozens of temples springing up after she was brought to the notice of the nation. Until then only an occasional pamphlet gave the brief story of Satyavati, the devotee who overcame her misfortunes by observing her vow to Santoshi Ma of eating chick peas every Friday. The film begins by showing the creation of the goddess, acknowledging her novelty. Ganesha's two sons lament the absence of a sister when it is the festival for sisters tying a protective wristlet on their brothers, and their father graciously accedes to their request. The girl is born instantly from a lotus. After she has performed the ritual for her brothers, the film then switches to the image of a full-grown Santoshi Ma, in a red sari and holding a large trident, worshipped in her temple by a bevy of rural dancing-girls. Satyavati undergoes much ill-treatment from her husband's family, but the goddess acts forcefully to protect those who worship her, and all ends satisfactorily, thanks to the goddess of satisfaction, the meaning of her name.

Sarasvati and Ganga

The river Sarasvati in north-west India was the most famous river in the *Rig Veda*: 'best mother, best of rivers, best of goddesses', but now only the dried-up riverbed remains. The mantle of the river was taken up by Ganga, but Sarasvati, clad in white and holding a *vina* (lute), remains popular as the divinity of learning and music.

The nine-night festival in the autumn, at the end of the monsoon, includes celebration of Sarasvati in addition to Lakshmi and Durga, though the last-named dominates, and the festival in many places is called Durga *puja*. Sarasvati is sometimes the daughter of Brahma, sometimes his wife. But whether or not Brahma is in evidence, she is completely benign, and in this she is unique among major goddesses. Schools, universities, and public offices enthusiastically celebrate Sarasvati. Factory workers worship her in addition to the forceful monkey god Hanuman and Vishvakarma, the god of smiths, for she symbolizes their hope of seeing their children rise to higher things through education.[14] Her connection with music is shown by her *vina*; and her white goose represents the pure knowledge of the spiritual nature of the self. In Tamilnadu a rival to Sarasvati has arisen in the form of the deified Tamil language, Tamilttay, who has adopted aspects of the iconography of Sarasvati, especially the most noticeable feature, the *vina*.[15]

Many rivers have some connection with divinity. Particular rivers are locally considered to be deities, with their own small shrines, and receive the kind of ritual offerings that are made to an auspicious married woman: turmeric and red kunkum powder, or more elaborately, as in Maharashtra, what is called 'filling the lap': a coconut, some grains of rice or wheat, turmeric powder, kunkum powder, a piece of blouse, a betel nut, and sometimes dried dates, whole almonds, pieces of turmeric root, and some fresh fruit. Sometimes the femininity of a river is made fully obvious in ritual by stretching a string of saris that have been tied together across its width. Rivers may be inhabited by female water spirits, sometimes by a group of seven, who parallel the Mothers (Matrikas), and whose dangerous powers may be placated by parents floating their baby or child on a raft across the river's surface.[16]

Ganga, 'Swift-Goer', since the time of the epics has been the number one river in India, and has enjoyed the undivided loyalty of all Hindus, bestowing both prosperity and salvation. Rising in the Himalayas, she flows through the North Indian plain and into the Bay of Bengal. All rivers in India partake of her qualities, and she is their prototype. All running water purifies, but bottled Ganga water is better. Ganga is divine in origin. Rival myths of Vishnu and Shiva claim Ganga. When Vishnu in his dwarf *avatara* progresses to gianthood in three steps, he cracks open the cosmic egg, allowing access to the cosmic waters that are Ganga. Again, when Agastya drinks up all the ocean the sage Bhagiratha practises extreme asceticism to win from Shiva the boon of that god interposing his head to break the fall of the Milky Way to the earth, so that the divine Ganga still pours from Shiva's head – the Himalayas – to the earth. Southern bronzes of Shiva show Ganga as a mermaid in his hair. In poetry she is considered Parvati's rival for his affections. But, above all, Ganga washes away sins, and one should end one's days by bathing in her waters; failing that, one's ashes should be deposited in her.

Parvati

Parvati corresponds to Lakshmi in that she is the consort of the other great Hindu god, Shiva. Both are queenly, loving brides, mistresses of the house-hold. But whereas Lakshmi diverges into the differing consorts of the greatly differing *avataras* of Vishnu, Parvati indulges in changes of shape, colour and aspect while remaining in some sense herself. This shape-changing is strik-ingly manifested in what is called the Woman-Lord, when Shiva merges half his body with hers. This is no androgyne of ambiguous sexuality, but super-man joined with superwoman, half and half, though the exigencies of iconog-raphy and the human form itself mean that the erect linga is fully manifest. One full breast, narrow waist and curving hip mark out Parvati's half of the joint body. Her close identity with Kali is shown by the classical story of Shiva teasing her about her blackness, provoking her to practise asceticism until her skin turns golden.

Often Parvati is perceived as the local goddess who attains universality by marrying Shiva. One myth, perhaps originating as a partial authorization of widow-burning (sati), accounts for the presence of goddess temples all over the earth by saying that these shrines house body parts from Sati, who is said to be Parvati's previous incarnation. Sati is made the daughter of Daksha, a son of Brahma. Daksha will not invite Shiva to his Vedic sacrifice because of his way-out character. Angered by this lack of respect for her lord, Sati jumps into the fire. Nevertheless her body remains, and Shiva, distraught, carries it about with him, until Vishnu cuts it up with his discus, and the various pieces fall to earth. The most powerful bit, the yoni, falls to earth at Kamakhya in Assam. The tongue falls at Jvala Mukhi in Kangra District, Himachal Pradesh, and is manifested in the form of a flame which devotees preserve by feeding it ghee and singing devotional songs to it.[17]

Kali

The most widely travelled Hindu goddess is Kali, in that it is she of all Hindu deities who has captured the Western imagination, first horrifying and then enthralling. For the West, in the nineteenth century, Kali epitomized an alien other; in the twenty-first century she symbolizes the Western revolution in gender and religious imagination. The fierce black goddess whose first textual appearance is in the *Devimahatmya* has long been known in many parts of India. A favourite deity of, for instance, the Chola dynasty in south-east India, on the west coast it was probably her form as Bhadrakali that first greeted Vasco da Gama when he entered what he thought was a church. The theology of this goddess is especially worked out in the tantras of Kashmir. The goddess herself straddles several discourses – sculpture, myth, and tantra – taking differing forms and names in each. It was in Bengal that Westerners first got a detailed knowledge of Kali, a Kali whose cult had been revived as part of the independence movement, but her worship is far older and wider than her history in Bengal might suggest. Her power ranges from personal black magic, when she is sought to harm others, to the grandest cosmic scale.

Kali was a problem for the British, as was clearly stated by Macaulay in his 1843 speech condemning Lord Ellenborough's attempt to restore the gates of the Somanath temple, carried off in the eleventh century by Mahmud of Ghazni. Macaulay cannot bring himself to name Kali, but the notorious thugs (who strangled travellers before robbing them) make one of the climaxes of his diatribe against the religion of the Hindus, 'this superstition . . . of all superstitions the most irrational, and of all superstitions the most inelegant . . . of all superstitions the most immoral': 'It is by the command and under the especial protection of one of the most powerful goddesses [i.e. Kali] that the Thugs join themselves to the unsuspecting traveller, make friends with him, slip the noose round his neck, plunge their knives in his eyes, hide him in the earth, and divide his money and baggage.'[18] Macaulay had read many examinations of thugs, and particularly remembered 'an altercation between two of those wretches':

> One Thug reproached the other for having been so irreligious as to spare the life of a traveller when the omens indicated that their patroness required a victim. 'How could you let him go? How can you expect the goddess to protect us if you disobey her commands? That is one of your North country heresies.' . . . it is a difficult matter to determine in what way Christian rulers ought to deal with such superstitions as these.[19]

It has been suggested that the thugs were a figment of the British imagination, a misunderstanding that served to justify the Raj: according to Friedhelm Hardy, 'Practically all information about the *thugs* was gained from "Approvers" or, in modern parlance, "supergrasses" who might well have phrased their information in terms corresponding to the preconceived ideas that they knew their masters had.'[20] Parama Roy speaks of 'an almost fatal lack of empirical detail': 'All natives were potentially thugs, since the system of *thuggee* was remarkably inclusive; the most seemingly innocent objects, like handkerchiefs [used for strangling] or *gur* [unrefined sugar, ritually consumed at the commencement of an expedition], could participate in a diabolical signifying system.'[21] She concludes by identifying the thug with the thug-hunter: 'wherever there is an Englishman there is a thug'.[22] But there is some post-colonial sleight of hand on her part, for the thugs were not entirely an invention of the British. For instance, in the eighth-century Sanskrit adventure story *Brihatkathaslokasamgraha* we find a typical passing reference to robbers and Kali. A prince's auspicious arrow is worshipped by his friends 'in the same way as a man who has strangled a successful merchant worships Ambika [Kali] who has granted him the boon he desires'.[23]

Hardy is correct to speak of thugs as the topic that 'perhaps more than any other fired the British imagination'[24] in the nineteenth century, but it was by no means only the British imagination that was fired. Caleb Wright's American bestseller of 1849, *Lectures on India*, went through many editions. Wright travelled to India and then lectured throughout the United States on his findings; the basis of his presentation was a series of engravings. He began with macabre ascetics. 'No 1 Portrait of a Devotee who had been standing eight years, day and night . . . No. 2 A devotee who had kept the left arm elevated in the position represented until it had become stiff, and the finger-nails had grown six or eight inches in length . . . No. 3 A devotee who had kept both arms elevated until they had become stiff and immovable.' The first 127 pages comprise two general lectures, based on the various engravings, which also include the standard themes of the juggernaut car and religious murder; Wright then describes the lamentable condition of women in India 'and other Pagan and Mohammedan countries'; his third lecture is on the 'Habits and Superstitions of the Thugs', and the last is 'a brief description of two of the principal Hindu festivals' – namely of Durga and Kali.[25] The thugs and Kali are the culmination of Wright's account of Hinduism. They dominate the nineteenth-century view of Hinduism from the outside.

Among several nineteenth-century French novels that treat of thugs, Pont-Jest's long serial novel *The Trial of the Thugs* (1877) stands out, with its many pictures and circulation of almost half a million copies. Feringhea, chief of the thugs, is brought to justice in Madras in 1850. In the courtroom crowded with every nationality and every Hindu caste, an ascetic holds up his arm, and when admonished by Lord Bentinck explains that he has held it up for two years and cannot now lower it – like the second picture in Wright's book. Feringhea's son vows to avenge his father and goes to London in disguise, joins the Irish Fenians and fights against British capitalism before returning to India to educate the Hindu people.[26]

In Lieutenant-General Sir George Macmunn's *The Underworld of India* (1933), things go from bad to worse, as we might expect, and it is in the eleventh chapter, 'Darkest India', that the author turns to Kali and thuggism.

Thuggism 'is most illustrative of an underground side of Indian character' a side which 'may easily return in an India that has lost the resolute mainspring from its policy'[27] – that is, an India not blessed by British rule! Macmunn moves on to modern variations, to the 'seditious and secret murder cult in Bengal' and indeed throughout India, to the '*bomb-parast*', one who consecrates his bomb at a Kali shrine, so that he may 'gloat with hungry Kali on the blood that may flow when he shall throw it'.[28] Macmunn prefaces this chapter with a section on eunuch transvestite prostitutes, and refers to sexual perversity throughout his account of Kali and violence. Thus the heroic students who tried to win independence for their country are for Macmunn not only 'sour super-minds' but 'depraved and often injured by too early eroticism' – and it is this 'too early eroticism' that somehow leads them to worship 'the nitro-glycerine bomb as the apotheosis of his goddess'.[29] Kali did indeed inspire the freedom movement in Bengal, and was often seen as trampling not on Shiva but on the British.

The American adventure film *Gunga Din* (1939), set in the nineteenth century, links thugs obsessed with killing for the love of Kali with massed ranks of well-organized Indian troops ready to win independence. Brave Gunga Din, the water-carrier, alerts headquarters, and the Raj is saved. Kipling's poem in his praise is read as Gunga Din dies from his wounds. *Indiana Jones and the Temple of Doom* (1984), set in the 1930s, imagines a revival of thuggee, but primordial evil practice is linked with modern efficiency. Kali's victims become slave workers in mines with an extensive railway system underneath the Kali temple. Tunnels with horrible insects and sliding doors lead to the giant womb where a monstrous Kali image is bowed down to by massed ranks of the heathen. Glowing within the image are the seven lingas established by the Vedantin Shankara, light sources that enable the idol, like some science fiction superpowered robot, to function.

Altogether more authentic is John Masters's novel *The Deceivers* (1952), made into a film of the same name in 1989. Masters's hero William Savage closely relates in time and place to William Sleeman, the actual discoverer of the thugs. Savage disguises himself as a thug, to bring the miscreants to justice, but finds himself strangely drawn to Kali. Masters's partly sympathetic approach to Kali worship offers a more open and objective view than is usual. The producer of the film notes that he 'was fascinated by Savage's journey into a "Heart of Darkness"; not just his journey through India with the thugs, but his journey into himself'.[30] Whereas *Gunga Din* and *Indiana Jones* join Kali with a modernity (military efficiency on the one hand, industrial efficiency on the other) that is at the same time alien, *The Deceivers* hints at a universal horror within that the sensitive may become aware of.

The American horror novelist Dan Simmons began his career with *Song of Kali* (1985), in which an American poet with his Indian wife and their baby daughter (called Victoria, after Bombay's Victoria terminus!) go to Calcutta to look for a missing Bengali poet. It transpires that the Kapalikas, the famous skull-carrying ascetics who worship Shiva and Kali, are still active. The missing poet had been resuscitated by Kali and become a creature of the Kapalikas The hero finds him and helps him to commit suicide. His daughter is murdered by the Kapalikas in revenge. Snippets of poetry to Kali punctuate the novel, which vividly raises the unanswerable question of human sacrifice in India today, a question raised for a West that is obsessed with serial killers.

Kali and modern India

Kali was a problem for Nehru's new secular India, just as she had been for the British. Satyajit Ray's film *Devi* (1960), set in the 1860s, tells how a widower landlord, worshipper of Kali, comes to believe that his daughter-in-law is an incarnation of the goddess. In an early scene, as a good daughter-in-law, Doyamayee massages her father-in-law's feet, while he leans back in his chair, smoking his hookah. Her husband is away, studying English literature in Calcutta. His father has a vision that Doyamayee is Kali, and arranges public worship of her. She seems to cure the dying son of a villager. When her nephew falls ill, her father commits him to her care, saying that a doctor is unnecessary. The boy dies. Her husband comes back and takes her away, but she returns to persist, it would seem, in her 'divine' role. When released the film was seen as an attack on Hinduism and there was an attempt to stop it being shown abroad, though it later won the President of India's Gold Medal. 'For Nehru, who released the film to foreign audiences, it must have read in the nature of a proclamation declaring the old order dead.'[31]

Kali is often closely associated with Durga, and the iconography of both may be found in the same temple. In the *Devimahatmya* Durga appears in the central episode. In the next episode two demons have taken over heaven, and the gods pray to Durga for assistance. Parvati walks by on her way to bathe in the Ganges and asks who they are praying to. Then Durga under the generic name and form of Ambika, 'Mother Goddess', springs forth from Parvati's body and tells her that they are praying to her, Ambika. Parvati's body – Ambika having left her – becomes dark, that is to say she becomes Kali. But subsequently Kali springs forth from Ambika's frowning forehead. This readily changing form of the goddess finds perfect expression in the computer graphics of the film *Ammoru* (1995), a great box-office success, where the shapeless mound that is the goddess Ammoru in a village shrine transmutes into the beautifully formed multi-armed destroying goddess. These seamlessly flowing and extensive changes in precise three-dimensional computerized rendering, familiar from such films as *Terminator II*, are the exact visual representation of the kind of change envisaged long ago in the *Devimahatmya*. Films from South India such as *Ammoru* (1995) and *Devi* (1999), directed by Kodi Ramakrishna, show that the ancient forms of Kali are as strong as ever.

Affirmation of Kali in the West

The Psychedelic Venus Church was an outgrowth of Willie Minzey's Shiva Fellowship. Formed in San Francisco in 1969, it was a pagan fellowship dedicated to the worship of Kali as 'the sex-goddess Venus-Aphrodite'. It described itself as 'pantheistic nature religion, humanist hedonism, a religious pursuit of bodily pleasure through sex and marijuana'. It had disappeared by 1980.[32]

More arbitrary than the conflation of Kali and Venus is that of Kali and Gaia. Rae Beth comes up with the following prayer to Kali: 'Divine Goddess Kali, purifier and renewer, take from our lives all the ways in which we cause harm to ourselves and others and to the Earth.'[33] Kali, we are told, has become angry because people have used each other and the earth cruelly. Indeed Kali *is* Gaia: although she is portrayed as 'vengeful, unforgiving and violent', yet 'if, for Kali, we read Gaia, the inner spirit of our Earth, She whose presence manifests in Earth's ability to protect natural balance, even if She must act ruthlessly to achieve this, then it becomes clear why She appeared in a time of great evil and did what She did . . . If we disturb the balance of nature too far then She must appear. She has no choice.'

But this eco-Kali is very much a modern transmutation of the Indian Kali who, if an outsider wishes to connect her with nature, should surely be seen rather as the terrible forces of nature, burning summer heat, and destructive monsoon flood, that are the inherent and regularly recurring nature of things, especially in the extremes of the Indian climate. Kali is more in accord with Camille Paglia's view of nature: 'Civilized man conceals from himself the extent of his subordination to nature . . . let nature shrug, and all is ruin. Fire, flood, lightning, tornado, hurricane, volcano, earthquake – anywhere at any time.'[34]

More applicable perhaps to the nature of Kali, is the attempt to use her as motivation to cut away unwanted aspects of a person's personality. Thus the Kali ritual devised by Victoria Luna Circa and the Rainbow Connection[35] offers the possibility of pledging to Kali that one will cut out the rotten parts within, or fight evil on the earth. The first part of this ritual involves meditation on an India of starving children that would strike an Indian as a Western tourist view of India; and strange is the claim that one is dancing with Kali. As things draw to a close, taking of cakes and fruit juices precedes announcements, and the final words are 'Merry meet, merry part, and merry meet again.' The wild power of Kali is hard to find here.

Rachel McDermott, in her account of the Western Kali, points out that 'goddess spirituality is attractive for women because it makes possible an affirmation of the female body, of women's anger and aggression, and of the changing cycles of life which menstruation and birth so readily illustrate'. And it is especially through Kali that the traits 'that patriarchy repressed and demonized – her potent, sexual, dark side – can be claimed as liberating for women, within a context of wholeness and balance'.[36] Alexandre Chandra uses her Ph.D. thesis to celebrate her own engagement with the dark goddess as Kali. She assists a Kali priest in his temple in Orissa, and offers her own menstrual blood to Kali at Hirapur in Orissa and at the Kalighat temple in Calcutta. She studies 'the ways in which the Dark Goddesses such as Kali and the Black Madonna serve as catalysts within the entire transformational process and the ways in which they are themselves converging into a new global consciousness.'[37] Kali, and other dark goddesses, are speaking today through Western women, she claims, quoting Starhawk, 'She exists, and we create Her.'[38]

Varieties of form

The opening work of the 1999 exhibition 'Devi: The Great Goddess' at the Arthur M. Sackler Gallery of the Smithsonian Institution was an abstract sculpture by the contemporary British artist Anish Kapoor. Entitled *At the Hub of Things* (1987), it is a hollow half-sphere of cast fibreglass covered with dark blue pigment, and is said to represent Kali. The artist wanted 'to make an object that isn't an object, to make a hole in space, to make something that does not exist' but that at the same time is there 'due solely to its own volition.' Inspired by the piles of coloured pigment for sale outside temples, the artist has expressed not only the beauty of the goddess's darkness, a darkness that the poets say shines, but also her all-swallowing thirst.

The goddess thirsts for blood, and she has a long tongue for that purpose; but the thirst is also theologically developed in the medieval Krama theology, which sees Kali as a kind of black hole which swallows the universe, indeed a succession of Kalis, each swallowing the other up to the thirteenth and final Kali. The goddess thirsts, she carries a bowl full of blood. Often her ravening thirst and hunger are shown by her reduction to skin, bone, and sinew. The artist Kapoor reduces all these factors to the hollowing out of his art object.

If Kali today can be portrayed as a hollow hemisphere, natural boulders have long been seen to be manifestations of the divine. Thus in Bhaktapur in Nepal the eight Matrika goddesses that protect the town are represented by unhewn stones 'that seem to emerge from the ground', and these goddesses 'have to be considered as the most basic manifestation of place, with a radiating energy of their own'.[39]

These boulders and the fibreglass concavity of Kali remind us of Simmel's striking characterization of woman as lying like an immovable prehistoric boulder in the landscape of modernity: 'woman seems to be untouched by the fractures and conflicts of modern culture and to remain close to the "primeval grounds of being (Urgrund des Seins)"'. But this biological essentialism from a contemporary of Max Weber's has least of all relevance to Hindu India – save only the incident in the Ramayana where the unfortunate Ahalya, wife of a forest sage, seduced by Indra disguised as her husband, is subsequently turned into a boulder by her angry husband. The touch of Rama's foot subsequently restores her to her true form.

India's most famous contemporary artist, the Muslim M. F. Husain (b. 1915), who recently obsessively painted the film star Madhuri Dixit, has several times been in trouble with right-wing Hindu organizations for representing Hindu goddesses in the nude. Over several decades, after beginning as a painter of cinema hoardings, he has painted hundreds of Hindu deities with sympathy and imagination. But because he painted Sita, Sarasvati, and Drapaudi in the nude, he was prosecuted for obscenity, and his home was attacked. Picking on him because he was a Muslim and charging him with raping Hindu goddesses, his opponents showed a rigidity that savoured more of Islamic iconoclasm than anything else.

In contrast with the usually naked Kali, most Hindu deities, goddesses and gods, now appear in a form that springs from Victorian costume painting, for Ravi Varma's realistic oils in the form of poster prints defined Hindu iconography for most of the last century. Brightly coloured and true to life in shape and garment, his divine figures no less than his human heroes and heroines demonstrate the actuality of Hindu myth, legend and iconography, and have continued life as models for film actors and their costumes in 'mythologicals'. These posters are found everywhere, including in places of work and vehicles. They are essential features of rudimentary temples and home shrines. The pictures themselves often set the deities in their temple situation with oil lamps burning beside them and food offerings in front of them.

For the worshipper and the Hindu theologian, the deities' specific forms really exist. Concrete images of goddesses and gods are called their 'form' and their 'reflection'. Form (*murti*), the commonest term, means a corporeal form enclosed or condensed within a defined area. Reflection (*pratima*) is the image as replica, portrait or reflection. The *pratima*, reflection, is only a copy of the original. Although a secondary version, the form, the reflection, is a reproduction of the divinely existent figure of the goddess or god. When the image is worshipped – which is continuously the case in a temple – it *is* the deity.

The most basic form of the goddess is the ground, the earth. It is fitting to close with the Guhya ('secret') Kali of Nepal, the goddess of the secret, whose temple is not far from the famous Pashupatinath temple. Her sanctum is simply a open hole filled with water. The hole is covered by a metal plate in the shape of a lotus, with a Shri Yantra marked upon it, and also a silver pot. This hole is considered to be a vulva or an anus. It is called Parvati, Durga, Kali, or other names. In his study of this shrine, Axel Michaels repeatedly asks: Who then is the goddess of the secret? Why does she have many contradictory identities but not an identity in Western terms? Why is the identity of goddesses 'such an oceanic, almost unlimited identity'? This is his answer:

In my view, goddesses reflect, in sharp distinction to Western concepts of identity, the Hindu belief in the power of primary, pre-verbal, preconscious experiences of reality . . . What makes goddesses powerful is beyond words, theories, analysis, separations, boundaries – beyond identity. In other words, it is the Secret that provides the goddess's identity.[40]

In fact, we end where we began, on the bedrock of physiology.

Chapter Nine

The Gods of Hinduism and the Idols of Modernity

Surely we have not spent so much time and labour in rooting out the old Grecian and Roman mythologies, to have their places thus filled up by the older system of Indian polytheism?[1]

The worship of 'the many gods' is in this country not just dead tradition or evocative poetry but part of the life of many, a living reality of their world, not yet overpowered by modernity. Does this so-called polytheism, this worship of the graven image, not have a profound truth of its own? Is there not here something to understand, something which we can make our own? Is not such understanding likely to make us more explicitly aware of those presuppositions or prejudgments which have been responsible for relegating such experience of Divinity to an inferior level of the religious consciousness?[2]

As we have seen, the current revolution in understanding of gender has given a new relevance to Hindu goddesses, but Hinduism has many gods as well as many goddesses. The traditional number of gods (and goddesses), 330 million, was a figure that originally approximated to infinity, but is now less than a third of the present population of India, and half the number of Hindus. If religion and modernity are opposed, the ultimate divergence from modernity must be this extravagant proliferation of divine bodies, this 'long and splendid catalogue' as James Mill ironically termed it.[3] Christianity, sufficiently rational – in its own view – to have only one god, is in the form of some of its theologians prepared to concede to modernity the lack of reality of even that god; but Hinduism, despite the criticism not only of Christians and Muslims but also of nineteenth-century Hindu reformers, has remained resolutely polytheistic: the gods are as popular as ever.

Full accounts of Hindu polytheism are relatively few. Most Hindus have a chosen deity, and worship a handful of others on special occasions or for special purposes. Though they are aware of many deities, they normally have no reason to survey the whole range, and so it is the outsider who has attempted summation, though one early classical text lists the gods of the Vedas. Image-makers have pattern books for the gods they manufacture. The music scholar Alain Danielou wrote a valuable summation and affirmation of Hinduism under the title *Hindu Polytheism*. A more recent phenomenon has been the attempts of anthropologists to sum up the gods in a particular area, such as Babb's *Divine Hierarchy* and Levy's *Mesocosm*, for every locality has its own versions of a selection of the pantheon. Levy, in his excellent account of Hinduism in one Nepalese town, speaks of its divinities as 'a collection of divine South Asian flotsam that has drifted into the Valley' and has been subjected to local usage. 'Flotsam' lacks dignity, but certainly it is helpful to think in terms of an ebb and flow of divine forms across South Asia, forms that collect in some areas more than others, but are broadly similar everywhere.

We are now in a position to turn our attention fully to the Hindu gods, to the exaltation of masculinity, though even here femininity is not entirely lacking. The neuter deity, Brahman, who is nothing but consciousness and bliss, who is, in a word, the self, will be left to the next chapter. Brahman is formless; the gods have form. Philosophically Brahman is the highest, the supreme, but is inexpressible. Our concern here is the gods about whom a great deal has been expressed.

Brahma, Vishnu and Shiva

Presentations of the Hindu gods usually begin with a schema found in the Puranas. There are three gods at the heart of the kaleidoscopic elaborations of Hindu theology. Two of these, Vishnu and Shiva, predominate, and each of these is supported by schools of thought which claim their god's supremacy. The two gods were often in competition, and this rivalry led to new myths and new iconography.

According to the Samkhya philosophy, in a formulation that was very widely accepted in Hindu thought, the universe is made up of three threads or fundamental qualities: light, activity, and darkness. These threads run through everything that is not consciousness. In this formulation of the deities, consciousness is left out of account. Each of these threads is identified with a male deity: light with Vishnu, activity with Brahma (not to be confused with Brahman), and darkness with Shiva. As this distribution would suggest, it is mainly of Vaisnava inspiration. It is highly factitious. Brahma, despite corresponding to the activity thread, accomplishes little in myth, while Shiva and Vishnu are each the supreme deity for their worshippers, subsuming the qualitylessness of Brahman in addition to their individual characters and paralleling monotheistic gods. However, keeping to the terms of the tripartite formulation, three functions are distributed among the three gods: Brahma creates, Vishnu protects, and Shiva destroys.

This division is prefigured in naturalistic terms in the *Maitrayani Upanishad*'s statement of creation. The initial absolute darkness starts to revolve, then

> it became unbalanced, and the form of the revolving tendency appeared. Stimulated, this revolving tendency became unbalanced, and out of it the tendency toward disintegration, the centrifugal tendency, appeared. Stimulated, in its turn it became unbalanced, and the tendency toward cohesion appeared. (*Maitrayani Upanishad* 5.2)

Vishnu, then, is the cohesive principle, all that tends towards light, towards the centre. Shiva is the centrifugal principle, fleeing the centre, moving outward to darkness, to dispersal. Brahma is the equilibrium of these two forces, the fundamental quality of activity, of the state of being of the created universe. In the formulation of the triple gods, of the Trimurti, Hinduism attempts to set out the universal laws of existence. This logical and intellectually very powerful statement has always attracted attention, at first for the superficial reason of its resemblance in number to the Christian Trinity.

These are, however, intellectualizations of the living reality of the Hindu gods. In worship, in mythology, in ritual, Brahma is of relatively small account. In appearance a four-headed brahman, his caste made conspicuous by the water-pot he holds – for brahmans are always anxious to maintain their purity – his work of creation is low-key in the mythology. He is first produced by Vishnu, being seated in the lotus that springs up from Vishnu's navel, and, from that lotus, holding the four Vedas, Brahma begins the periodic process of the creation of the universe. His four heads correlate with the four Vedas. He was originally five-headed, but Shiva cuts off one of his heads, in one version because Brahma seeks to make incestuous love to his own daughter. Seated in the lotus, he is vulnerable to attack by demons, and is all too ready to grant whatever boons they demand. This complaisance brings about situations that have to be remedied by Shiva or Vishnu. Because he has lied to Shiva, claiming to have seen the top of Shiva's linga when in fact he has not, Shiva curses him never to be worshipped. Although a handful of temples dedicated to Brahma exist, he has been replaced there as the main god by Vishnu or Shiva.

Brahma, then, is an equal on the level of cosmological explanation but is of no consequence as a god in relation to humanity. Two great gods command the Hindu universe. As we have seen, the goddess is enormously important, but in terms of extent of texts, of size of temple, of wealth, the gods win hands down. In their great temples the goddess is not absent, but she is subsidiary. Both gods glory in their masculinity. Shiva is worshipped in the form of the phallus, the linga. There is a tendency among Hindus today to see the linga as 'the formless' and to deny its sexuality. As the sign of the absolute, there is no theological problem in seeing it as formless, but myth and iconography make its phallic nature certain. Shaivites claim the superiority of Shaivism over Vaishnavism on account of its naturalness: had men been meant to worship Vishnu, whose emblem is the discus, they would have had discuses rather than penises! In human form, Shiva is the great lover, his potency huge on account of long ages spent as an ascetic; his love-making with his wife Parvati shakes the universe.

Whereas Shiva's roles oscillate between the sexual and the non-sexual, Vishnu is a mighty warrior male in nearly all his incarnations. In his primal form as Vishnu, he has two wives – not only Lakshmi, goddess of prosperity, but also Bhumi, the earth. As Rama, he loses his wife, and banishes her again after winning her back, but as Krishna, testosterone-charged adolescent, he makes love to many married cowgirls, and goes on from there to have 16,000 wives of his own. So attractive is this form of Vishnu that a Shaiva version has been generated, with Shiva as naked ascetic making love to the wives of sages in the pine forest, or at least with them overcome by lust for him.

In the cosmological framework, Vishnu and Shiva are opposites. There is a joint form of the two gods, arising by analogy with the joint form of Shiva and Parvati, but normally the two males are not equivalent.

Although Vishnu was originally a sun god, and the discus he holds first represented the disk of the sun, he becomes closely associated with water, floating on the cosmic, undifferentiated waters in the interval between the destruction and re-creation of the world. He holds a conch, symbol of the ocean, and also a feminine symbol – his nature is in some respects feminine as well as watery. Floating on his back, he gives birth to the universe, inasmuch as it is from his navel that springs the lotus on which Brahma the creator god sits. To steal the nectar from the demons after the churning of the ocean he takes on the form of a beautiful woman. Indeed, Shiva falls in love with this woman, and begets the god Ayyanar from her. Like Parvati, Vishnu merges with Shiva to form a joint body of two halves joined vertically down the middle – in this case two male halves.

Then again Shiva, though he is the god of fire – holding fire in his hand when he dances as Nataraja, 'King of Dancers', and emitting a fiery ray from his third eye when angered – at the same time he holds Ganga in his hair, a rival woman to Parvati, but contained within his person. The crescent moon on his head casts its cooling rays. In one southern myth he appears as a sow with many piglets.

We are confronted by the richness of myth and icon. The more fully each god is explored, the less each can be narrowly delimited.[4] Shiva as yogi-ascetic, clad usually in a tiger-skin wrapped round his loins, adopts contradictory roles. Although he is ascetic, he is nevertheless erotic, and also a family man. In the eighteenth century miniature painters loved to show him sitting with his wife and two sons at ease in the burning ground.

Vishnu, usually a kingly figure, descends successively and regularly as various *avataras* ('descents' or incarnations) to fight evil. The two most worshipped are Rama and Krishna. Rama is a relatively straightforward deity, a quality that may have endeared him to the Islam-influenced north of India, as the nearest thing to a mirror-image of Allah. There has been a paradigm change in modern India from the play of Krishna (Krishna-*lila*) to the kingdom of Rama. 'Krishna as the god of erotic mystical love has virtually disappeared from the public sphere of reformed Hinduism. He remains, though, as the child (*bala*) and as the hero of the *Bhagavad Gita*.'[5] It is true that the second half of the nineteenth century saw a reaction against the erotic Krishna, but growing Western interest in Krishna in painting and poetry feeds back into Indian film and video. Notwithstanding the Hare Krishna movement's pious abhorrence of sexuality, Krishna continues as a richly various deity.

Ananda Coomaraswamy introduced Krishna painting to the West; he also made known Shiva as the King of Dancers, Nataraja. The famous Chola bronzes of Shiva dancing in a ring of fire on the demon of ignorance, now common on the dust-jackets of books on Hinduism, were unknown outside India before Coomaraswamy's writings at the beginning of the twentieth century. Both Krishna with his flute and Shiva with his hourglass drum as he dances are prime examples of a key Hindu theological notion, that of play. Both gods lose themselves in the practice of their art, and they entrance the world. The process of creation itself is the result of their play. All supreme forms of the two gods are credited with the desire to play, with desire as the motor of creation, but it is in the flute-player and the dancer that this is most graphically stated.

Both Krishna and Shiva are also associated with the play of childhood, which is after all the most natural instance of play. Krishna in the stories and iconography of his childhood from the *Bhagavata Purana*, and Shiva not from himself but from his two sons, Ganesha and Skanda – above all Ganesha.

Gods as sons: Krishna, Ganesha and Skanda

Krishna, though one of his commonest names is Son of Vasudeva, has little to do with any father. Brought up by foster-parents because of the threats of his wicked uncle, his lovable nature, not to speak of his divinity, allows him to roam unchecked. His heroism enables him to kill the demons his uncle sends against him, and finally to kill the uncle. His foster-mother figures largely in his life as a boy. Grown up, he will be a father-figure, or more precisely guru, to Arjuna, but his wilful nature continues to manifest itself in the *Mahabharata* despite the weight of divinity upon him. Shiva himself is father-figure to his sons, of course. Note that he and Parvati are unique among the major pan-Indian deities in having children. Having children makes it harder for the gods to be convincingly immortal – children would age even the gods – so usually they don't; and in Shiva and Parvati's case, their conception and birth is somewhat remote. Parvati makes Ganesha from a fold of her sari, or from some dirt from her body; Shiva's seed reaches the six Pleiades to beget the six-headed Skanda. When Shiva first meets Ganesha guarding his mother's bed-room he doesn't know who he is and naturally enough cuts his head off, so father–son strife is apparent at the beginning. An elephant provides the first available replacement head. Later they get on well, and Ganesha is frequently shown dancing in imitation of Shiva. Skanda takes after his father in becoming an ascetic. Some myths say that, after losing in the contest for the mango, when Ganesha wins the race round the world by simply walking round his mother and father, Skanda out of pique goes off to the far south, to Palani, a major Skanda pilgrimage site, to practise austerities, and his father concedes that he is the real victor and his true heir, by punning on Palani and *palam* (meaning fruit) and saying, 'You are the fruit (*palam*/Palani).'[6]

Oedipal themes have been found in the story of the race round the world. The mango is a symbol of the vagina in Sri Lanka and in Tamilnadu; it might also be a symbol for the breast. 'In the symbol of the mango, then, both oral and sexual satisfaction are suggested. This allows for the expression of a con-sciously unacceptable sexual desire for the mother in the sublimated form of a desire for food.'[7]

Furthermore, Ganesha, the devoted son, in his essential iconography – his extreme pot belly – is an embodiment of oral satisfaction and maternal over-indulgence. According to Kakar, he 'embodies certain "typical" resolutions of developmental conflicts in traditional Hindu society . . . In effect, the boy expresses his conviction that the only way he can propitiate his mother's de-mands and once again make her nurturing and protective is to repudiate the cause of the disturbance in their mutuality: his maleness.'[8] The very fact that he has an elephant's trunk is due to the displacement of his penis from its natural position to his mouth.[9] The common presence of images of Ganesha at public bathing places in Tamilnadu has been interpreted as an instance of his fixation on his mother, since 'people said that Vinayagar (Ganesha) is con-tinually looking for a woman as beautiful as his mother, but since he never finds one, he remains a perpetual bachelor'.[10]

Both Ganesha and Skanda clearly relate in one way or another to a strong father as well as a strong mother, to their divine parents. Krishna is much more free-floating, his parents are not divine. As Bala Krishna ('Boy Krishna'), he is the complete centre of attention. He has an elder brother, but there is no rivalry; this brother incarnates Shesha, the snake on whose coils Vishnu re-poses. Shiva's sons do experience rivalry; even their sibling status is not cer-tain, for in some myths it is Ganesha who is the elder of the two. Krishna is the centre of his foster-mother's universe and of the whole universe: when he has been eating mud and she looks in his mouth she sees the cosmos there. Krishna is an incarnation of Vishnu, he is the lord of the universe, so of course the cosmos is within him. A well-known representation of Krishna has him as a baby, lying on his back on a banyan leaf, his big toe in his mouth; sometimes included in the scene is a bearded old man. The old man is the immensely old Markandeya, who will never die. Endlessly wandering, during the night of time when sleeping Vishnu floats over the cosmic waters on Shesha, Markandeya enters the giant mouth of Vishnu and journeys through his body. After an immense time he comes across a baby on a leaf. The helpless baby who calls forth parental love from all who see him, the helpless baby Krishna sucking his toe in lieu of the maternal breast, declares himself to be the Lord of the Universe.

There is one Shaiva myth which comes close to being a parallel to the Oedipus myth. This is the story of Andhaka, the 'Blind One', who is so morally blind as to want to make love to his mother. But this is stopped by the all-powerful father. One day Parvati playfully creeps up behind Shiva and places her hands over his three eyes. The universe is at once plunged into darkness, for Shiva's eyes are the sun, moon, and fire. From the erotic heat of Parvati's touch a drop of sweat from Shiva's forehead takes life and on account of the universal night of its birth becomes a blind, black creature. They give him to an ascetic demon who wants a son; by his own austerities the young Andhaka gains sight and lordship of the universe. Thus empowered, he seeks to make love to Parvati, his mother. She bewilders him by making multiforms of herself, and Shiva puts an end to him by impaling him on his trident. Andhaka is then either reabsorbed into Shiva's body or becomes a fervent devotee.[11]

Chosen deity (*ishta devata*) and cinema

The devotee has the freedom to choose where they place their devotion. Their chosen deity is known as the *ishta devata*. A very real relationship develops, with a concrete object to focus the emotions and intellect upon. For serious devotees with time to spare, various mental rituals exercise the mind: an extensive repertoire of epithets sums up all possible attributes of the deity, and the physical form is carefully mentally reconstructed, with such rituals as libations and flower offerings being exactly performed in the virtual reality inside the head. This virtual world is also expressed by the cinema. It might be said that Hinduism had long been waiting for the cinema. Like film stars, the gods manifest both the unreal and a surcharged reality. The gods mirror the human world, but the mirror is a magic mirror, that shows hopes and fears and the world of dreams in graphic reality. Segal argues that Hollywood film stars are the modern secular version of gods: like gods, the stars live for ever in their films, reappearing in new roles, larger than life, seldom seen by ordinary people, with superhuman powers.[12] In Bollywood, Indian film stars have that and more when they take the role of gods on film. In modernity the make-believe of Hollywood is a separate world of play, and arguably a continuation of mythology in the secular world, enchantment amid disenchantment. In Hinduism modernity's technology gives renewed vigour to the continuous tradition of divine forms.

Modernity and the gods

For his doctoral dissertation, Marx took as his motto a line of Aeschylus: 'In a word, I hate all the gods.' These sentiments were shared by C. N. Annadurai, the founder of the Tamil DMK political party, who in 1967 banned portraits of gods and goddesses from state government offices and schools. The 1970 census showed that Tamilnadu was India's most urbanized state. At the beginning of 1971, the DMK party held, as it had held before, a 'superstition eradication conference', but this time a large number of posters mocking the gods were carried out in procession. For example, the origin of Murugan, the Tamil name for the region's favourite god, Skanda, born from Shiva's semen shed into fire, was represented by brahman priests crowding round Shiva, seeming to masturbate him, while Parvati stood by with her hand held out to receive the seed. As well as such posters, an effigy of Rama was beaten with sandals during the procession.

Atheism has always been a feasible stance, even within Hinduism. Did not the ultra-orthodox philosophical school of Purva Mimamsa, devoted to the interpretation of the Veda's instructions on sacrifice, declare that it was irrelevant whether or not the gods existed? All that mattered was to understand the rules of sacrifice. Western-educated Indians sometimes credit some kind of scientific efficacy to the Vedic sacrifice, while seeing the gods as an illusion of the common man. Nehru, the creator and first prime minister of independent India, was moved by the Buddha statue at Anuradhapura in Ceylon, but said that 'some famous temples in South India, heavy with carving and detail, disturb me and fill me with unease'.[13] It is precisely this unease that lies between modernity and Hinduism, this inability to understand Hinduism on the part of modernity. Harrow- and Cambridge-educated Nehru shrinks before the rich specificity of the Hindu divine.

For Ram Mohun Roy (1772–1833), polytheism was the source of all India's social evils. First impressed by Islamic monotheism, he went on to the deism of the Enlightenment. In Rabindranath Tagore's words, 'Unsparingly he devoted himself to the task of rescuing from the debris of India's decadence the true products of its civilization, and to make our people build on them, as the basis, the superstructure of an international culture.'[14] For Roy the Hindu gods were only a product of the human imagination. He gives a good – though highly unsympathetic – description of mental worship, and shows the difficulty of the process:

> The gods on which you meditate are but the fictions of your own mind. For you form in your mind the head of such and such a god – give him mouth, nose etc. – endow him with hands, feet and other limbs – deck him with clothes, beads and trinkets – and prepare in your mind various presents which you offer to him. When your attention is engrossed by some worldly affair, some limbs are finished, and other limbs remain unfinished. In the meanwhile, if anybody should enter into a conversation with you, or if the mind should become engaged in anything else, then this whole fancied image is all at once destroyed, and you are obliged to form it again in your mind . . . This mental image of yours is only a mental play. You form such an image at what time and in what manner you wish, and then you expect salvation and happiness from such a destructible thing of your own formation.[15]

Outside India virtually all discussion of modernity in relation to religion has been in terms of the monotheist religions: Christianity, Judaism, and Islam. Hinduism's polytheism puts it at odds with those religions, and with Buddhism which has no gods at all. This account must be at once qualified, by recognizing the parallels between the Hindu gods and the multiple saints of Catholicism and the multiple buddhas, bodhisattvas and other beings of Mahayana Buddhism. Voltaire brings out the absurdity of Catholic claims to truth when he ironically puts their case thus: 'The difference between them and us is not that they have images, and we do not have them; that they should pray before images, and that we don't: the difference is that their images represent fantastic figures in a false religion, and that ours represent real beings in a true religion.'[16] But, generally speaking, polytheism is little appreciated, and has long been held to be inferior to monotheism in countries where the principal religion is monotheistic.

However, though Enlightenment thinkers reasoned that polytheism must be older than monotheism, and its philosophers were mainly concerned with the sceptics and atheists of ancient Greece and Rome, they often found the pagan gods more congenial than the Christian one.[17]

The Enlightenment itself has, in its turn, been interpreted as the rise of modern paganism. It is important to remember that most thinkers, from the Enlightenment to the end of the first half of the twentieth century, studied Latin and Greek, and were often as familiar with the texts of classical polytheism as with Christian texts. This is by no means to suggest that they believed what the former texts had to say, but they did know them. Gibbon, the Enlightenment historian of the Roman empire, spoke of the 'easy temper' of polytheism. As the philosopher Hume put it, 'The tolerating spirit of idolaters, both in ancient and modern times, is very obvious to any one, who is the least conversant in the writings of historians or travellers . . . The intolerance of almost all religions, which have maintained the unity of God, is as remarkable as the contrary principle of polytheists.'[18] The young Hegel played with the idea of the revival of the Greek gods.[19] Nietzsche made a full affirmation of polytheism, declaring that it alone gave full scope to human freedom: in polytheism lay the freedom of the human spirit, its creative multiplicity. The doctrine of a single deity, whom men cannot play off against other gods and thus win open spaces for their own aims was, he thought, the most monstrous of all human errors.[20]

Even the sociologist Max Weber, who stressed the disenchantment of the world of modern man, once or twice turned naturally to the idiom of polytheism, in particular in his address on science as a vocation. For Weber, we live in a world of warring forces, but the world is disenchanted because one can, 'in principle', master all things by calculation. There is no longer any need to treat these forces as personalities, as gods, yet Weber chooses to call them gods. Christianity, he says, is challenged. 'Many old gods ascend from their graves; they are disenchanted and hence take the form of impersonal forces. They strive to gain power over our lives, and again they resume their eternal struggle with one another.' Life is 'an unceasing struggle of these gods with one another.' In French and German culture, 'different gods struggle with one another, now and for all time to come'. 'The various value spheres of the world stand in irreconcilable conflict with each other. The elder Mill [James Mill] . . . was . . . right when he said "If one proceeds from pure experience, one arrives at polytheism."'[21]

Weber's references to the gods seem to spring from a profound sensitivity to the variety of forces at play in human culture. At the same time, he was aware like all his scholarly contemporaries of the revived gods of classical antiquity. There was a profound affinity between German modernity and classical antiquity, the latter becoming, in Hofmannsthal's words, 'a magic mirror in which we expect to glimpse our own faces in a strange and purified guise'.[22] But by and large Weber rejected these gods. He dismissed the embryonic New Age movement of his time, scorning 'the need of some modern intellectuals to furnish their souls . . . they play at decorating a sort of domestic chapel with small sacred images from all over the world, or they produce surrogates through all sorts of psychic experiences to which they ascribe the dignity of mystic holiness, which they peddle in the book market'.[23]

An etching by Max Klinger, Weber's favourite artist, serves as a dramatic portrayal of the general attitude of modernity towards the gods. The giant figure of Time sits as master of the world, legs astride it, one hand for the moment sealing a volcano, the other holding an hourglass. Beneath him we see civilizations and their industries; to the right is a cliff edge to which a man, mankind, naked, walks blindly. Already over the edge of the cliff and tumbling down are the gods, Moses for Jahweh, Christ, Buddha, and Zeus. Klinger's best known art work, the series of etchings that comprise the Glove sequence, shows an amazing succession of male fantasies arising from picking up a woman's glove on a roller-skating rink. Klinger shows how deeply the fetish is embedded in modern consciousness. Consciousness skates uneasily over subterranean images.

Freud had little to say about Hinduism and nothing about Hindu gods. But his desk was thronged with images of gods and other beings, among which was an ivory statuette of Vishnu, presented to him for his seventy-fifth birthday by the Indian Psychoanalytic Society. In thanking the society, Freud wrote 'As long as I can enjoy life it will recall to my mind the progress of Psychoanalysis, the proud conquests it has made in foreign countries and the kind feelings for me it has aroused in some of my contemporaries at least.' He also said, 'I gave it the place of honour on my desk.'[24] But this was only temporary – Athena, Greek goddess of wisdom, held the central place.[25] Vishnu was on the periphery of Freud's vision. Vishnu was, indeed, an inter-loper among those massed ranks, not just because he was from the East – there were two or three Chinese images – but because he alone was not a product of archaeology, a dead image recovered from the darkness of the earth. Vishnu alone was from a living religion, Vishnu alone was, so to speak, alive.

Bacon's idols of the mind and the idols of modernity

Right at the beginning of modernity, Francis Bacon categorized what he saw as the 'idols of the mind'. Although he does not directly refer to the common meaning of the word idol – the image of a false god – for Bacon, as Reinhardt Brandt puts it, 'the idols are also gods; like the old idols [Bacon's new idols are] a bungling work of men, a product of illusion that wins its own life and obtains dominion over its producer'.[26] For Bacon, 'The mind of men is rather like an enchanted mirror, full of superstition and imposture, if it be not delivered and reduced.'[27] Schopenhauer quotes Bacon – 'Passion influences and infects the intellect in innumerable ways that are sometimes imperceptible'[28] – and says that most men lack judge-ment, abandoning themselves to 'every conceivable chimera' into which they can be talked by anyone. 'Ideas are implanted which afterwards cling so firmly, and are not to be shaken by any instruction, just as if they were innate . . . we can accustom [people] to approach this or that idol imbued with sacred awe, and, at the mention of its name, to prostrate themselves in the dust not only with their body, but also with their whole spirit.'[29] Schopenhauer also instances here vegetarianism in India and sati. But the incidental mention of India by Schopenhauer must not distract us from Bacon's crucial point that these errors of the mind, these manifestations of lack of judgement, are found everywhere among most people. In the Enlightenment Bacon's theory of the idols of the mind was expanded into a general theory of prejudice, in which idols and superstition were merged into an anti-rationalism that originated in arbitrary deformation of the intellect, and religions were thought to originate in the fraud of greedy priests.[30]

Consideration of Bacon and his influence on the Enlightenment raises two important points that can only be dealt with very briefly here. In the first place, the role of priests in the promotion of religion, and above all in relation to the gods, is crucial. Bernier, in his attitude to Hindu priests, foreshadows Enlightenment execration of the Catholic priesthood. Nineteenth-century Hindu reformers such as Ram Mohan Roy were opposed to polytheistic worship, but the living force of 'idolatry' was strikingly compared to the primary instance of Indian modernity, the railway, by J. N. Bhattacharyya. Referring to Dayanand's attempt to 'replace idolatry by the ancient Vedic cult', Bhattacharyya declares, 'idol-worship is a much more effective and useful weapon to the priest than fire-worship, and is no more likely to be superseded by it than railways of modern times by the ancient means of locomotion like . . . the bullock-cart'.[31] The closed communities of priests have as yet received little in the way of sympathetic study. But mention must also be made of the countless storytellers and artists who have given the gods form in India. 'The Gods and Goddesses [of Hinduism] are neither remote nor really frightening or incomprehensible, as in many other religions. Their adventures are real enough for us to empathize with them.'[32]

The second, and more important, point is that idols, chimeras, are a constant of the human mind, and that they are therefore to be found in one way or another in modernity. Kipling's story 'The Bridge-Builders' has the Hindu gods dismiss Christianity and modernity as temporary entities: 'Their Gods! What should their Gods know? They were born yesterday and those that made them are scarcely yet cold', proclaims the crocodile god; 'Tomorrow their Gods will die.' Ganesha adds: 'It is but the shifting of a little dirt. Let the dirt dig in the dirt if it pleases the dirt.'[33] Prior to Marx and Freud's discovery of regimes of fetishism in the modern world, Coleridge declared that only familiarity prevented us from realizing that there were 'as numerous tribes of fetish-worshippers in the streets of London and Paris, as we hear of on the coasts of Africa'.[34] For Marx, the colonial system 'was "the strange God" who perched himself on the altar cheek by jowl with the old Gods of Europe, and one fine day with a shove and a kick chucked them all of a heap. It proclaimed surplus-value making as the sole end and aim of humanity.'[35] In capitalism, the products of men's hands appear as 'independent beings endowed with life' as soon as they are produced as commodities – this Marx calls fetishism. Colonialism and capitalism parallel or reproduce the supernatural in the distortion of human reason. So too the nation:

The nation, as a culturally defined community, is the highest symbolic value of modernity; it has been endowed with a quasi-sacred character equalled only by religion. In fact, this quasi-sacred character derives from religion. In practice, the nation has become either the modern, secular substitute of religion or its most powerful ally.[36]

The nation as God will be considered after we have looked at the self and at godmen.

Chapter Ten

The Image of the Self

A popular chromolithograph shows the gods Shiv and Parvati and their two sons, Ganesh and Kumar (also known as Kartikey), having their photograph taken. Shiv, clad in a leopard skin and with a writhing cobra around his neck, sits comfortably with Ganesh, his beloved elephant-headed prodigy, seated on his right knee. Parvati clasps Kumar [Skanda], who has insisted on bringing along an arrow, and we can almost hear the cosmic photographer politely urging her to squeeze closer to her husband to fit into the picture. Shiv and Parvati clearly visited this studio some time after their marriage, but it is marriage, and the fruits that flow from it, which is celebrated here.

(Description of a chromolithograph, painter unknown, c.1980)[1]

Like humans, the gods visit photographers' studios; for them also, their family is codified and enshrined within the photograph. No less than for the gods, identity for humans is concentrated, strengthened and preserved by the photographic portrait. What people as well as gods are is made apparent by photograph, film and video. Shiva and Parvati marry and have children; when humans marry and have children they do so in the context of the mirror-image of the divine world. In modern times, the mirror-image is redoubled by the world of film, where superhuman humans, larger than life, act out their scripted individualities in a way that reverberates through the lives of their audience. 'From the very beginning, the acceptance of photographs – the ease with which photographs made their way into even very orthodox Hindu families – was rather unusual. No other product of . . . nineteenth-century Western technology was given such a welcome.'[2] Pinney describes a world where photography is so dominant that even a painter is called a photographer, for photographic exactitude is what he aspires to.

In photographic studios, the client can be captured on film in the company of film stars, and even within their bodies by inserting his head into a cut-out. This temporary illusion is all the more valued on account of the notion that the body is the expression of the inner self, that 'the state of the body . . . provides an index of the state of the soul . . . [for] a whole and perfect body is both a sign of one's moral state, and a prerequisite for making sacrificial offerings to the gods and ancestors'.[3] The photographer can enable his client to attain a higher level of being that will be preserved in the photograph. No such artifices are necessary for the gods – their bodies are perfect, the usual norm for their representation being that of a 16-year-old human.

The social self

The human being as conceived by the Enlightenment and by modernity is an ideal abstraction: abstract because abstracted from the extreme variety of the human condition, ideal because accorded equality and equal rights with all other human beings. Here Hinduism, as usual, is realistic: such equality may well be desirable, and indeed is enjoyed by the spiritual self, but does not apply to the human condition as we actually find it in ourselves and the people we live amongst. And, of course, the notion of karma makes equality all the more unlikely. Since our present lives are largely dictated by the effects of previous ones, and we have an infinity of past lives behind us, acting upon us, human circumstances, abilities, and level are necessarily going to be all the more varied than if we were all the product of only one lifetime. People are infinitely varied because they have infinite life-histories, even though recollection of past lives is rare. However, the importance of karma must not be overstated. Although frequently referred to as the explanation of misfortune, karma is otherwise most favoured as a concept by those social classes who have the most to thank it for.

While karma is theory, people's lives are circumscribed by the complexity of the social situations they find themselves in. The joint family and the caste system form webs of great complexity. As we saw in chapter 3, the earliest Hindu scripture, the *Rig Veda*, gives a cosmic explanation of the fourfold caste system: the bodily parts of the cosmic giant whose sacrifice produced the universe formed the castes. The mouth became the brahmans, the arms the warriors, the legs the farmers, and the feet the peasants. All are essential parts of a unity, but vary in value. Taking the cosmic giant as a standing figure, the higher the better. The head is higher and of higher value than the feet. The parts are ranked in relation to the whole; they form a hierarchy, a religious ranking. This is the great difference from the Western view of the person – a ranked system as opposed to individualism. As the head of the social body, the brahmans have the theoretical knowledge (the Vedas) to control the cosmos, but it is only the arms, the Ksatriyas, that can actually act and wield weapons. The arms are superior to the lower parts of the body, but inferior to the head. The thighs, the Vaisyas, who have dominion over cattle and production, are inferior to the arms and the head, but are superior to the feet, the peasants. In the *Bhagavad Gita* (3.35) Krishna explicitly associates himself with the caste system: it was he who created it and it is everyone's duty to carry out the roles their caste assigns them. Emphatic and dogmatic is the statement that 'Better to do one's own duty [*svadharma*], however imperfect, than another's duty, however perfect. Better to do one's duty, even if it leads to death. What is dreadful is to perform the duty of another.'

Although the caste system is hierarchical (as is the joint family), an important part in the system is played by the simple dichotomy between purity and impurity. Indeed, the French anthropologist Louis Dumont claimed that this dichotomy is at the root of caste. How this is so is most apparent by looking at the top and bottom of the caste system: at the pure brahman and the impure outcaste. But we must first note that the terms pure and impure are not in themselves to do with morality; they refer to a physical condition. Impurity in Hinduism in this context refers to raw nature, to intrinsically dangerous and alarming natural forms: blood, especially menstrual blood, semen, urine, faeces, sweat, nail clippings. These bodily products are of the body but leave the body. They are dangerous and they contaminate. They must be contained as much as possible within rigid bounds. They are the stuff of life, but they are impure. The pure person and the pure caste are removed as far as is possible from the presence of impurity. Those who deal with the removal of impurity are necessarily the most impure and form the bottom of the hierarchy. The orthodox brahman is concerned at all times to maintain his purity. He is vegetarian and is very careful about who cooks and serves the food he and his family eat, he does not permit the remarriage of widows, and so on. His state of purity is maintained by frequent baths and elaborate religious rituals. The outcaste, such as a sweeper (emptier of latrines) or a remover of carcasses, is through his work continually impure. What is most apparent at the two extremes of the hierarchy of castes, according to Dumont, underpins them all, for each caste is less pure than the one above, and purer than the one below.

A consideration of the factors taken into account by a high-caste person evaluating offered food will show how the dichotomy of pure/impure easily generates an elaborate hierarchy. A high-caste person is offered food by an unknown person. Meat would be impure, vegetarian food would be pure. If that vegetarian food is safely secured with a hard shell, such as a coconut, then it is pure; otherwise it may be impure. If it is cooked food, fried food will be more pure than boiled food, for the frying is considered a more thorough alteration of the original food source. But what sort of pot was the food cooked in? An earthenware pot would accrue impurity in its pores; a brass pot can be thoroughly cleaned and is inherently purer on that account. Who cooked the food? Was that person of the same caste as or a higher caste than the recipient of the food? This question explains why professional cooks are always brahmans (so concerned are highly orthodox brahmans about the source of food that, at least in the past, men, when travelling without their womenfolk, would cook their own food, giving rise to the saying, 'Twelve brahmans, thirteen cooks'). Furthermore, what is the state of purity of the cook? If a woman, she must not be menstruating; in any case, no one should have died recently in the cook's family, for that too would have given risen to a condition of impurity. It will readily be seen that the consideration of pure/impure in each case generates a long list, a hierarchical list, of possible foods, from the coconut to boiled food cooked by a low-caste person in a state of impurity. In a somewhat similar way, it may be argued that the opposition of pure and impure generated and helps to maintain the hierarchy of the thousands of castes and sub-castes.

We can get a better understanding of the Hindu notion of impurity by considering saliva. Like blood and other bodily products, saliva is intrinsically impure because of its uncertain status, being both of the body and separate from it. In the explanatory words of the anthropologist Mary Douglas, it is matter out of place. When eating, Hindus like to drink water only at the end of the meal, so that the transposition of saliva between vessel and lips happens only once. But what is really bad is contact with another's saliva. One must not eat food touched by another. This does not matter within the nuclear family, between parents and their children. The wife routinely eats the husband's leavings, for he is in the position of a deity regarding her. All Hindus eat the leavings of the gods. Food offered to a god, and partaken of by the deity as smell, is the purest of food. A parent may eat a young child's food, for the child is not yet a fully formed separate person. But an adult male may not eat an adult's leavings. In the film *Jai Santoshi Ma*, there is a moment of shocking horror when the hero discovers that he is being fed his elder brothers' leavings by his sisters-in-law in the joint family.

Saliva-contaminated food is the transference of bodily substance. The wife eats the husband's leavings so that she may be incorporated into the new family to which she is initially alien; and indeed she may eat the leavings of her husband's father and mother, and his brothers. She is thus incorporated into the body of the family. Another way in which this incorporation is sometimes shown is by the ritual cooking of boiled food by the new wife. That the family can absorb from her this less pure form of cooking marks her proper membership of the affinal family, the family she has married into. Food does not simply involve bodily subsistence, but also transference of body substance from the preparer to the recipient. Families who eat together share a common body. The anthropologist McKim Marriott argued that the Hindu individual is in fact a 'dividual' – not an indivisible bounded unit, but a divisible unit particles of which can be absorbed by other 'dividuals'. 'To exist, dividual persons absorb heterogeneous material influences. They must also give out from themselves particles of their own coded substances – essences, residues, or other active influences – that may then reproduce in others something of the nature of the persons in which they originated.'[4] The parents physically create their children, but this process of creation continues with the mother's milk and then the food she cooks.

Life-stage rituals

The social self is physically formed by its parents and its substance further developed ritually within the family. Particularly important are the life-stage rituals which polish and refine the self. These rituals are called *samskaras*, the refining rituals. This word is connected with Sanskrit, the 'refined, polished' language. (It also has a second meaning, 'traces'. We can understand this better if we think of the traces or scouring marks that a grinding polish leaves on metalwork. *Samskara* in this sense means the traces left on a person by previous lives.) *Samskaras* as life-stage rituals begin before conception and end after death with the funeral. Sixteen are laid down in the classical texts, but the number actually performed varies according to region and caste.

The series begins with ritual to help ensure that a male is conceived. After intercourse the husband helps conception by reciting Vedic verses with similes of creation and invoking the gods. This is followed in the second month of pregnancy by a ritual to produce a male child. The ceremony of the husband parting the wife's hair is said to ensure easy delivery. After birth, the naming ceremony is followed by rituals marking the first going outside the home and the first eating of solid food, and the first hair-cutting. These *samskaras* of the first year of life are followed by the investiture of the sacred thread for boys of the three higher castes (*varnas*), the second birth that gives them the title of twice-born.

Marriage is the most important of all the *samskaras*. Traditionally the twice-born should marry as soon as he has finished his studies, and become a householder. The law books sing the praises of the life of the householder, for he is the basis of the whole social structure:

> And in accordance with the precepts of the Vedas, the householder is declared to be superior to all of them; for he supports the other three. As all rivers, both great and small, find a resting place in the ocean, even so men of all orders find protection with the householders.[5]

The funeral (*antyeshti*) is no less important for a person than any other *samskara* – 'It is well known that through the *samskaras* after birth one conquers this earth; through the *samskaras* after death one conquers the next world.'[6] After the cremation, all the relatives of the deceased undergo a period of impurity, traditionally 10 days for a brahman, 12 days for a Kshatriya, 15 days for a Vaishya, one month for a Shudra. The death of a child causes less impurity. There are rituals to convert the marginal ghost of the deceased (*preta*) into an ancestor (*pitri*), and to facilitate the arduous journey of the deceased to 'the abode of the ancestors' (*pitri-loka*) where he arrives on the anniversary of his death.

Bodily contact, manipulation of the body and development of the body are especially important in Hindu culture. The prolonged intimacy of bodily contact with the mother, the frequent massaging and oiling of the body, have their counterpart in the rituals of *abhisheka* of the gods, where the divine bodies are similarly oiled, massaged and shampooed by the priest. The precision of posture demanded in the art of love and in dance as well as in yoga bear witness to the thoroughgoing and multiple incorporation of the body into the Hindu world-view.

The body is set off by clothes, jewellery, and flowers. The prime paradigm is the auspicious married woman, but both genders and all ages have their appropriate dress code that affirms and confirms their status, both inner and outer. In some villages incorrect dress by low castes, such as wearing sandals and having upturned moustaches, can lead to violence. Men's dress has been Westernized, women's has not.

The spiritual self, the body, and ideal types

The *Bhagavad Gita* associates the castes with the threads (*gunas*) that the Samkhya philosophy sees as running all through the material world (Prakriti), though it is left to commentators to spell out how three threads – light (*sattva*), activity (*rajas*) and darkness (*tamas*) – relate to the four castes. The idiom of the threads is still used, though turned to one's own advantage. Thus a farmer might claim that farmers are *sattvik mat*, 'inclined to goodness', while higher castes are *rajasik mat*, 'royally inclined' or 'high and mighty'. Rowdy young men, of whatever caste, might be called *tamasik*, of the darkness thread.[7] However, the goal of the Samkhya philosophy is to enable the conscious individual self to leave off watching the dance of Prakriti and achieve the isolation of its individual consciousness for ever. In the *Bhagavad Gita*, when Arjuna refuses to fight against his teachers and his relatives, Krishna explains to him that the self is eternal, assuming body after body in just the same way that an individual changes clothes. For as long as it is contained within the body, the self has to perform its karmic duty. And God too has a body that likewise expresses his nature; in the *Bhagavad Gita* he has a superbody, brighter than a thousand suns, swallowing up the worlds, with the bodies of gods and men entering into it, some caught between his teeth.

The representation of the individual in art

Hinduism likes to define people as ideal types, hence Zimmer's claim that the gods are the only individuals within Hinduism. Much extant pre-modern Hindu painting relates to *rasa*, the aesthetic creation of specific emotional states, above all in relation to Krishna. Krishna's love sports with the wives of the cowherds amongst whom he was brought up, as described in the *Bhagavata Purana* and subsequent poetry, are the pre-eminent theme of Hindu miniature painting of the seventeenth and eighteenth centuries. With the demise of imperial ateliers, artists schooled in the realism of Mughal art played a significant part in the formation of a Hindu courtly art, in which kings and princes amid their harems saw themselves as Krishna with the *gopis*. The calm and orderly re-creation of desire, whether in enjoyment or most powerfully in separation, produced a powerful conjunction of painting, music, poetry and dance. The classical *rasa* system, however, is only a small part of artistic endeavour in theatre and dance, which varies from region to region, sometimes based on the mainline tradition, sometimes on local folklore.

The Hindu self is akin to the divine self in its appreciation of these arts; both human and divine individuality are expressed and defined in art. The human situation is also indirectly portrayed by somewhat inchoate sculptural forms. Shiva's *gana*s, the chubby and boyish monsters, roly-poly forms blown about by an inner breath, are representations of childhood, and also unstable masculinity. As dwarfs, their shortness denoting stability and strength, they support structures, but at the same time they directly express the playful nature (*lila*) of the phenomenal world, lacking proper human order just as the latter lacks proper divine order.

The *vyali*s, half-lions and half-mythical creatures that rear from pillars in southern temples, flanking images of the gods but larger and more crudely powerful, must be expressions of royal power, of vaulting ambition and desire for glory, indeed of the will to power. Such figures express more fluently what is sometimes spelled out by poets. The Sanskrit poet Bana (*c*.600) compares the strength of a royal warrior to that of a lion and his gait to an elephant's. His forearm is likened to that of a tiger, his eyes, wide and round, are like a deer's, his nose is like the snout of a boar, his lusty shoulders like the mighty back of the buffalo.[8] Analogous to the half-lion composite animal is the monstrous Face of Time that is placed above doorways and windows, with bulging cheeks and eyes, filled with breath like the *gana*s but spewing forth matter and swallowing it up. This face lacks a lower jaw. In one view it is the eclipse demon. At all events, not unlike the other forms, it embodies a certain monstrousness in the very heart of things. Then there is Apasmara, the *gana* who lies or sits beneath the dancing Shiva. This figure is usually called Ignorance, but often supports Shiva, and arguably has strong affiliations with the universal phenomenon of possession.[9] Forgetfulness rather than ignorance, Apasmara like the *gana*s, the *vyali*s and the Face of Time, may be read as representing the unknown within, the submerged part of human experience, the forgotten past lives, the subconscious.

Such figures are analogous to some of the dream figures that appear in Western art. Examples are to hand in Max Klinger, with the same kind of desperate precision we find in Hieronymus Bosch and Goya. Klinger is more significantly modern in his extensive thinking out of fetishism in narrative terms. But dream and nightmare figures are legion in Western art. In Hindu art they are set within the order of a coherent iconography without losing their power; in Hinduism a calm rationality retains overall control of artistic expression.

One function of the Face of Time is to protect against the evil eye. The beneficent sight of the gods and holy people has its opposite in the harmful gaze of people who might have reason to feel jealous, though this harmfulness may well be involuntary. Children's eyes are marked with lamp black, and black string is tied on their wrists to make them less attractive to the jealous gaze of the childless. Abbott gives an extensive range of diagrams used in western India in the 1920s to ward off the Crow's Eye, or Eye Pollution, as the phenomenon of the evil eye is sometimes called.[10] It is transmuted into myth as the destructive force of Shiva's third eye, for this third eye is not only the mark of superior insight but also the source of a beam of fire which destroys Kama the god of love when he attempts to disturb Shiva's meditation. Strangely, Lacan claims that, while the evil eye is universal, 'there is no trace anywhere of a good eye, of an eye that blesses'.[11] The power of sight in both directions is expressed in the key notion of *darshana*. The devotee sees the god or the guru and is blessed by the simple act of vision. The gaze is returned by the divine object, though it is true that that is not crucial, since for instance looking only on the divine object's feet can be sufficient for one to be blessed. But not only a living guru returns the devotee's gaze, for when an image is installed in a temple, the final process is giving it its eyes. At this moment a mirror is held in front of it so that the first thing it sees is itself. The sudden irruption of sight would be harmful to a non-divine recipient.

Spiritual physiology

The comatose sprawl of Apasmara beneath Shiva's foot noted above, and perhaps also the often contorted form of *gana*s, may be seen as artistic forms of an important expression of the Hindu self, namely trance, voluntary or involuntary.[12] The subordination demanded of the social self severely curtails freedom of expression, but becoming possessed permits behaviour that would not otherwise be sanctioned. But beyond possession, like the evil eye a universal phenomenon, Hinduism has its own very detailed physiological explanation of higher states of consciousness.

The human ascetic, like Shiva, acquires an inner heat, known as *tapas*. *Tapas* is synonymous with asceticism. *Tapas* is that general energy which manifests in the heat of the sun and fire and in the heat of animals when they procreate or fight, and which in Vedic speculations on the origin of the cosmos is the very energy that started the process of creation. But ascetically produced within the human being *tapas* saturates the body, making it a reservoir of hot power. This power is a sexual and fecundating energy which can also be destructive. Walter Kaelber remarks that 'much of the dramatic tension of post-Vedic mythology is provided by world-threatening tapas produced from ascetic ardor':

> Gods, goddesses, demons, kings, heroes, married sages, celibate yogins, young children, even animals perform tapas. The god Brahma produces by tapas; Shiva's tapas and magical fire alternately create and destroy; Parvati maintains tapas for 36,000 years; a host of demons . . . concentrate on world domination by *tapas*.[13]

It is the ascetic *tapas* of Shiva that gives such creative force to his mere sweat and produces the creature Andhaka, for instance. The very generalized power of *tapas* is the product of asceticism. Specific powers are produced by the specific procedures of yoga, as defined by Patanjali. These powers, *siddhis*, 'demonstrations of achieved power', often referred to as 'the power of becoming small etc.', from the first one in the list, include several abilities often credited elsewhere to shamans and seem to point to an original connection of yoga with shamanism, especially the ability to fly through the air, to read people's thoughts, and to understand the language of animals. The ability to know one's own past lives and those of others is seen as confirmation of the truth of rebirth. For the early Upanishads, power is inseparable from knowledge: it is to be expected that someone who knows has power. Knowledge is power.[14]

A new category of Hindu art was revealed to the West in London in 1971 in the Tantric Art exhibition set up by Philip Rawson in collaboration with Ajit Mookerjee.[15] In fact a melange of several different art forms, it did bring to light secret and professedly dangerous images that are definitely tantric. Thus Chinnamasta, the goddess who has cut off her own head, was the subject of several paintings in the exhibition. Herself in the form of a *yogini* (female yogi) of 16 years, Chinnamasta is attended by two younger *yoginis*, 12-year-olds, who join Chinnamasta's cut-off head in drinking the blood that flows from her headless neck. Beneath these three is the copulating couple of the god of love and his wife Rati, the latter on top. This image is so powerful according to tantric texts that the practitioner employing it should think of it only in abstract terms, and its power is said to be used to harm others. Should a woman employ it, she will become a powerful *yogini* but her husband and son will die. Such images as this are not designed to hang on walls.[16]

Not at all tantric is the linga in the yoni, the quintessence of Shaivism, its standard and public form. Here again the inchoate sexual forces that worry other religions, and are expressed in modern art in infinitely varied and mindless mutations, find calm exactitude. The yoni holds the linga; genitalia achieve divine certainty.

One form of tantric art, already briefly mentioned in chapter 8, is the diagram (*yantra*), and the *yantra* called the Shri Chakra with its nine interlaced triangles often graces book covers on Hindu topics. It is in fact not Shri or Lakshmi, but Rajarajeshvari, queen of the universe. It is not a representation of her, but actually embodies her. It is not a circuit-board, but a fully working 'mother-board', so to speak, a goddess-board of the universal computer. The nine triangles, five downward-pointing, four pointing upwards, are contained within a double set of lotus petals set within a square with four gateways. Only the central small triangle uncrossed by any other triangle is significant in itself. The other triangles form multi-angled enclosures where they intersect. The *yantra* is a series of enclosures, each within the other. Each enclosure contains a set of mantras and *yoginis* and a presiding deity. The meditator usually works inwards from the exterior. Each enclosure is associated with part of the process of cosmic evolution and devolution. Each is also associated with a particular body part. Well known as part of hatha or tantric yoga, the centres of concentrated power within the body, the six *chakras*, are each associated with a particular enclosure of the Shri Chakra.

Colourful paintings of the *chakras* within the human body formed part of the Tantra Art exhibition. Each *chakra* is a lotus. Four-petalled at the base of the spine, six-petalled behind the genitals, ten-petalled at the level of the navel, twelve-petalled in the heart, sixteen-petalled in the throat, and just two-petalled between the eyes. Each of these lotuses has it own special colour and presiding deity. At the top of the head, is the thousand-petalled white lotus. Connecting all these is a subtle vertical channel called the Sushumna, which intersects with two subsidiary channels which criss-cross its length. In the lowest *chakra* a female snake coils around a linga, and successful meditation will cause this snake to rise and break through all the *chakras* till she reaches the thousand-petalled lotus. The lowest *chakra*, as stated above, is at the base of the spine, and its internal linga is quite distinct from the meditator's own linga. Inspired by this formal and technical imagery, some modern Indian painters produce imaginative variations which they claim are 'tantric' painting, but this is the whimsy of modernity since exactitude in relation to tradition is essential for meaningful representation.[17]

Oceanic feeling

While their exact history is unknown, the *chakras* would seem to be a development of the *Chhandogya Upanishad*'s declaration (8.1.1–3) that the centre of consciousness within the human body is a small lotus which is the heart. Within it are earth, sky, sun, moon and stars. Brahman is within it. Later Upanishads refer to the heart as the hanging cup of a lotus flower. It must have been on the analogy of the lotus of the heart that there developed the more extensive mystical physiology noted above. If these lotuses are modelled on the original heart lotus of the *Chhandogya Upanishad*, what was the heart lotus modelled on? The concavity of the lotus, explicitly said to be inverted in later Upanishads, is a natural and obvious symbol of the vagina and the womb. The Upanishads, then, necessarily eschewed the womb, place of physical birth, as a symbol of spiritual rebirth, but embraced it indirectly as the lotus, symbol of the place of Brahman, giving us a physical representation of the place of the spiritual self and its bliss directly analogous to the womb, transposed from the original site of bliss which was the womb.

Another image of the female container is used by the *Taittiriya Upanishad*, which speaks of the self as having five sheaths (*koshas*) of progressive subtlety: the bodily sheath, the vital sheath, the mental sheath, the intellectual sheath, and the blissful sheath, the last being the place where the spiritual self resides. In later developments of esoteric doctrine, the whole universe is divided into zones corresponding to these sheaths, the macrocosm paralleling the microcosm. The decreasing density of these sheaths or zones shows Hindu thought's preference for relativism and interdependence over logical oppositions, and for physical complexity over idealized simplicity.

Within the heart, Brahman is bliss. In deep, dreamless sleep, we all have a foretaste of the supreme bliss that is the pure objectless consciousness that is Brahman. This sort of sleep, since it dissolves subject and object, is a temporary union with Brahman. The *Brihadaranyaka Upanishad* explains:

'It is like this. As a man embraced by a woman he loves is oblivious to everything within or without, so this person embraced by the self [*atman*] consisting of knowledge is oblivious to everything within or without.

Here a father is not a father, a mother is not a mother, worlds are not worlds, gods are not gods, and Vedas are not Vedas . . . Neither the good nor the bad follows him, for he has now passed beyond all sorrows of the heart.

He becomes the one ocean, he becomes the sole seer! This, Your Majesty, is the world of *brahman*.' So did Yajnavalkya instruct him. 'This is his highest goal! . . . This is his highest world! This is his highest bliss!' (*Brihadaranyaka Upanishad*, 4.3.21–3)

In the *Chhandogya Upanishad* (6.13), Shvetaketu's father uses the analogy of salt dissolved in water: the salt cannot be found, there is no separation between the two, salt and water. In the same way, the self is everywhere, though it cannot be seen.

This passage is the ultimate source of Freud's notion of oceanic feeling. In 1927 Roman Rolland, then working on his study of Ramakrishna, described the latter's spontaneous state of limitless sensation in a letter to Freud. Despairing of seeing Kali, Mother of the Universe, Ramakrishna seizes a sword to kill himself, when suddenly:

I saw an ocean . . . boundless, dazzling. In whatever direction I looked great luminous waves were rising. They bore down upon me with a loud roar, as if to swallow me up . . . they engulfed me. I was suffocated. I lost all natural consciousness . . . Round me rolled an ocean of ineffable joy. And in the depths of my being I was conscious of the presence of the Divine Mother.

In explaining this experience Ramakrishna gives a rather more elaborate analogy than Shvetaketu's, though clearly referring to the Upanishad:

A salt doll went to measure the depth of the ocean, but before it had gone far into the water it melted away. It became entirely one with the water of the ocean. Then who was to come back and tell the ocean's depth?[18]

We might wonder, why anyone, least of all a salt doll, should want to measure the depth of the ocean; presumably this is modern man, seemingly the opposite of the full consciousness that is the ocean, and concerned to measure. When one understands the true nature of reality, there is no call to measure anything. At all events, it was Ramakrishna's description of the experience of being unbounded within the ocean which Rolland passed on to Freud, and which Freud refers to as 'oceanic feeling' in his *Civilization and its Discontents*.

Freud was willing to allow that the oceanic feeling exists in many people and was inclined to trace it back to 'an early phase of ego-feeling', but was unwilling to regard that feeling as 'the source of religious needs'. He could not think of any need in childhood 'as strong as the need for a father's protection'.

Thus the part played by the oceanic feeling, which might seek something like the restoration of limitless narcissism, is ousted from a place in the foreground. The origin of the religious attitude can be traced back in clear outlines as far as the feeling of infantile helplessness. There may be something further behind that, but for the present it is wrapped in obscurity.

I can imagine that the oceanic feeling became connected with religion later on. The 'oneness with the universe' which constitutes its ideational content sounds like a first attempt at a religious consolation, as though it were another way of disclaiming the danger which the ego recognizes as threatening it from the external world. Let me admit once more that it is very difficult for me to work with these almost intangible quantitites.[19]

In his letter in reply to Rolland's, Freud declared, 'I shall now try with your guidance to penetrate into the Indian jungle from which until now an uncertain blending of Hellenic love of proportion, Jewish sobriety, and Philistine timidity have kept me away. I really ought to have tackled it earlier, for the plants of this soil shouldn't be alien to me; I have dug to certain depths for their roots. But it isn't easy to pass beyond the limits of one's nature.'[20] From the perspective not just of Hinduism but virtually all cultures it is altogether remarkable that Freud should so overlook the bond between mother and child as to write that he could not think of any need in childhood as strong as the need for a father's protection.

Scarcely less remarkable is the conclusion to his brief discussion of the oceanic feeling:

> Another friend of mine . . . has assured me that through the practices of Yoga, by withdrawing from the world, by fixing the attention on bodily functions and by peculiar methods of breathing, one can in fact evoke new sensations and coenaesthesias in oneself, which he regards as regressions to primordial states of mind which have long ago been overlaid. He sees in them a physiological basis, as it were, of much of the wisdom of mysticism . . . But I am moved to exclaim in the words of Schiller's diver: –
>
> > 'Let him rejoice
> > Who breathes up here in the roseate light.'[21]

Indian thought, then, rests at too deep a stratum of being for Freud. He fears to descend to such depths! But the monsters that the young diver in Schiller's poem sees in the 'womb of the ocean' remind us of the monsters, the *vyalis* and the Faces of Time that are everywhere in Hindu temple architecture, upfront manifestations of the depths ready to be confronted and passed by as one circumambulates the deities. As for the oceanic feeling, it is only later on in *Civilization and its Discontents* that, in passing and without reference to the oceanic feeling, does Freud refer to the true and obvious source of that feeling:

> If we go back far enough, we find that the first acts of civilization were the use of tools, the gaining of control over fire and the construction of buildings . . . the dwelling-house was a substitute for the mother's womb, the first lodging, for which in all likelihood man still longs, and in which he was safe and felt at ease.[22]

The Upanishads sing the praises of Brahman that is consciousness as the ultimate reality, and declare it to be the inner witness that is the self. They extol the state of dreamless sleep that may be fairly called the oceanic feeling, and which may equally fairly be taken to be a reminiscence of the perfectly content life in the womb – a time of life that comes to be incorporated within the scope of Hindu ritual. But at the same time, all this is accompanied by a new fear of the womb, fear that follows from the new doctrine of rebirth, and the ever continuing re-entry into the womb the doctrine implies. In the Vedic sacrificial texts which preceded the Upanishads, performance of the sacrifice involved the symbolic return of the sacrificer to the womb, so that he could be reborn into the world of the gods. A special hut represented the womb, in which he was to crouch like a foetus. Now this physical imitation is replaced by the exaltation of what is covertly the condition of the foetus, the bliss of dreamless sleep, of consciousness without objects.

Conclusion

In this chapter the self has been followed from the family photograph to regression to the womb. Not unlike the worshipper beginning at the doorways of the square container of the Shri Chakra working backwards to the beginning of creation, the principal lineaments of the social self and the spiritual self of Hinduism have been set out, while moving back to the womb and Brahman. Some passing references to modern Western art, its deformation and defamation of the self, have been made, but the trail of the Hindu self has led us to Freud. Thus concludes the presentation of some of the general features of Hinduism that have persisted over centuries. This presentation has been contaminated, unavoidably, by modernity, but it has attempted in a limited way to set Hinduism at a critical distance from modernity, to show that Hinduism can stand on its own feet in opposition to modernity, but also that they have features in common.

Part IV

Hinduism Today

Chapter Eleven

Gurus

Nothing better characterizes the gulf between Hinduism and modernity than the guru, but gurus have brought Hinduism to the West and given modern times a saffron tinge. Many Hindu gurus are teachers and exponents of a spirituality they claim is relevant to the modern world. The British pop group the Beatles took up Maharishi, and George Harrison then supported the Hare Krishna movement. Swami Satchidananda made a dramatic appearance at the 1969 Woodstock festival in the USA, bringing Indian spirituality to the American people – for them to give to the rest of the world! The spiritual peace that these and many other gurus claimed to bring from India coincided with the peace movement that wanted to end the Vietnam war, and with the spread of consciousness-altering drugs in the West.

In complete contrast to the watchword of the Enlightenment, 'Dare to reason for yourself', the guru requires submission from the disciple, whose own limited power of reason might inhibit understanding of superior truths. An element of daring to contravene normal knowledge and behaviour is sometimes necessary in following esoteric teachings, but submission to and worship of the teacher are usually inevitable. From the standpoint of Hindu psychology, a key factor is the importance of forging a new relationship outside the established order of joint family and caste. Choosing a guru in India is sometimes almost the counterpart of choosing a spouse in the West, or, more accurately, a parent. Kakar, in his invaluable study of the psychology of the relationship between the guru and his disciple, stresses the surrender of the disciple to the guru, and also the intimacy that the disciple feels he or she enjoys with the guru.[1] Guru and disciple in India enjoy an exceptional freedom from official and social control, a freedom that has good and bad aspects, giving the guru more power for good and more power for harm.

The guru is a figure of the greatest importance in Hinduism. The best single account of the guru is that given by the previous Shankaracharya of Kanchi in his *The Guru Tradition*.[2] However, there is no thorough academic study of the Hindu aspect of what is often called the guru phenomenon. One reason is perhaps that people sympathetic to the notion of the guru might be drawn to consider only one guru; and those who are unsympathetic turn aside. There are many individual studies, mainly of particular gurus in the West, but almost no overviews, certainly no extensive academic survey of gurus.[3] Gita Mehta's *Karma Cola* (1980) is a series of sharp sketches of Westerners and Indian gurus in India; but the guru is too significant a figure to be only a topic of popular journalism. A useful academic study of several contemporary gurus is Lise McKean's *Spiritual Enterprise*, though she is unable to disguise her distaste for her subject-matter; her primary concern is the 'business and politics of spirituality'.[4]

Both poles of approach to gurus, either enthusiasm or scorn, were displayed back in the seventh century by the great Sanskrit prose-poet Bana. His description of what seems to be a fictional contemporary guru-priest in his prose-poem *Kadambari* is referred to in chapter 6 above – this would-be wonder-worker is a figure of fun. At the other extreme, Bana, in his *Deeds of the Emperor Harsha*, vividly describes a mighty spiritual teacher who brings about the founding of an imperial dynasty while himself going on to attain even greater power in the celestial world. Similar extremes are found today. Some gurus are rogues, some are spiritually elevated, some are extremely powerful. Sathya Sai Baba is venerated by many of the most important people in India; his organization is immensely wealthy, and criticism of him is held to be dangerous in India.

Politicians have a special need for gurus: the tradition of spiritual adviser to the ruler goes all the way back to the Vedic notion of the priest as *purohita*, 'standing before the king'. Dhirendra 'Brahmachari' was the guru of Indira Gandhi; the infamous Chandraswami (b. 1949) was the guru of Narasimha Rao (prime minister 1991–6); Bhagwan Ram (d. 1992) was the guru of Chandra Shekhar (prime minister in 1990). Chandra Shekhar's surprise and very brief premiership was said in his home state to have been due to the favour of his guru. Bhagwan Ram had a much better reputation than is usual for gurus who associate with politicians; the leprosy hospital he set up is in the *Guinness Book of Records* for the maximum number of leper cures. A less personal relationship was that of Vinoba Bhave, Gandhi's successor, appearing as the 'Sarkari ("Government") guru' of the Republic of India into the 1970s. Jaffrelot speaks of the contemporary fundamentalist organization the RSS acting as a guru to the government, as 'a collective *Rajguru*'.[5]

The lawyer and president of the brahman council of Bengal, J. N. Bhattacharyya (1850–99), whose work on Hindu sects was extensively used by Weber in his study of Hinduism, noted the growth of the institution of guru: 'since the commencement of Mahommedan rule . . . the absence of a strong central authority . . . in ecclesiastical matters, and the ignorance of the masses, have enabled many a clever adventurer to play the role of "incarnations", and to carve out independent religious principalities'.[6] In Weber's words, 'It was first the foreign domination of Islam shattering the political power of the higher Hindu castes which gave the development of guru power free rein, permitting it to grow to grotesque heights.'[7] Some institutional gurus have long enjoyed golden or silver thrones, but enthronement is now commonplace for successful gurus. The Shankaracharya of Kanchi was seated on a throne while he was showered with 200 kilos of gold coins on his hundredth birthday in 1993.[8] On his silver throne, Sathya Sai Baba sits above the prime minister and president of India when they share a platform.

In 1896 Bhattacharyya, in the tones of Macaulay, described what a would-be guru required. Not much training, some tact, some skill in speaking, and 'genius for inventing unexplodable legends' – with these the profession brings 'not only power, money, fame, and honour, but everything else that the most wicked lust of the most depraved of human beings can have a craving for'. 'He must, through his disciples, circulate the most extravagant stories about his miraculous powers; but, at the same time, must avoid their exhibition.' Bhattacharyya says that most important is the choice of the guru's closest disciples, for a traitor would spill the beans. Success is difficult. There are many competitors.

> Even when a great religious kingdom is successfully established on an apparently sound footing, it usually proves quite as ephemeral as the secular monarchies founded in the last century by political adventurers of the type of Hyder Ali. But in spite of all the checks on the overgrowth of the sects, their number at the present time is not at all inconsiderable.[9]

Today there are said to be tens of thousands of gurus. The comparison with 'secular monarchies' is appropriate and significant: gurus do set up spiritual kingdoms. It is natural for Indian ascetics to aspire to dominion. The Buddha was destined to be either Buddha or Universal Emperor. There are many ancient stories of ascetics who aspired to Indra's throne in heaven. Indra usually thwarts them by sending celestial dancing-girls to seduce them, the consequent expenditure of their semen draining away their ascetic power. Bernier in the seventeenth century tells us that the ascetics he met expected to return as great kings in their next rebirths. Many ascetics are motivated by a will to power either now or later. But only some ascetics become gurus.

B. Premanand, head of the Indian Rationalists Society, president of the Committee for the Scientific Investigation of Claims of the Paranormal (CSICP), and editor of the *Indian Skeptic*, has spent 50 years going round Indian villages exposing fake miracles. The guru as trickster is presented, along with a demonstration of the value of the institution in A. K. Narayan's novel,

The Guide. The hustling hero resting destitute in a temple is taken by the villagers to be a wandering *sadhu*. At first living comfortably on the proceeds of his deceit, he is led by their adulation to offer to end a drought by fasting. It rains when he dies. This novel was made into a successful film, helped by the fact that the hero's companion is a talented dancing-girl.[10] A more sombre view of gurus is taken by the film *Jadugar* ('Magician', 1989), where a wealthy and powerful guru, in fact a criminal whose success lies in simple magical tricks, is overthrown by a stage magician pretending to greater powers.

The great innovation in Hinduism in modern times has been the assumption of a dominant position by the guru as godman, but the institution of guru has always been an essential feature of Hinduism. The classical position, the guru in brahmanic Hinduism, is set out in the Laws of Manu:

> That *brahman* who performs in accordance with the rules of the Veda the rites, conception rite and so forth, and gives food to the child is called the guru . . . That man who truthfully fills both his ears with the Veda, the pupil shall consider as his father and mother; he must never offend him . . . Let him consider that he received a [mere animal] existence when his parents begat him through mutual affection, and when he was born from the womb. But that birth which a teacher acquainted with the whole Veda, in accordance with the law, procures for him through the Gayatri, mantra of initiation, is real, exempt from age and death. That *brahman* who is the giver of birth for the sake of the Veda and the teacher of the prescribed duties, becomes by law the father of an aged man, even though he himself be childless.[11]

The word guru means 'venerable', 'venerable teacher'. Traditional etymology explains the word as the one who removes (*ru*) ignorance (*gu*). A traditional verse declares that the guru is Brahma, is Vishnu, is Shiva, is Supreme Brahman in visible form. On the same lines, Badarayana, foremost of teachers in the non-dualist lineage, is described in a verse as 'Brahma without four heads, Vishnu with only two arms, Shiva without a third eye on his forehead'. The guru is the direct and immediate representative of God. An often quoted verse says, 'The guru is father, the guru is mother, the guru is God, the guru is the refuge. If Shiva is angry with you, the guru will come to your rescue. But if the guru is angry, there is no one to help you.' This last point hints at the dangerous power of the guru. Holy men are notoriously bad-tempered in myth and story. But the main thing is the link between temple and school, the link between deity and instruction, and between parenthood and instruction. Intellectual and spiritual formation take place within a lineage, indeed create the most important sort of lineage. The gods themselves are pupils as well as teachers, so pervasive is the idiom of the guru. Shiva has his specific form as teacher, Dakshinamurti; but his son Skanda teaches him the mantra OM and is therefore his guru. Both Rama and Krishna are humble pupils of their gurus. The idiom and discourse of the one-to-one guru–pupil relationship is absolutely crucial to Hinduism.

There are many gurus and many gods, but the gods mutually reinforce each other, their multiplicity confirming the existence of the divine world, while the gurus, all the same basic shape with only two arms and one head, are rivals. With regard to gods, Chandrasekharendra makes the point that no one wants to eat the same dish every day, or hear a musician play only one raga. The variety of deities in a temple allows the devotee to concentrate on each for a little while. 'It is in realisation of human nature, our desire for change, that our religion has so many forms of gods and goddesses, so many different forms of each deity, so many different ways of decorating them, so many different vehicles for them, and so many different ways of worship.'[12] One's interest is aroused, he says, when a number of deities are brought together like musical ragas strung together in a garland. But the guru has nothing to gain from comparison with other gurus. Once the choice has been made, the spiritual parent should be as fixed as any other kin. Where there is a tradition behind the guru, then of course one should be aware of and meditate on the lineage, on the guru's guru, and so on backwards if feasible.

General characteristics of gurus

Various parameters may be usefully applied to the phenomenon of gurus. First and foremost, a guru is a spiritual person, with spiritual powers, who attracts and accepts disciples. He has a spiritual teaching, though this teaching may be formal or informal. But he may genuinely possess special powers (from reading people's thoughts to control over the physical world) – and such powers are for many Hindus inseparable from spirituality – or merely falsely lay claim to them. This is the great problem in studying gurus. Everything hinges on the spirituality they possess and impart to their disciples. Experience of this spirituality is all-important. Often it is difficult for an outsider to reach a just conclusion about the value of a guru and his teachings. Narayan's novel *The Guide*, mentioned above, shows the strength of the institution, a false guru becoming a true guru. The reverse is perhaps more frequent, genuine gurus becoming corrupted by the power they hold over disciples. In any case, a guru's career may consist of highs and lows, spiritual heights and depths.

A guru necessarily has followers or disciples. A standard procedure is the process of initiation (*diksha*) in which a disciple is given a secret Sanskrit phrase (mantra). Such mantras have fixed and standard form, but being imparted by the guru gives them a unique power. A disciple greets a guru by touching his feet, if not prostrating himself before him.

Gurus may claim to be the supreme deity or, what is little different, an *avatara* of the supreme deity. Sathya Sai Baba claims to be both Shiva and

Shakti. A guru may claim to be an *avatara* of a previous guru, which was the initial position of Sathya Sai Baba, namely that he was a reincarnation of Sirdi Sai Baba. Or the guru may make no such claims, but his followers do. It is well-nigh inevitable that followers worship the guru, and this is the norm, though the degree and formality of such worship vary considerably.

The guru may behave like a king. He usually has the title Swami ('Lord'). He is often addressed as Maharaj ('Great King'). He may have great wealth at his disposal, sit on a throne, and spend extravagantly. Rajneesh was famous for his 80 Rolls Royces, the kind of empty extravagance maharajas used to be notorious for when the British had taken their power and left them with a purse. Chandraswami has a palatial ashram in the capital. Followers of Prabhupada, the deceased founder of the Hare Krishna movement, provide his replica with palatial quarters in their temples, and a full-scale palace in Virginia, USA. As noted above, Bana describes a guru providing terrestrial power for a king and celestial royalty for himself. Like the *purohita* of old, the guru may advise a king or a prime minister, and be a Raj guru, closely connecting his status to that of the ruler. Gurus usually maintain retreats called ashrams, which are, so to speak, their spiritual kingdoms.

The guru may simply assert his status, and convince people by his charisma. Alternatively, he may be initiated into a long-established spiritual lineage, chosen by the current guru to be his successor. Very important are the five institutions (*mathas*) which are said to have been set up by Shankaracharya, and whose heads each take the title Shankaracharya. There are thousands of parallel institutions on a smaller scale. Where householders form a spiritual lineage, as in some Vaishnava sects, the guru might inherit his status from his father; he may claim that a deceased guru appeared in a dream or vision to initiate him; or he may say that a mysterious and otherwise unknown guru initiated him, and then departed.

The guru is usually a renouncer, though a guru who inherits his status will be a householder like his father. A tantric guru may have sexual relations with his disciples. Normally the guru asserts his celibacy, but allegations of abuse are not uncommon, and are perhaps inevitable. Jealousy or other motives may lead disciples to make accusations; and power corrupts. Few gurus are exempt from such accusations. Gurus are usually practitioners and teachers of yoga or some other spiritual discipline. They may write down their teachings, or these teachings may be oral. Their teachings may be entirely traditional, traditional with a new emphasis, or, as in the case of Rajneesh, entirely new.

Gurus are commonly held to have special powers. They may flaunt these powers, or leave it to their disciples to spread their fame. At the least, the guru will claim to be able to read the thoughts of his disciples. Often he reads the character of his disciples and tailors his discourse to suit them. The guru's powers may include magic tricks, which are a manifestation of his divinity. On the other hand, gurus frequently claim scientific validity for their teachings.

The guru may be a healer, able to cure the body as well as the mind. He might take into himself the ills of the person he cures, and be temporarily inconvenienced thereby.

The guru may act as a priest. Ramakrishna was a priest in the Dakshineshvar temple. Sathya Sai Baba has produced large quantities ashes for the anointing (*abhisheka*) of Shiva's linga at the Shiva Ratri festival, and also small lingas from his mouth. Hereditary temple priests may aspire to the role of guru.

The guru may be a social worker, a doer of good works. Successful gurus may replicate the work of governments and NGOs by building and running schools and hospitals.[13]

The guru may have only Indian disciples, or Western disciples as well; he may travel abroad, within the diaspora, or around the world. He may restrict his attention to Hindus, or he may seek to act as missionary to the West.

A few gurus are women; their numbers may well be increasing. They may be the wives, widows, or disciples of established gurus, or they may be self-manifestations. There are several instances of female gurus being accepted by their followers as manifestations of the goddess as supreme deity. Although veneration continues for medieval women saints such as Mirabai (late fifteenth century) who took nothing from their spouses, the first women gurus/saints in modern times tended to be wives of gurus who took over their husband's role after his death or retirement: examples include Saradamani (1853–1920), widow of Ramakrishna, and Mira Alfassa, 'the Mother' (1878–1973), the wife of Aurobindo. A more modern phenomenon is that of women who are believed to embody the highest godhead. Instances are Anandamayi Ma (1896–1982), highly regarded by many important Indians; Amritanandamayi Ma (b. 1954), who individually touches and blesses vast crowds of devotees; and Meera Devi (b. 1960), who does the same on a much smaller scale in Germany.

Gurus are in fact difficult to summarize; a brief account of the most important modern gurus will now be given, to give some idea their variety.

Ramakrishna (1836–1886)

Apart from Mahatma Gandhi (see chapters 2 and 12), who is completely atypical, the most famous and the most important modern guru remains Ramakrishna, not least on account of the durability of his fame.[14] Ramakrishna is revered for his varied and intense mystical experience and his ability to express that experience in his body language as well as verbally. Max Müller not only published the text of the Veda for the first time – his book on Ramakrishna established him in the West as a saint. Ramakrishna knew neither English nor Sanskrit. His vivid sayings in rustic Bengali on the topic of *bhakti* and the religious life have been published under the title of the Gospel of Ramakrishna. He inspired the second most famous guru, the charismatic organizer, Vivekananda. Vivekananda founded the Ramakrishna order of monks, and preached Vedanta to India and the West. An important aspect of this movement was its involvement in social work, and this Western-inspired practical assistance came to be a feature of many later Hindu movements. The Ramakrishna Mission has centres round the world, and publishes many key Hindu texts.

Ramakrishna experienced trances from an early age and liked dressing up as a woman. He became priest at a new Kali temple, set up outside Calcutta at Dakshineshwar in 1855 by Rani Rashmani, a low-caste widow. The temple comprises shrines to all three major strands of Hinduism: the lofty central shrine with nine pinnacles to Kali, the extensive shrine to Krishna, and the 12 Shaiva linga shrines. Ramakrishna was in a position in which he could have gained wealth and a degree of power, but his destiny was to be acknowledged as a spiritual giant.

He saw Kali everywhere, so much so that he was first taken to be insane, but his religious experience was richly varied. He was initiated into Advaita Vedanta and Tantra. In 1866 a Hindu Sufi initiated him into Islam, a faith he held for three days:

> I devoutly repeated the name of Allah, wore a cloth like the Arab Moslems, said their prayers five times daily and felt disinclined even to see images of the Hindu gods and goddesses, much less worship them – for the Hindu way of thinking had disappeared altogether from my mind. I spent three days in that mood, and I had the full realization of the *sadhana* [ritual practice] of their faith.[15]

Before this his devotion to Rama led him to imitate Hanuman, Rama's faithful servant, whose picture hung in his room. For several days he jumped about, part of his *dhoti* (lower garment) hanging like a tail. He claimed the lower end of his spine lengthened, forming a proto-tail. This practical meditation on Hanuman was rewarded by a vision of Sita, who then entered into his body.[16]

Ramakrishna's mystical experience was manifest to those who saw him: he was living proof of higher states of consciousness, and this immediacy is preserved in the few photographs of him that exist, complementing the several detailed first-hand accounts of his maturity. The editor of a 1981 souvenir booklet remarks that he 'was the first incarnation of God who has been photographed'.[17] According to Roy, Ramakrishna himself believed that 'photographs of holy people were not merely symbolic but were living and spiritually vibrant'.[18] The three photographs of the living Ramakrishna show him in his characteristic state of *samadhi* ('ecstatic bliss'), mouth open and eyes half-closed. The best known of the three, which shows him seated cross-legged, is known in the Ramakrishna movement as the 'Worshipped Pose', and hangs in all its shrine rooms. The same photograph is also used in poster prints which set him beside the image of Kali.

Vivekananda (1863–1902)

The second guru figure we have to consider, for ever linked with Ramakrishna, is Vivekananda. Possessed of a very different charisma from that of Ramakrishna, he ensured the perpetuation of Ramakrishna's fame along with his own. Vivekananda, handsome and a good singer, neglected his family duties to form a 'monastery' of his fellow disciples, where, after their leader's death, they continued to associate and beg for their livelihood. Thanks to patronage, Vivekananda got to Chicago for the World Parliament of Religions in 1893 and had a great success. Vigorous and dynamic, he returned to India to call for a muscular Hinduism, declaring 'India must conquer the world'.[19]

Whereas Ramakrishna dramatically asserted image worship in the face of the Christian-inspired monotheism and communal worship of such reform movements as the Arya Samaj and the Brahmo Samaj, Vivekananda took up the non-dualist Vedanta as a hammer to smash the pretensions of Christianity and Islam. Vedanta's spiritual hierarchy and levels of truth enabled it to encompass all religions without leaving any doubt as to its own superiority. This relaunching of Vedanta was extremely successful and was to become the master doctrine of the innumerable gurus who followed in Vivekananda's footsteps.

The ample funds that Vivekananda brought back to India enabled him to set up the Ramakrishna Mission mentioned above, which undertook social service as well as the promulgation of the divinity of Ramakrishna and the philosophy of the Vedanta. Ramakrishna's child bride, with whom he never established sexual relations, long survived him and took on divinity of her own as the Mother.

The strong organizational set-up of the Ramakrishna Mission led to the establishment of missions in other parts of India, and in the West. Without plotting the details of this growth, the picture is not complete without mention of the Mission's attempt in 1985 to argue that it was not a Hindu organization but was 'the cult or religion of Sri Ramakrishna'. This came about because special privileges are accorded by Indian law to minority religions, including the right to run their own schools and colleges. The Supreme Court found against the Mission in 1995, decreeing that it was indeed Hindu.

Ramana Maharshi (1879–1950)

Ramana Maharshi is one of the most widely respected gurus of modern times. As a boy he read the stories of the Shaiva saints, the Nayanars, and at the age of 17, after a near-death experience, he felt called to Arunachala. He stayed there until his death, enjoying a continual state of bliss. An ashram was established, in which he played some part in administration for a while. Numerous people came to see him. In 1931 he was visited by Paul Brunton, and was then made known to the world in that author's *A Search in Secret India*. Arunachala, the Red Mountain, is supposed to be the place where Shiva manifested himself in a column of fire to Vishnu and Brahma. The Tamil poets and saints sang of it in the seventh and eighth centuries. The base of the hill is ringed around with shrines, and there is a major Shiva temple there. Ramana Maharshi was the latest of a string of saints who have lived there over the centuries, but by far the most famous. He was renowned for his simplicity, his silence, and his public manifestation of supreme bliss.

Aurobindo (1872–1950)

Aurobindo, at first a freedom fighter, was an independent thinker who claimed that his 'integral yoga' was the spiritual technique for the higher evolution of all mankind. India was the guru of the nations, and had been set apart by the divine as the eternal fountainhead of holy spirituality. India was to send forth from herself the future religion of the entire world, the Eternal Religion which was to harmonize all religion, science and philosophy and make mankind one soul.[20] The ashram he set up in Pondicherry, continued by his wife, is still active and well known.[21]

Jagadguru Shri Chandrasekharendra Sarasvati (1894–1994)

Chandrasekharendra Sarasvati was installed as the sixty-eighth Shankaracharya of the Kamakoti Pitha of Kanchi in 1907, in direct line of spiritual descent from the original Shankaracharya. An important feature of the spiritual rule of the Shankaracharyas, whose title is Jagadguru ('Guru of the World'), is that, like Hindu kings of old, they spend much time touring the country, and the term for these tours, *vijaya-yatra*, has implications of spiritual conquest. Chandrashekharendra's first tour was to the Shiva temple at Jambukesvaram outside Trichy. The form of Parvati there is held to have been very fierce until the original Shankaracharya gave her earrings in the form of the Shri Chakra. The maintenance and repair of these earrings has long been the responsibility of the Shankaracharya of Kanchi.

Chandrashekharendra was deeply and widely learned as well as being a charismatic teacher. He promoted the traditional study of the Veda, and tirelessly lectured on the classical spirituality of Hindu India. Active and deeply reverenced throughout his long life, he was without question the most respected

traditional Hindu of modern times. He was the living incarnation of Adi
Shankara, the great exponent of non-dualist Vedanta and of all the traditions
that had accrued around that historical figure. By contrast, Ramakrishna, the
most famous guru, had richly varied mystical experience, modern in its eclec-
ticism and, thanks to Vivekananda, became the divine founder of the
Ramakrishna Mission (discussed above). Gandhi was also eclectic, but was
intellectually original and politically active. He was deeply influenced by the
ahimsa, non-violence, that is most thoroughly adopted by Jainism, but was
also influenced by Christianity.

Chandrashekharendra's successor Jayendra Sarasvati (b. 1934), the current Shankaracharya at Kanchi, is widely respected, and a national figure.
He has attempted to mediate between Muslims and Hindus in the continuing crisis over the (re)building of the Ayodhya Rama temple. The *math* at
Kanchi makes full use of modern technology, offering automated telephone
advice and an elaborate website. On taking over as leader he said the new
watchwords were 'culture of one's own land and technology from abroad'
(*svadesa samskriti, videsa vijnan*). He has founded a university which offers
advanced degrees in business administration, computer science, and Sanskrit.

[handwritten annotation: S and d puja popular in US. — Tamil Brahmin (Smarta) communities)]

Shivananda (1887–1963)

Shivananda may be regarded as a typical example of hundreds if not thousands of gurus, though he is particularly successful. Shivananda simplified yoga
and combined it with devotional mysticism. A big, strong man, he nevertheless radiated love. He wrote almost 350 books and pamphlets, including large
commentaries on the *Bhagavad Gita* and the key text of Vedanta, the *Brahma
Sutra*. He founded the Divine Life Society with its first ashram in Rishikesh; it
now has several branches round the world. His work is continued by his disciples Chidananda (b. 1916) and Krishnananda (b. 1922). There are also Western successors such as the Canadian woman Swami Radha (b. 1911), who was
initiated by Shivananda in a dream.

Satchidananda (b. 1914)

Satchidananda, after varied experiences, including time in the Ramakrishna
Mission, was initiated by Shivananda, and went on to the USA where he teaches
a yoga simplified for Westerners which he calls 'integrated yoga'. He set up a
successful community called Yogaville in Virginia in 1979: a major feature is
the Light of Truth Universal Shrine (LOTUS), lotus-like in outline, with a
column of moving light at the centre; it is dedicated to all religions.

A. C. Bhaktivedanta Prabhupada (1896–1977)

Prabhupada founded the International Society for Krishna Consciousness (ISKCON) in 1966, an authentic form of Krishna worship based on the *Bhagavata Purana*. His innovation was to make the sect a missionary one. When he met Nikhilananda, head of the Ramakrishna-Vivekananda Center in New York, he was told he would have to abandon Indian dress and strict vegetarianism to succeed. Prabhupada made no concessions, but his traditional Hindu movement swept round the world, with centres in all the major cities. He made 14 world tours and wrote more than 80 books. Western devotees took on the role of brahmans, and temple cars, like that of Jagannatha, progressed through New York and other Western capitals in Krishna festivals organized by the Hare Krishnas. ISKCON continues, and is respected in India, but there have been many squabbles about leadership among the Western initiates since the founder's death.

Maharishi Mahesh Yogi (b. 1911)

Maharishi studied physics at Allahabad University before taking to the spiritual life as the disciple of the Shankaracharya of the Jyotir Math in North India. In the 1960s Maharishi founded Transcendental Meditation™, a technique of relaxed meditation on a personal mantra. Notoriety followed when in 1976 the TM Siddhi programme claimed to teach meditators to levitate. Perhaps less easy to disprove was the Maharishi effect, that when at least the square root of 1 per cent of the population engages in meditation practice then measurable benefit such as reduction in crime follows in the general population.

Rajneesh/Osho (1931–1990)

The most notorious of modern gurus, Rajneesh/Osho, claimed to have experienced all religions in previous lives, and to have synthesized them in his current life. His followers say that he was never born, never died, but merely visited the planet earth for the period of his life. In his *Discipline of Transcendence* he describes his achievement of enlightenment at the age of 21: 'For many lives I had been working on myself . . . and nothing was happening.' At last he stopped searching and struggling: 'It started happening. A new energy arose.' He took an MA in philosophy, and then taught philosophy at the University of Jabalpur for nine years, before giving himself full-time to the religious teaching he had already started. In 1974 Rajneesh set up an ashram in Pune that in a few years claimed to attract as many foreigners to India as the Taj Mahal. He freely invented yogic and tantric practices for his disciples. The move of the ashram to the USA ended in failure. The organization in Pune continues, sustained by videotapes of the master.

Sathya Sai Baba (b. 1926)

By far the most famous godman living today is Sathya Sai Baba, whose picture, smiling under a round mass of hair, and clad in an ochre robe, is everywhere in India, in temples and in home shrines. He backs up his claim to be an incarnation of both Shiva and Shakti by a wide variety of well-publicized miracles. He produces sacred ash magically from his hands or at a distance, from pictures of himself, and, for the favoured few, jewels and watches. Apart from his miracles and the affirmation of his divinity, his teachings scarcely differ from those of the *Bhagavad Gita*: one should be pure, one should do one's duty and dedicate one's actions to God in loving devotion. His divinity and miracles are accepted by many important Indians, and his charitable works are extensive, including the founding of hospitals and a university. His worldwide following is in millions, but he has only once left India. It is in India that he belongs, as he explains:

> Only in India are Avatars born, because only in India are the Shastras understood. And only in India do the sages constantly experiment and practise. It is like a gold mine. Where gold is found, there gather the geologists, engineers, and experienced miners. Gold is mined and stored there, and then it is taken all over the world.[22]

Conclusion

The term guru, as all-knowing personal guide in a particular discipline, or in respect of life in general, has been readily adopted in the West. In many areas of life, an arbitrary choice of guide is made and long kept to, as in the case of child care, economics, or nutrition. Keeping to a single favoured teacher is probably a common human phenomenon. The special features of the Hindu guru stem perhaps from the Hindu family system, with its readiness to accept a father-figure rather than rebel against him, and its readiness to introduce a strong emotional element into what is essentially, at least elsewhere, an intellectual arrangement, namely instruction. On the one hand, the disciple asserts his autonomy by striking out for himself, downgrading family ties, learning new things. On the other hand, the autonomy is then surrendered to the guru, who inducts the disciple into a new family of fellow aspirants.

Again, the Hindu guru differs from the Western teacher by his proximity to an active and extended pantheon, whose visible forms are worshipped and are perceived to benefit their worshippers. The guru, no less than the gods, is the object of *darshana* – seeing him can be enough in itself. For the guru, modernity can be a profitable home, encouraging his entrepreneurship, spreading his ideas more easily, fostering innovation in techniques and doctrine. From the point of view of traditional Hinduism, gurus are generally maintaining traditional spirituality, but packaging it attractively for the modern world, and also spreading it beyond the shores of India. They are living exponents of the truths of Hinduism. However, unlike the gods, they gain nothing from being considered *en masse*. One has to sit at the feet of the guru for the system to work.

The movement of forms of Hinduism round the world through the efforts of travelling gurus is an important event in modern times that has taken place alongside the emigration of South Asians and South Asian culture. However, although an enthusiastic account of this world-wide permeation would have been a high note for a final chapter, looking forward to the day when India attains the global influence its population and civilization deserve, when, to modify Nirad Chaudhuri's wish, England might be one of the jewels in India's crown, such a prospect must here be put aside. In the next chapter we must consider the rise of Hindu nationalism in India.

Chapter Twelve

Modernity and Hindu Nationalism

A scene from the film *Satya* ('Truth', 1998), provides our opening. We see Ganesha, elephant-headed god of auspicious beginnings, as a large festival image on the shore of the Indian ocean, a Mumbai beach, Ganesha's immersion slowly beginning. Viewed from behind the huge, seven-headed temporary image of the deity, a man's corpse rolls in the incoming tide. This dead devotee of Ganesha is in fact the arch-villain of the film, a politician who has taken over Mumbai through mobster control of the elections. Satya, the eponymous gangster hero, has killed the politician to avenge the politician's murder of his comrade; we have previously seen Satya advancing through the crowds on the beach thronging round the many Ganesha images to seek out the politician, and finally, as the politician leads devotions to one of the Ganeshas, Satya holding him in a tight embrace while stabbing him repeatedly. The victim's bodyguard's absorption in devotion to Ganesha aids the assassination.

The name of the politician in the film is Bhau, the top politician in Mumbai. The credits of the film stress the absence of connection with any living person; there are many famous gangsters in Mumbai, and the best-known individual there is Bal Thackeray, leader of the 'Army of Shivaji' (the Shiv Sena), associate of criminals, and fascist persecutor of Muslims. Bhau's appearances in the film are backed by the suggestion of Sanskrit chanting; in his home he stands before a huge wall panel of the *Bhagavad Gita* showing Krishna and Arjuna in their chariot. In contrast, Satya, the hero of the film, is clearly dissociated from religion. When, at the beginning of the film, he is shown the Mumbai flat allocated to him by the gangster boss who has befriended him, the flat's amenities are listed: TV, fridge – 'there's even a god [Bhagvan]'. The camera refuses to show us this particular amenity, no doubt a poster print, and Satya declares, 'I don't believe in God.' The only consequence of this assertion seems to be the thunder and heavy rain in the immediately following scene.

Gangsters play a large part in Indian political life, not just in films. One in 10 of election candidates for the 1996 election had a criminal record of murder, rape, theft or extortion; at least 40 of them managed to be elected as MPs in the eleventh Lok Sabha; one out of every 14 sitting MP in that Lok Sabha had a criminal record.[1] For Satya, coming to the city to seek work, maintenance of his dignity leads to prison, and thence friendship with a gangster leader. Among his group of gangsters he finds friendship and fulfilment. The brotherhood of crime replaces distinctions of caste. He kills, and ultimately dies violently himself. The hero of this film, an orphan who comes from nowhere, whose name, Truth, asserts his universal validity, as modern man can but perform his share of the universal violence.

The worship of Ganesha was reinvented in Maharashtra by the great independence leader, B. G. Tilak (1856–1920), who also began the modern promotion of Shivaji, leader of Maratha independence; the Ganesh festival today is the largest Hindu public religious performance in Maharashtra.[2] The scholar-activist Tilak, author while in prison of a vast commentary on the *Bhagavad Gita*, has been succeeded by the ex-cartoonist Bal Thackeray, himself lampooned by Salman Rushdie as the Frog King. The murderous gangster who is Truth (Satya) shows the homeless plight of the individual in modernity, bereft of family, but able to make friends, and – in the hyper-reality of film – able to dispense justice prior to his demise. We have here a world-view where the action of the film star – archetypal individual – is primary, and religion is irrelevant, and possibly also intrinsically corrupt. Undertaking violence oneself is the only sure course. The autonomous individual, freed from the constraints of caste, makes the action film the site of modernity. The avenging heroes on the screen provide the illusion of fulfilment for India's unemployed youth.

According to Zaiuddin Sardar, the modern Indian film embodies the traits of the modern world – alienated ideas and ideals – so completely in its one-dimensional characters that it cannot be construed as a comment on modern times;[3] Steve Derne argues that Indian films 'celebrate strong masculine bodies that are able to withstand the threats of modernity';[4] Ashish Nandy speaks of popular film as 'Indian modernity at its rawest' and as 'the disowned self of modern India returning in a fantastic or monstrous form to haunt modern India'.[5] But we now have to examine a confrontation between India and modernity over the last decade that is as fantastic and monstrous as a popular film, a confrontation that is also a collusion. I refer to the rise of Hindu nationalism. What at first sight is fundamentalism, tradition fighting back, turns out to be malignant modernity.

Nationalism

Indian nationalism arose from the need to drive out the British, and it produced Nehru's secular India. Hindu nationalism was an important part of the growth of Indian nationalism, but was held in check by Gandhi and Nehru. In the 1980s Hindu nationalism took on renewed vigour, but before considering this growth, it will be helpful to consider nationalism more widely, and to bring to the fore the modernity of all nationalism.

The fairy story of Sleeping Beauty provides Jackie Assayag with a handy metaphor for the various theories of nationalism.[6] The simplest version is that she – the nation – wakes under her own steam, so to speak. The ethnic unit comes to realize its geographical and historical unity and awakes to national consciousness. The second theory sees her woken by the kiss of modernity: it is modernization that causes the nation to emerge; Sleeping Beauty has no prior history, the nationalists invent her. The third theory sees her as the bride of Frankenstein: the nation awakes to find itself married to the monster that is the industrialized nation-state. The fourth version has a European Prince Charming waking a non-Western Beauty: the colony creates the nation. Assayag goes on to say that none of these models applies to Indian nationalism. India has invented its own nationalism, transforming the products of colonization while building on the old patriotism: 'Indians have Indianised Europe [within India] and Westminsterised South Asia.'[7]

For old-style patriotism Assayag refers to Bayly's *Origins of Nationality in South Asia*. Bayly does discern evidence of 'a fluctuating sense of loyalty to homeland, or *deshbhakti* ("devotion to one's country")' in pre-modern India, as distinct from the more common *swami-seva* ('loyalty to the ruling dynasty').[8] But surely nationalism is something other than this natural love of native place. Kedourie shows that nationalism is a doctrine invented in Europe at the beginning of the nineteenth century.[9] The key point is that, as Ernest Gellner puts it, 'Nationalism is a political principle which maintains that similarity of culture is the basic social bond.'[10] The trouble is that often the unity of culture that nationalism needs for its existence calls for a conjuring trick. The illusion of an immemorial antiquity is necessary for that unity to be asserted. The nation awakes only because it has dreamed up a history. Sleeping Beauty awakes thinking that she is very old. Nairn makes a convincing diagnosis, based on his theory of the pressures of the uneven development of capitalism:

> 'Nationalism' is the pathology of modern developmental history, as inescapable as 'neurosis' in the individual, with much the same essential ambiguity attaching to it, a similar built-in capacity for descent into dementia, rooted in the dilemmas of helplessness thrust upon most of the world (the equivalent of infantilism for societies) and largely incurable.[11]

The pathological side of nationalism might stem from its being a reaction against the universal reason of the Enlightenment. Then again a clear starting point of nationalism is the French Revolution, when the people of France were equated with the French nation, an equation that ended in the Terror.

Anyway, in the final analysis the success of nationalism in the modern world is due, as Josen Llobera says, to 'the sacred character that the nation has inherited from religion. In its essence the nation is the secularized god of our times'.[12] In modernity much of religion has transmuted into nationalism.

Gandhi and Mother India

Independent India began in the Enlightenment mould forced on it by Nehru, but nationalism obsessed with primordialism has now shattered that mould. Mother India has become a bemused Sleeping Beauty awoken to a dangerous world. Two images sum up the change in India from the tolerance of Nehru's secular India to the Hindu nationalism of today. The first image is extremely well known: Gandhi, the statue of the Mahatma placed at the crossroads of every town, striding forth across India, staff in hand.[13] The second is a political cartoon of unknown provenance: 'Mother India under attack by Islam, Christianity, Marxism and Macaulayism', from the web page of a right-wing publisher, Arvind Ghosh, showing Mother India as a woman in chains, stabbed in the heart by a Muslim, and, as if the spurting blood from that wound weren't enough, also about to be attacked by the Marxist with his hammer, the mitred bishop with his cross, and the Macaulayite, stooge of the former colonial master, with a cudgel – their weapons yet to fall upon their victim.

Gandhi's image dominated India from the 1930s to the 1950s or even 1960s, the Father of the Nation leading the people from colonial subjection to leadership of the unaligned free world. In Ghosh's paranoiac picture, India is surrounded by a world in league against her: she is seen as female, subjected to males; in chains, just as she was in the political posters of the 1930s under British rule. Her hair is wild and unbound, like Kali's. Is she to become an avenging destroyer?

The Macaulayite would be hard to identify were it not for the caption. It's almost a century and a half since Macaulay died. It was he who opted for English-language education for India in 1832; he too who famously sneered at the traditional Hindu geography of India as the central continent surrounded by concentric continents set within seas of milk and treacle. But it was this English education that provided literary models for literatures in the regional languages, and it certainly in no way hindered achievement of the world's largest democracy. Spurred on by the Orientalists' portrayal of a great Hindu India in the past, and educated in politics by the colonial government, independence was ultimately aided rather than hindered by Macaulay. Nevertheless, Macaulay has acquired demon status, and the secular views of English-language-educated Indians are dismissed by Hindu nationalists as Macaulayism:

The British took over our education and taught us to look at ourselves through their eyes. They created a class Indian in blood and color, but anti-Hindu in his intellectual and emotional orientation. This is the biggest problem rising India faces – the problem of self-alienated Hindus, of anti-Hindu Hindus . . . In India, Macaulayism prepared the ground for Marxism – early Marxists were recruited from Macaulayites. Marxism in turn gave Macaulayism a radical look and made it attractive for a whole new class.[14]

For the Hindu fundamentalist, the Indian education system is 'a hybrid of Macaulayism and Marxism'.[15]

The most notable feature of Ghosh's picture is the expression of hatred, hatred of the enemy for India, and India's hatred of the enemy. No one would object to hating Macaulay. His hatred of Hindu idolatry, his complete incomprehension of Hinduism, has led to well-justified obloquy today. The contemporary attitude to British rule is shown in the 1994 Hindi film, *1942 – A Love Story*, where the only Englishman is a general, quintessence of evil, modelled on the general of the dark forces in the Star Wars films, down to the harsh voice echoing as if from an empty helmet.

From the perspective of the beginning of the new millennium, the British empire seems little less distant than the Roman empire. Yet more than 2 million Indians participated on Britain's behalf in the First World War. It was unrest in the Punjab at rising prices after the war that led to increased repression and General Dyer's massacre of nearly 400 unarmed Indians in Amritsar in 1919. Any hope of a gradual Indian accession to self-rule as a British dominion vanished for ever.

Gandhi, as the only Indian lawyer in South Africa, developed the method of passive resistance to oppressive and discriminatory laws. While there, Gandhi wrote his first book, *Hind Swaraj* ('Independent India'). For Gandhi, independence meant not only freedom from foreign rule but also freedom from all forms of injustice. For true self-rule, Hindus and Muslims had to respect each other's religion and treat each other as equals. With regard to caste, the fourfold *varna* system was natural and essential, but untouchability was a crime against humanity. No less essential than the removal of untouchability was the equal distribution of wealth. *Swadeshi*, the use only of what is produced locally, was the solution to India's poverty – hand-spinning was the key example of this. The spinning-wheel affirmed the dignity of India's rural way of life, and symbolized Gandhi's rejection of modernity. The wearing of hand-spun cloth, *khadi*, would provide a national uniform for rich and poor alike.

The name Gandhi coined for the political technique of non-violence was *satyagraha*, 'holding fast to truth'. For Gandhi God was Truth; indeed, truth was prior to divinity: Truth was God. For Gandhi, the attainment of national independence was a search after truth, and the interests of his country were identical with those of his religion, but his views on religion were very much his own. He learned about Hinduism in the constrained and confrontational limits of South Africa. In Bhikhu Parekh's view, Gandhi's knowledge of Hinduism 'was largely based on reading and reflection, and remained shallow and abstract . . . he made up his brand of Hinduism as he went along'.[16] Several close friends were Christians; he was deeply attached to the British missionary C. F. Andrews. The suffering love depicted in the crucifixion was integrated into his own redefinition of Hinduism. He was deeply impressed by a life-size crucifix when he visited the Sistine Chapel in 1931. One of his favourite hymns was Isaac Watt's 'When I survey the wondrous Cross'. This provides a stark contrast to Ghosh's picture considered above, where the bishop is using a crucifix to prod, if not stab in the back, the hapless Mother India.

It is also instructive to contrast Ghosh's rabid polemic with a 1930s poster print of Gandhi as Protector of India, which sums up the political situation of the time by building on traditional iconography. Provided with four arms, Gandhi is here modelled on Shiva the Destroyer of Death, with the 16-year-old Markandeya replaced by Mother India. The story goes that a childless couple, offered the choice between a good but short-lived son and a long-lived bad one, chose the former. But Markandeya so fervently worshipped the linga of Shiva that when Death on his buffalo came for him, Shiva surged out of the linga and killed Death. In the poster Gandhi rises up from the linga, holding a spinning-wheel and khadi cloth in lieu of weapons. In Markandeya's stead Mother India clasps the linga, and a rope goes from her to a British political officer, who is riding the buffalo of Death.[17] The nationalism of Ghosh's picture throws aside the traditional imagery of Hinduism, and has no divinity other than the dishonoured nation.

Gandhi conquered his opponents by non-violence, but his ultimate weapon was the threat to fast to the death. In this way he made the colonial government withdraw its proposal to make the outcastes a separate electoral constituency as the Muslims were at that time; and again he used fasting to stop Hindu–Muslim fighting in Calcutta in 1947. Mountbatten, the Viceroy, said that 50,000 soldiers were needed to calm the Punjab, but one man did the job in Bengal.

Gandhi's last fast was undertaken to force the government to pay Pakistan its share of the former India's cash reserves, withheld because of the dispute over Kashmir. This fast led to a small group of Brahman nationalists, followers of V. D. Savarkar, plotting to kill Gandhi. He was shot dead by N. Godse in 1948. In the ensuing fury of the population, prominent Hindu nationalists were lynched, and in Maharashtra, the home state of the plotters, brahmans were murdered almost at random. It was Gandhi's living presence, not his teachings, that had restrained the masses.

In Ghosh's picture, the major assault on Mother India is that of the Muslim, though it is partly muted by being in association with the other assailants.

As noted at the beginning of chapter 4, which discussed aspects of the relationship of Hinduism and Islam, once it became clear that independence was inevitable, there was increasing rivalry between Hindu and Muslim elites, rivalry that ended in wide-scale rioting and ultimately in partition. Far from paralleling Shiva as destroyer, Gandhi wrought miracles in restraining Hindu Muslim violence, but they were only temporary miracles.

V. D. Savarkar (1883–1966)

Gandhi's assassin and his comrades had been inspired by the writings and example of Savarkar. As a 15-year-old, Savarkar vowed to Durga to drive the British out of India. He became known as 'the Hero' on account of his terrorist activities. Shortly before his death, he was urging India to acquire the atom bomb. Savarkar was put in the shade by Gandhi in his lifetime, but his ideas have now reached centre-stage. Whereas Gandhi spent his life exploring the application of Hinduism to politics, and the relationship of *sanatana dharma* to other religions, Savarkar had little to say about the nature of Hinduism, which he saw as only one element of Hindu nationalism. In 1923 he published *Hindutva: Who is a Hindu?* Whereas one of Gandhi's favourite maxims, from the *Rig Veda*, was 'May noble thoughts from all over the world come to us' Savarkar looked to the Veda as an early statement of a 'religious, racial, cultural and political unit' – the nation was Savarkar's supreme truth. He declared that the Hindu nation was 'not a mushroom growth . . . It has grown out of this soil and has its roots struck deep and wide in it. It is not a fiction invented to spite the Moslems.' But this language is revealing. Nationalism is precisely the mushroom growth of modernity, springing up overnight from nowhere. Savarkar himself admitted that he was willing the Hindu nation into being: 'we Hindus will to be a Nation and, therefore, we are a Nation'.[18] In similarly revelatory language he refers to Hinduism as a creature from the deep, from what may be seen as the primordial depths of the imagination: 'During the course of the last 5,000 years of its continuous growth and consolidation, this gigantic Octopus of Hindudom has clutched and crushed within the formidable grip of its mighty arms a number of Shakasthans, Hunasthans [kingdoms set up by invaders in India]'. Addressing himself to Muslims, he continued, 'the Marathas swallowed and gulped down your very empire entirely and altogether before it knew what was happening'.[19]

In 1937, after being allowed to leave Nagpur jail, he was invited to become president of the Hindu Mahasabha, the leading political organization for Hindus. He remained president until 1944, travelling throughout India and mobilizing opposition to Congress and Muslim leaders. Savarkar promoted Hindu missionary activities, and fiercely denounced Muslim and Christian missionaries. A new ceremony called Purification brought Untouchables and Indian

Christians and Muslims back to Hinduism. Some temples open to all Hindus, including outcastes, were established. But Savarkar's main contribution to Indian politics were his writings and his speeches. The Hindu Mahasabha was never successful at the polls, but another organization founded by a Maratha brahman attained considerable power and influence outside the political process.

The Rashtriya Swayamsevak Sangh

The Rashtriya Swayamsevak Sangh (National Volunteer Corps, RSS), founded by K. B. Hedgewar in 1925 after reading Savarkar's works and meeting him in person, sought to bring cohesion and strength to Hindus. Adopting khaki shorts like the British police, and later white rather than khaki shirts, its militarism had an initial affinity with the traditional wrestling ground of northern India, the *akhara*, which was led by a guru and dedicated to the strong god Hanuman. Members of the RSS consecrated themselves to their organization in front of an image of Hanuman. The saffron flag of Shivaji, the 'Sacred Flag', became the 'guru' of the RSS. In 1940 Hedgewar was succeeded by M. S. Golwalkar – author of *We, our Nationhood Defined* (1931) – who led the movement until 1973. The backbone of the RSS were, and are, the 'preachers or missionaries' (*pracharaks*) who give up their jobs and become celibate, austerely devoted to the cause. They see themselves as *karma yogis*, making actions their yoga. The tradition of asceticism levelled out social distinctions, and Hedgewar and Golwalkar used it as a means to develop a nation that was united and egalitarian. 'While iron discipline prevailed, the atmosphere of sociability and camaraderie . . . was truly remarkable . . . The question of caste, for instance, was simply conspicuous by its absence. We all played together, sang together, ate together . . . We were all Hindus and children of the Bharat Mata.'[20] 'To anyone who wanted theoretical explanations, the standard reply was, 'You don't require intellectual arguments to love your mother – the same thing is true of the motherland.'[21] Despite the organization's past links with fascism, including meetings with Mussolini, Jaffrelot argues that its lack of emphasis on a supreme leader, and the central position it gives to the social system rather than race, mean that the term fascist is inappropriate here.[22]

The Sangh Parivar

Grouped around the RSS are several other organizations that together with it are known as the Sangh Parivar, the 'Family of right-wing organizations'. Tapan Raychaudhuri scathingly remarks that the term family has a 'Sicilian resonance'.[23]

The Bharatiya Janata Party

The RSS is not a political party, but it has close connections with the Bharatiya Jana Sangh, founded in 1951 by S. P. Mookerjee and renamed the Bharatiya Janata Party (both names meaning 'Indian People's Party') in 1979. Mookerjee's draft manifesto spoke of the 'Hindu' nation, but the RSS and others objected to this. The party has as its objective the building up of India as a nation 'which is modern, progressive and enlightened in outlook and which proudly draws inspiration from India's ancient culture and values'.[24] The party's key theorist is D. Upadhyaya (1916–68), author of *Integral Humanism*, first published in 1965. According to Upadhyaya, above monarch and state are the *dharma* and the genius (*chiti*) of a society, though his book does not make it clear who is to define *dharma*, which is just taken to be self-existent. In fact, national identity is the source of meaning: 'Without this [national] identity there is no meaning . . . The Nation too, like the individual, becomes a prey to numerous ills when its natural instincts are disregarded.'[25] No less than a human being, the nation is a single being. Although Upadhyaya stresses the importance of integrating the four ends of human life as set out by Hinduism – sensory gratification (*kama*); material well-being (*artha*); religious behaviour (*dharma*) which leads to heaven or higher rebirth; salvation, escape from rebirth (*moksha*) – the nation which lacks these clear parameters takes precedence over the individual in his system. The nationalism of modernity overrides the original Hindu model.

The Vishva Hindu Parishad

Neither the BJP nor the RSS includes the word Hindu in its name. That omission was remedied in the creation of another organization affiliated to the RSS. The Vishva Hindu Parishad (VHP), was founded in 1966 to counter secularism, with Swami Chinmayananda as president and S. S. Apte of the RSS as general secretary. It was first mooted at a conference in 1964 convened by Golwalkar, head of the RSS. The five Shankaracharyas were present, along with Jain and Sikh leaders, and the Dalai Lama. Golwalkar explained that the aim was to unite all faiths of Indian origin, 'all those faiths and beliefs that have sprouted from the banyan tree'. The word Hindu applied to the followers of all those faiths.[26]

Those present were told by Apte: 'The world has been divided into Christian, Islamic and Communist; all these three consider the Hindu society as a very fine rich food on which to feast and fatten themselves. It is therefore necessary in this age of competition and conflict to think of, and organise, the Hindu world to save it from the evil eyes of all the three.'[27] Up to 1980 the VHP worked mainly among scheduled castes and tribes, setting up schools and clinics, and also temples.[28] While the RSS restricts theism to Bharat Mata, along with Hanuman in the training ground, temples in VHP offices add icons of Rama, Sita, Lakshman, and Hanuman to that of the national goddess. Many gurus and wandering ascetics are associated with the VHP.

The Bajrang Dal

In July 1984 the youth wing of the VHP, the Bajrang Dal ('The Force of Strong-Bodied Hanuman') was formed to implement the policies of the VHP. Its chief, Vinay Katiyar, drew a gruesome parallel with the *Ramayana*: Hanuman had no option but to burn down Ravana's city when the demons tied a burning rag to his tail – so too the members of the Bajrang Dal, whom demons have offended.[29] In 1999 even the RSS backed away from this force: 'All the riff raff, the rejects of society, and the discards of the Sangh Parivar, these are the people who find refuge in the Bajrang Dal.'[30]

Thackeray's Shiv Sena, an independent organization founded by him in 1966, is a parochial version of the Bajrang Dal, fighting for the interests of the Marathi-speaking population of the city. Thackeray, its commander, who has called himself 'emperor of the Hindu heart', directed his forces against South Indian and Gujarati migrant workers. The left-wing trade unions of Mumbai's mills were attacked. Shiv Sena is implicated in protection rackets, as well as doing good works.[31]

Rama and the temple at Ayodhya

The symbol of the Shiv Sena is Rama's bow and arrow. We need to look more closely at King Rama, and the way in which he has been used to turn Hinduism into something like a mirror-image of Islam. Previously, Rama had been viewed as a restorer of moral order, not an avenger. He was a compassionate king, the ideal king, and the traditional iconographic texts said simply that he should be represented as a king. When Gandhi visited a branch of the leading Hindu nationalist organization the RSS, the National Volunteer Group, he saw pictures of Shivaji and other Hindu heroes on the walls, and asked why they didn't have a picture of Rama too; he was told 'No, that we cannot do. Ram is too effeminate to serve our purpose.'[32] But now his image is that of a warrior in the midst of battle, his bow drawn and aimed – and appropriated as the symbol of the Shiv Sena. Jaffrelot asserts that the Rama of the Hindu nationalists 'shares many things in common with stereotypical heroes of Hindi popular cinema. For urban youths, these films often provide role models which enable them to sublimate their daily lives. Most of the time such youths are unemployed and to a large extent devoid of self-esteem.'[33] Rama taking aim with his arrow provides a point of focus for the unfocused.

According to Sudipta Kaviraj, 'this wrathful Rama is wholly ungrammatical', by which he means that it is incorrect iconographically; but he also finds fault with the use of plastic for god images in vehicles.[34] That drivers want their favourite deities on the dashboard is not in itself a bad thing, except blind faith can lead to bad driving. That iconographies and materials of images change is not in itself a bad thing. The claimed unchangeability of Hinduism up until now is in large measure due to the absence of sufficient material historical evidence to plot the extent of change. It is not so much the facts that the iconography of Rama has changed and that his chariot is manufactured by Toyota that should concern us, but rather the fact that all the other gods seem to have been pushed over the cliff into nothingness as far as the central definition of political Hinduism is concerned.

But why has Rama been chosen? No one, except Kali, is fiercer than Shiva, and Krishna's epiphany in the *Bhagavad Gita* is modelled on Shiva; then there is Narasimha, man-lion form of Vishnu, the immensely powerful inspirational deity of the last great Hindu empire at Vijayanagara. Why pick Rama? Well, Muslim numbers were greatest in the Hindi-speaking states after partition, so it was natural for the locus of dissension to be in the Hindi belt. And Rama was the most popular deity in the Hindi belt. But at this point, we should take a step backwards. Why was he so popular there? It was precisely in the area longest and most fully under Muslim rule that he became the principal Hindu deity. It is striking that, of all the Hindu gods, Rama is the most straightforward, a two-armed warrior, the ideal king – it is he among Hindu gods who least contradicts the Islamic notion of the deity. The cult of Rama worship centres on the name of Rama, paralleling the role of the name of Allah. More generally, the competition from Sufi doctrines and Muslim egalitarianism led to a democratization of brahmanic institutions and to the simple emotional type of *bhakti* directed to Rama.

Early in the independence movement, Hindu nationalists had picked three key sites where mosques had been built on Hindu temples devoted to the three most popular gods of India, Rama, Krishna, and Shiva. Of the three temples in question – the temple of Rama's birthplace (Janmabhumisthana temple) at Ayodhya, the Keshava Rai temple at Mathura, and the Vishvanatha temple at Varanasi – the last was incomparably the most important, and had been destroyed many times by Muslims. The Keshava Rai temple at Mathura, though not old, had been extremely popular and very wealthy when it was destroyed by Aurangzib and a mosque built on top if it.

The question as to why it was the Rama site that was picked rather than the others has already been answered, inasmuch as Rama was the mirror-image answer to the problem of Islam. Those asserting Hindu nationalism were only too well aware of Islamic and Christian criticisms of Hinduism. Rama was the least problematic from those alien perspectives. Further, though no fewer than three temples in Ayodhya had in the past been replaced by mosques, the Babri mosque was the logical choice because it was said to be built over the birthplace of Rama. The reconstruction of this temple would affirm the historical reality of Rama in a way that paralleled the vaunted historicity, the modernity even in some sense, of Islam and Christianity too. India would be given a single point of holy focus parallel to Mecca and Jerusalem, in wanton disregard of thousands of other Hindu holy places.

When in 1989, three years before the destruction of the mosque, the foundation stone of the new temple was laid on a piece of ground in front of the mosque, all Hindus were called on to face Ayodhya at the exact moment, 1.35 p.m. on Friday, 10 November, and make a flower offering. Nationalist propaganda strove to make Ayodhya Hinduism's most important historical site. Back in 1924 Swami Shraddhanand, leader of the Arya Samaj, urging the need for organizing Hindus, had called for the building of one 'Hindu Rashtra Mandir' in every city and important town in India. Educated Hindus, he said, were reluctant to mix with each other because 'they have no common meeting place'. Each mandir was to have a compound capable of holding an audience of 25,000, and a large hall for recitations from the holy texts and epics – in other words, Hindu mosques! What did catch on was his further suggestion for these national temples – 'Let a life-like map of Mother Bharat be constructed in a prominent place, giving all its characteristics in vivid colours so that every child of the Matri-Bhumi may daily bow before the Mother and renew *his* pledge to restore *her* to the ancient pinnacle of glory from which she has fallen.'[35] Such images were made as poster prints, and then in 1936 a Bharat Mata temple in Varanasi was inaugurated by Mahatma Gandhi, with a horizontal marble relief map of India, viewable from above from a surrounding gallery. A second Bharat Mata temple was built in Hardwar by Swami Satyamitrand at a cost of 10 million rupees, and inaugurated in 1983 by the prime minister, Indira Gandhi. This innovatory eight-storey temple has the map of India set out on its ground floor.[36]

One of the founder members of the VHP was K. M. Munshi, who in 1938 was the founder-president of the Bharatiya Vidya Bhavan (Institute for Indian Culture) in Mumbai, an organization promoting 'the reintegration of the Indian culture in the light of modern knowledge and to suit our present day needs and the resuscitation of its fundamental value in their pristine vigour'.[37] This dynamic view of Indian culture stressed reform and renaissance rather than the status quo. The permanent values of Indian wisdom, which had flowed 'from the supreme act of creative life-energy as represented by Shri Ramachandra, Shri Krishna, Vyasa, Buddha, and Mahavira', were expressed in modern times by Ramakrishna, Dayanand Saraswati, Vivekananda, Aurobindo, and Gandhi. However, in the field of practical politics he rejected the grassroots democracy favoured by Gandhi and argued for a strong central government.

Munshi was not only an active politician and lawyer; he was also the leading Gujarati novelist. Convinced that his fellow Gujaratis were ignorant of 'the greatness of their ancestors' he reconstructed the golden age of Gujarat in his novels. In 1937 Munshi published a historical novel about the sacking of the Somanath temple by Mahmud of Ghazni in 1026, presenting it as 'an unforgettable national disaster'.[38] When Munshi wrote his novel the temple had been sacked many times, and was in ruins: 'Reconstruction of Somanath was then but the nebulous dream of a habitual dreamer.'[39] The temple was in the princely state of Junagadh, ruled by Muslim nawabs. At partition the nawab wanted his territory included in Pakistan, despite a population that was 82 per cent Hindu. The majority rose up; the nawab fled to Pakistan. Munshi pushed for the reconstruction of the temple, and the powerful home minister, Sardar Patel, backed him: 'The restoration of the idols would be a point of honour and sentiment with the public.' The government was going to provide the money for this, but at Gandhi's suggestion it was left to the public to pay by subscription.[40] Nehru was alarmed when the ritual preparations for rebuilding involved Indian ambassadors round the world being asked to provide river water and soil for the ritual consecration of a linga, a linga that would thus have a global character. It was not appropriate for a secular government thus to allow a Hindu site to symbolize 'the unity of the world and the brotherhood of man'.[41] When half a century later in 1995 the temple was finally completed, the president of India, Shankar Dayal Sharma, dedicated it to the nation, declaring that all faiths taught the same message of unity among all and placed humanism above everything else:[42] nationalism was altogether absent. In an ideal world Somanath as national temple might conceivably have sufficed for fundamentalist ambitions, but that was not to be the case.

Just as independence gave scope for Hindu aspirations in the matter of the Somanath temple, so too in Ayodhya, the birthplace of Rama, a temple was the centre of Hindu attention. But in this case the temple had not merely been demolished, but a mosque had been built on top of it 300 years earlier. Hindu Muslim riots in 1934 had led to the government closure of the mosque. In December 1949 Hindus entered the mosque at night and installed an image of Rama. Learning that Rama had appeared, large crowds gathered in front of the mosque. Nehru was concerned, and Patel, deputy prime minister, who had supported the Somanath reconstruction, did not disagree with the secular line. But the district magistrate refused to remove the image. The upshot was that a priest was allowed to maintain the image, and a group of Hindus permitted to entered once a year, on 22 December.

The cause of secularism was greatly helped by the death of Sardar Patel in 1950, and Nehru was able to take full control of India's destiny. However, Hindu aspirations did not die away. To understand current events and the significance of Ayodhya today, we must go back to 1981 when around 1,000 Dalits in Meenakshipuram, Tamilnadu, underwent mass conversion to Islam. During the following months thousands of members of the Scheduled Castes were converted to Islam in South India to escape their low position in the hierarchy of caste.[43] Hindu nationalists were deeply alarmed. India's tribals and Untouchables were at least nominally Hindu, but should they become Muslim or Christian the numerical superiority of Hindus would be gravely threatened. The Isha-ad-ul Islam Sabha of South India, which had brought about the Meenakshipuram conversions, claimed to be about to carry out 10 times more.

In 1983 the VHP arranged a triple procession to demonstrate the unity of Hindus: the Ekatmata Rath Yatra ('The Unification Chariot Pilgrimage') of Ganga water and Bharat Mata. Processions – from Gangasagar in Bengal to Somnath in Gujarat, from Hardwar in Uttar Pradesh to Kanyakumari in Tamilnadu, from Kathmandu in Nepal to Rameshwaram in Tamilnadu – all intersecting and meeting en route in Nagpur, home town of the RSS. The VHP installed images of Mother India and Ganga on a processional vehicle. Each procession carried Ganga water, which was sold and replenished by other holy waters on route, brought by linking subsidiary processions. Altogether 312 processions took place, and 4,323 meetings, affecting 531 of the 534 districts of India.[44] Members of the Scheduled Castes, along with Jains and Sikhs, carried the holy water. 'The message of the campaign was clear: Hinduism was in danger, and no danger was more sinister than the possibility of a concerted movement of Muslim and untouchable communities working together.'[45]

The VHP reorganized and expanded, for the first time building up a network throughout South India. Committees were formed for the renovation and expansion of temples and the organization of social work, raising funds from local traders. The system of local councils of spiritual guides (*margdarshak mandals*), set up in 1981, was expanded.

In April 1984 the VHP called for the liberation of the temple of Rama's birthplace in Ayodhya. The next month it established the Bajrang Dal, its Hanuman-inspired shock troops. In September a procession set off from Sita's birthplace in Bihar to 'liberate' the Ayodhya temple, with a lorry bearing large images of Rama and Sita under the banner 'Victory to Mother India'. They were due to arrive in Delhi in December, prior to the January elections, but the assassination of Indira Gandhi intervened. Continuing pressure from the VHP on politicians led to the district and session judge of Faizabad ruling on 14 February 1986 that the disputed site should be opened immediately to the public. There followed communal violence all over North India, and on 30 March 1987 in New Delhi Muslims staged their biggest protest since independence.

From January 1987 to August 1989 the *Ramayana* was broadcast on national television in 91 weekly episodes. Its popularity was unprecedented. The nation was glued to the screen, all timetables altered so that the episodes were not missed. The televising of the *Mahabharata* followed (1988–90, in 94 episodes). That too was highly popular. Video versions of both continue to sell well. Both serials brought the past to life in the vivid colours of religious poster art. The producer of the *Ramayana*, Ramanand Sagar, said all he had done was to 'take a cloth and wipe away the dust from the old treasures everyone knew about, but had lately ignored . . . Its production was therefore a simple matter, requiring no thought or skill'.[46] It is true that the enormous success of the serials was owing to the fact that they tapped a pre-existent religious feeling. But at the same time they brought home to every viewer the historical reality of an India of Hindus unconquered by foreigners, and made possible the illusion of an India without Islam.

Bricks to construct the new temple of Rama's birthplace were subscribed for and sent from all over India and from the Hindu diaspora, 'Shri Rama' written on each brick. On 9 November 1989 bricks were ritually placed in front of the mosque in Ayodhya. Some 300 people died in riots caused by the processions bringing the bricks across North India. Prime Minister Rajiv Gandhi did not accept an invitation to lay the temple's foundation stone, but expressed satisfaction that the ritual had taken place peacefully.

In 1992 the mosque was demolished by Hindu activists, triggering some of India's worst Hindu–Muslim riots, in which more than 2,000 people were killed. The campaign to build the temple forged ahead, and by 2002 the foundations had been laid and the stonework carved offsite. But actual construction is meeting with strong opposition, and is still stalled. In February 2002 some 40 people in a trainload of Rama activists en route to Ayodhya were murdered in an arson attack by Muslims, and in the ensuing riots at least 700 Muslims were killed.

Mani Rathnam's film *Bombay* graphically presents the horrors of the riots in Bombay in 1993 following the destruction of the mosque. At first seemingly a simple love film set in a Tamil village, with a young Hindu man falling in love with a young Muslim woman, when the couple elope to Bombay and marry they are caught up in the Hindu–Muslim riots, which burst forth in the film with the same unexpectedness as did the actual events.

An iconographic understanding of today's Rama-based Hinduism must not be restricted to Rama alone. This divinely royal figure is almost invariably complemented not only by his brother and wife, but also by that ideal servitor, the monkey Hanuman. Whereas Shiva has violent forms, sometimes considered as separate from himself, such as Virabhadra, Rama has his muscleman, the vigorous and powerful animal god. While Rama laments Sita's absence, it is Hanuman's initiative and enterprise that find her. In his hurry to get medicinal herbs for the stricken Rama on the battlefield, he has not the knowledge to pick the right ones, and with his animal might brings the whole mountain on which the herbs grow. The members of his new army, the Bajrang Dal, refer to his wilful destruction of Ravana's city as necessary violence. His power is not restricted to physical violence or its threat. Hanuman pulls apart the skin over his heart to reveal the presence of Rama, either his picture or his name written out many times in that worship of the name of God that has an Islamic parallel. Philip Lutgendorf reports the growth of tantric texts based on worship of Hanuman in cities over the last two decades. Meditational pictures of Hanuman as a source of power have a long history.[47] A striking painting by M. F. Husain has a nearly naked Sita with Rama beside the tail of a giant multi-headed Hanuman.

A recent story by the Urdu writer Kaisar Tamkeen encapsulates the ambiguity of Hanuman's joint role of animal and god as far as non-Hindus are concerned. A Muslim of good family, of Mughal descent, is taunted by the low-class Hindu boys in his street. They have trained a monkey to imitate Muslims. Their victim turns on the monkey, and kills it. A riot follows, two Muslims are killed, and the dead monkey is venerated by the Hindus as Hanuman. To placate his Hindu neighbours a Muslim tobacco vendor has to join in the worship of the dead monkey. The story is called 'A Ganga-Jumni Story', meaning a two-coloured, mixed, syncretic story, from *ganga-jumni*, the mixing of the two rivers Ganga and Jumna (meaning 'made of gold and silver'). The title is highly ironic, and subsequent events in the story are no less ironically handled.[48] The instant change in the monkey's status from live animal to murdered god shows – from a Muslim perspective – the impossibility, or at least difficulty, of the followers of two different religions being set beside each other in the satisfying way that gold and silver are in an ornament.

The Ayodhya mosque dispute was preceded in the nineteenth century by a dispute over the Hanuman temple, Hanumangarhi, in Ayodhya. This temple, like several others in Ayodhya, had been built by Hindu officials serving the Shi'ite rulers of the kingdom of Awadh. Hanuman was worshipped by Shaivite ascetics as Bhairava, a form of Shiva, and by Sufi fakirs as Hathile, 'the Obstinate'. 'The devotees of Rama, the Ramanandis, had to chase these competitors away before they could claim the place.'[49] In fact, it was Sunni Muslim disturbances about a mosque alleged to exist in Hanumangarhi that led to the capture of the Babri mosque by Hindu ascetics in 1855. When the British took over in 1856 the issue of the Hanuman temple had been settled.

This brief mention of conflict between Shaivites and Rama devotees must serve as marker for what has been a frequent type of occurrence over many centuries. Hindu tolerance is often only a theoretical position. Equally significant is the sharing of the object of devotion by Shaivas and Sufi, though under differing names. On a different plane, the interrelationship of Rama and Hanuman is also worthy of note. The animal god as devotee is the model for humans while also retaining his animality, in contrast to Ganesha, who is not at all animal in character and behaviour.

Finally, in contrast to the vivid variety of Hindu gods, for even the relatively straightforward character of Rama, as I have stressed, is inseparable from the extremity of Hanuman, we turn to the leader of the Dalits. The tension between Dalits and the higher castes is scarcely less important as a political issue than the tension between Muslims and Hindus.

B. R. Ambedkar (1891–1956)

The mass conversion of Dalits in 1981, noted above, was a worrying event for Hindu nationalists, since without the inclusion of the scheduled castes as Hindus, the Hindu numerical majority would be gravely impaired. It is appropriate to round off this account of Hinduism and politics with Ambedkar, the outcaste who became a lawyer and architect of the Indian Constitution, the patron saint of Dalits. It was he who chose the symbol of the Buddhist wheel for the Indian flag rather than Gandhi's quirky spinning wheel; Savarkar had wanted a lotus, sword, and swastika for his flag of Hindu India.

Relevant to this chapter is Ambedkar's attitude to Rama in his book *Riddles in Hinduism*, which was at first banned in Maharashtra. Rama holds no attractions for Ambedkar, for whom the most significant event in the *Ramayana* has to be Rama's decapitation of a Shudra for practising asceticism. Ambedkar calls this 'the worst crime that history has ever recorded'. He shows Ram Rajya, the ideal reign of the ideal king, to be in fact a life of dissolute indolence on Rama's part. He even refers to a Buddhist version of the *Ramayana* that claims Sita is Rama's sister, adding, 'If the story is true, then Rama's marriage to Sita is no ideal to be copied.'[50]

Ambedkar led the Mahar caste of Maharashtra to Buddhism in a mass conversion carried out just before his death. For Dalits, he is to some extent a parallel figure to Rama, since he is the ideal leader, commemorated now in a standard iconography, but a figure entirely pertaining to modernity, rather than a primordial warrior. Nevertheless, in Dalit eyes he is no less heroic, no less ideal, in his blue suit, white shirt and red tie, with fountain pen in his top pocket, neatly combed hair and black spectacles:

> The image is a simple but clear expression of the Mahar's own modest yet cosmic desires and potentiality. Here, those who had been forbidden a public presence announce both their presence and their newly claimed right to a place at the center of creation, by displaying an image of the Bombay statesman who pled their cause before the world and taught them that they were more than the 'children of god,' or Harijans, as Gandhi called them. They are the followers of Babasaheb Ambedkar.[51]

His image is an affirmation of modernity, while Gandhi's garb as a saint-peasant was a denial of it.

Ms Mayawati, a leader of the Dalit political party, when chief minister of Uttar Pradesh, had a golden statue of Ambedkar in her luxurious home, and put up in her state no less than 15,000 statues of him. More than a few of the new public statues there and in other states have been profaned by garlands of shoes. This insult, higher castes putting their feet on top of Ambedkar, is based on an ancient symbolism. Rama's younger brother, ruling in his stead while his elder brother is exiled in the forest, wears Rama's sandals on his head as sign of his subjection to the rightful king. Such insults to Ambedkar have caused riots all over India.[52]

Chapter Thirteen

Hinduism and the Global Future

In *Imagining India* Ronald Inden takes a painting by the fin-de-siècle painter Gustave Moreau (1826–98) as representing the European view of its own dominance over India. The painting is *The Triumph of Alexander the Great*, begun between 1880 and 1884 and left incomplete. Seated on an enormous throne, Alexander receives the submission of the defeated Indian king, Porus, in the fourth century BC. The Indian king is defeated, but the dominance of the West is not total in this painting, the background of which is Moreau's condensation of virtually all the known religious architecture of ancient India – Hindu, Buddhist and Jain – into a single structure. The images on the temples are not clearly represented, but one huge figure looms out distinctly: the statue of the Jain saint Bahubali, like all the other Indian details familiar to Moreau from drawings and photographs. Inden remarks, 'these religions of mysticism and dread are all summed up in the giant, dark statue that stands menacingly at the centre of the picture on a pedestal – he seems almost to levitate'.[1] The term 'dread' is applied by Inden to the Western view of Hinduism, Buddhism and Jainism. The statue is dark, being in the shade in Moreau's painting.

The cover of this book shows a young Jain seated at the feet of the same giant image of the Jain saint, Bahubali, which is carved from the living rock at Shravana Belgola in Karnataka. Bahubali was the younger son of a king who became the first Jina of this world age. His father renounced his kingdom and divided it between his two sons. The very strong Bahubali refused to submit to his brother, but the war that threatened between the two sides was averted by the two brothers agreeing to have a wrestling match instead. Bahubali was about to crush his brother when he suddenly became remorseful and decided to follow in his father's footsteps. He retired to the forest, pulled out all his hair, and, standing in the body-abandonment position, began to meditate. So absorbed was he, the years went by unnoticed. An anthill grew around his feet, vines and snakes began to embrace his body, his hair grew long and birds built nests in it. But only when he had completely forgiven his brother did he attain enlightenment and release. The 18-metre-high monolithic statue of Bahubali is one of the most popular Jain shrines. The boy in the photograph is performing *puja* of the giant's toes, with a *yantra* propped against the big toe.

The photograph, then, is a representation of ancient tradition today, with a giant form towering over the contemporary world. The most famous contemporary giant images are the two Buddhas at Bamiyan in Afghanistan, carved out of cliff faces in the late sixth century, and blown up by the Taliban in March 2001. Those giants were the cosmic Buddhas of the *Flower Garland Sutra*, universal Buddhas, teachers of all the myriad worlds in the universe, whose bodies were adorned with representations of those worlds. Ancient tradition is vulnerable. The Sanskrit university in Nepal was totally destroyed by Maoist terrorists in May 2002. Civilization is fragile.[2] We know that the giant Jain image stands on those feet though only they are visible on the book cover; nevertheless, the wheel of time – and the possibility of nuclear war – render Shelley's lines on the feet of Ozymandias, solitary and incomplete monument in the empty desert, not inapposite here:

> 'My name is Ozymandias, king of kings:
> Look upon my works, ye Mighty, and despair!'

But Bahubali was not a conquering warrior, he was a spiritual conqueror. It was his lower self that he conquered. He represents the conquest of spiritual tradition over mundane concerns; he represents the triumph of Jain thought and belief. Jainism is a religion parallel to and symbiotic with Hinduism, and no less Indian. Like Buddhism, its spiritual tradition is more focused than that of Hinduism; Jainism and Buddhism sprang from early Hinduism as reform movements. Jainism takes its name from the title of its founder, the Jina, literally 'the Conqueror', so it is literally the religion of (spiritual) conquest.

Bahubali withdrew from a life-and-death struggle with his brother over the kingdom they inherited. In May 2002 India and Pakistan, whose peoples had generally been good neighbours in kingdoms all over the subcontinent for centuries, had a million troops drawn up on their common border, and their nuclear weapons were ready: the once idyllic valley of Kashmir has been in dispute since the formation of the two countries. Hinduism shares with Jainism the doctrine of *ahimsa*, so emphatically exemplified by Gandhi, but it is also warlike. Perhaps the majority of Hindu gods and goddesses bear arms. Battle is frequent in Hindu myth and legend. Hindu ascetics – not unlike Buddhist and Jain ascetics – withdraw from the world into peaceful ashrams, but all too often Hindu ascetics are liable to fiery anger. The royal ascetic Vishvamitra, who became an ascetic to gain greater power because as king he failed to steal Vasishtha's all-giving divine cow Shabala, destroys the ashram of Vasishtha with magic missiles. A Mewar painting of this destruction's fiery radiance provides the cover picture of the first volume of the Princeton translation of the *Ramayana*.[3]

Alongside the fundamental truth that pure consciousness and bliss are all-pervading and are ultimate reality, strife and competition are the nature of things in Hindu myth and story. The classical Hindu view of time, as with Jainism and Buddhism, is of deteriorating conditions that end in the destruction of the world followed in due course by a new creation. The world is expected to end in fire. The televised *Mahabharata* ended with a warning of dread weapons that might be used when necessary to protect the motherland. It is well known in India that the atomic scientist Robert Oppenheimer quoted the *Bhagavad Gita* on the form of Krishna being brighter than a thousand suns when he witnessed the explosion of the first atom bomb. A certain insouciance is shown by India in code-naming its first successful nuclear explosion 'The Buddha Smiles'[4] and in speaking of the second set of tests in 1998 as 'The Buddha Smiles Again'. On both sides, these super-weapons have religious connotations. The Pakistani mid-range guided missile is called the Ghazni, after the eleventh-century Muslim invader Mahmud of Ghazni, destroyer of the Somanath temple. An earlier missile, the Ghori, was named after another invader of India from Afghanistan, perhaps the first Muslim destroyer of temples in Ayodhya. But the connection is more directly religious with India, which has missiles named after the god of fire (Agni) and Shiva's trident (Trishul). The latter is a short-range, surface-to-air missile, though the Puranas speak of Shiva's trident as a long-range missile that destroyed the triple cities of the demons in one blow. India's foremost missile scientist, A. P. J. Abdul Kalam (a secularly minded Muslim) is to be the next president of India.

More than any other religion, Hinduism welcomes science with open arms, and asserts its own scientific truth. (Gandhi was opposed to modern science, but he was influenced by Christianity and Tolstoy.) Without giving credence to the many extravagant claims that have been made about advanced Hindu science revealed in the Veda, there is an intuitive correctness in Hindu, Buddhist and Jain ideas concerning the scale of life-forms and the size of the universe that is light years in advance of other religions. At the same time, Hinduism, Jainism and Buddhism share the same profound awareness of higher states of consciousness, of levels of reality, and individual perfectibility. They also enjoy elaborate, often parallel, iconographies of divine images, revelling in the perfect visibility of the spiritual. These religions inspired, directly or indirectly, the work of Indological Orientalists (in the pre-Said sense), and partly through the Orientalists the ideals and ideas of these religions have

202 Hinduism and the Global Future

slowly permeated the West. If it is true as Gyan Prakash claims that Sir William
Jones's statue has, metaphorically speaking, 'tumbled down', one aim of this
book is to reaffirm the importance for the West of the Western attempt to
understand Hinduism.

I began with a metaphor from myth – the race between Ganesha and his
brother – and it should not be forgotten that this book's twin topics are in
themselves metaphorical in their imagined unity and cohesion, names for complex phenomena in reality too varied to take on a single shape or name. Where
is modernity when the Enlightenment loses itself in Romanticism or disap-
pears into postmodernism? Where is Hinduism amid the gods and gurus and
castes? Surely not Hindutva! More easily defined, sounder terms are the Enlightenment and India. But the title of this book expresses a complexity and a
tension that are profoundly exciting. Any portrayal of Hinduism – of the complex of religions that comprise Hinduism – is inevitably severely limited. I
have attempted a synthesis of the work of many scholars, and have produced
a reading that is in part a meditation, where in places I have chosen to let the
facts, some facts, speak for themselves.

My treatment of modernity has been of necessity all too cursory; and the
taut rationalism of Hindu/Buddhist/Jain philosophy has been passed over.
The rationalism of the Hindu four aims of human life (*kama*, *artha*, *dharma*
and *moksha*) is exemplary. There is much more that could be said about the
irrationality, the confusion, of modernity. I have said nothing here about the
postmodernity of Hinduism.[5] The hands of the Doomsday Clock of the *Bulletin of the Atomic Scientists* are closer than ever to midnight, but if there is a
global future, India has a significant role to play, leaving aside the fact that it
has recently brought Doomsday nearer.

Back in 1986, J. Duncan Derrett employed a benign and surely pardonable
essentialism when he declared, 'The genius of India . . . is peaceful coexistence
between groups, creative co-prosperity.' He elaborates: 'India has harnessed
the concepts of religion not to *activity*, nor to a meditative and self-absorbed
stagnation, but the creative co-prosperity of groups each recognising the other's right to contribute to the whole.' For Derrett, 'A balance of forces is still
needed and because it favours it, Hinduism still dominates.'[6] On the basis of
his profound knowledge of Hindu law and Indian history, Derrett has a notion – comforting and commendable to the modernity in us – of an India
above and beyond the religions it hosts.

Stressing the immense diversity of the subcontinent's social universe, the
French anthropologist Gérard Heuzé claims that 'India has become more
"advanced" than Europe. The perpetual nature of its crises proves it . . . The
India of today appears indeed one of the most explicit metaphors of the world
of tomorrow.' If Europe persists in tying itself to a model citizenhood and a
uniform mode of life, 'it appears more and more out of phase. Far from being
comparable to . . . a utopia . . . or even a boring suburb littered with super-

markets, this world is becoming a universe of . . . pitiless diversity.'[7] Not only, then, is Hinduism undiminished in modernity, but India is the most modern of countries in its variety and complexity.

Finally, there is this to be said. All ideas and ideals are in competition, seeking to colonize the mind and the world. The Mughal emperor Jahangir, 'Seizer of the World', liked to have himself painted astride the globe of the world, master of all countries, employing his artists' mastery of graphic realism to portray unreal, wished-for situations. Hindu art specializes in confident portrayal of the ideal. A contemporary poster image of Ganesha shows him sitting happily on the world, himself slightly larger than the globe.

Notes

Preface

1 Radhakrishnan 1968: 339. Note the wholly appropriate inclusion of a chapter on the contemporary installation of an image of Sirdi Sai Baba, a Hindu-Muslim saint, in a book on Egyptian and Mesopotamian image ritual of the 3rd millennium BC: Waghorne 1999.
2 Gombrich 1996: 3.
3 Wokler 1998: 307.

Chapter One: Modernity and Hinduism

1 Twitchell 1999: 70.
2 *Hinduism Today*, 18, 1 (Jan. 1996).
3 Denis Vidal, stressing the co–presence of the experiential and experimentation, sees here a linking of religion and science rather than opposition between them: 'Hinduism has once again demonstrated . . . the modernity that has always characterised it' (1998: 170).
4 See e.g. Alter 1991; Benjamin 1991; Frisby 1986; Heelas 1996, 1998; Lash 1992, 1998; Lash and Whimster 1987; Nagele 1991; Owen 1994; Scaff 1989; Turner 1992; Woodhead 2000.
5 Turner 1992 (the closing words).
6 Al-Azmeh 1996: 91.
7 Levinas 1988: 174.
8 Herzog 1974: 211, 222.
9 Appadurai and Breckenridge 1998: 1.
10 Appadurai and Breckenridge 1998: 15–16.
11 Miller 1994: 58.
12 Felski's summary of Charles Taylor's position in his *Sources of the Self* (Felski 1995: 12).

13   Cahoone 1988: 1.
14   Turner 1992: 12.
15   Habermas 1985: 9.
16   Gellner 1992b: 86.
17   Macaulay 1895: 400–2.
18   Mehta 1985: 4.
19   According to Samuel Sorbière (Pintard 1983: 152).
20   Hazard 1964: 145.
21   For the present study, the key parts of this most important work are: vol. 1 (pt. III, ch. 6), 'India in the Eyes of Europe: The Sixteenth Century' (also issued as a separate volume), and vol. 2.
22   Raynal 1781: 1: 47. Raynal had several collaborators, including most notably Diderot.
23   For Anquetil-Duperron, see pp. 39, 89, and 91. Haafner tells in his account how he was robbed of all his possessions by a British officer, and made friends easily with many Indians. He vividly describes the violent and unsettled nature of the times, when safe travel by land was almost impossible. He felt no animus against Hinduism, but when on Tirupati hill, site of one of the most famous and important temples, he preferred the 'sublime' aesthetics of the sunrise to the temple ceremony (Haafner 1811: 31–4).
24   Spinoza n.d.: 34, 33.
25   Kant 1983: 41.
26   Kant 1996: 69.
27   Olson 1992: 115.
28   Glasenapp 1973: 2.
29   Kant 1996: 69. 'His lectures on geography . . . contain more discussion of Asian ethnography and religion than of practically anything else' (Despland 1973: 103).
30   Olson 1992: 126–7.
31   Hegel 1975, in Gellner 1992a: 75.
32   Gellner 1992a: 77–9.
33   For Hegel and India, see Halbfass 1988: ch. 6.
34   See, above all, Halbfass 1988: ch. 5, 'India and the Romantic Critique of the Present'. Note the comment of Herder, 'If the East is the region from where come the regenerations of the human race, Germany must be considered as the Orient of Europe': cited in Gérard 1963: 132. French writers likewise took the view that Germans were the 'Indians of Europe' (Droit 1997: 151).
35   Hegel's view as summarized in Halbfass 1988: 93.
36   Hegel 1956: 142–3, cited in Inden 1992.
37   Taken up by Sartre and then Lacan, the distinction between self and other, dominant self and subservient other, has led feminists and other revisionists of the Enlightenment to reverse the polarity, to claim the other as sovereign territory, to be the supreme point from which one is mistress of all one surveys. The other of which one is ignorant, and of which one makes preliminary and necessarily incomplete summaries, becomes infinitely self-righteous and pours blame on the self that is ignorant of the other. The boot is on the other foot, but is not the later dichotomy as mistaken as the first?
38   Habermas 1987: 4.

39   For more details of Marx and India, see ch. 5 below.
40   For a critique of Weber's view of India, see ch. 5 below.
41   Hayek 1978: 30. According to the former editor of *The New Republic*, Martin
      Peretz, Marx + Freud = Truth: so he was said to have demonstrated in his seminar
      at Harvard (Andrew Sullivan, in 'News Review', *Sunday Times*, 6 Aug. 2000).
42   Mulvey 1996: 2.
43   For a careful but not exhaustive review of Nietzsche's knowledge of India see
      Sprung 1983; more up to date, and with valuable insights, is Hulin 1991. Conche
      writes of Nietzsche founding 'a new Brahmanism in opposition to the Buddhism
      of the future': Conch 1997: 40.
44   Parsons 1999.
45   Denis Wrong, cited in Gay 1997: 173.
46   Foucault 1977: 27.
47   Ahmad 2000: 129–66.
48   Foucault, cited in Droit 1992: 25.
49   Wolff 1985.
50   The French psychoanalyst Jacques Lacan is important in feminist and other cri-
      tiques of modernity. For Lacan, the self has no essential qualities, being con-
      structed rather than born. The self is always split, since the recognition of the self
      is inseparable from the recognition of the other, the not-self. When the child first
      recognizes itself in a mirror, it realizes its separateness from the mother and gains
      a sense of its own completeness. But the self remains a product of the imagina-
      tion, and is split. The notion of the constructed self is of course attractive to those
      who wish to deny what otherwise must be recognized as the biological realities of
      the human condition. Examples of the application of Lacan to South Asia include
      Hansen 1999: 61–5, 209–11 (the ultimate impossibility of producing 'full' iden-
      tities lies behind communal violence), and Hansen 2001: 197; more critically and
      more fully, Ewing says that 'Lacanian theory offers a powerful tool for explaining
      the power of ideologies to stimulate desire and move people to action and sub-
      mission without positing a cohesive ego as agent' (1997: 270). As so often, these
      exercises further understanding of the theory without adding to our understand-
      ing of the phenomena to which the theory is applied.
51   De Beauvoir 1968; Friedan 1963; Millett 1971.
52   Firestone 1979.
53   Brownmiller 1975.
54   Daly 1978; Dworkin 1981; Rich 1976.
55   Venn 2000: 49.
56   Loomba 1998: 66.
57   Gellner 1985: 5.
58   For a measured account, see Washbrook 1999.
59   In an essay written in 1977.
60   Shih 1937.
61   Clarke 1999: 7.
62   Kuspit 1993: 348–9.
63   Chomsky 2001.
64   Washbrook 1997: 412.

Chapter Two: India and the Juggernaut of Modernity

1   Fuchs 1994: p. ix.
2   Sankar Ray 1968: 64.
3   Coll 1994: 31, 28, 30.
4   Giddens 1991: 28, 30, 184.
5   Fuchs 1994: p. ix.
6   Their richly carved wood often makes temple cars mobile programmes of iconography. A temple car at Kumbhakonam has a pictorial summary of the *Ramayana* carved upon it.
7   Harvey 1985: 276.
8   Marx 1970: 280.
9   Marx 1970: 72.
10 Marx 1998: 817.
11 Benjamin 1999: 240.
12 Appadurai 1996: 333.
13 Ludden 1999: 176.
14 Forster 1952: 211.
15 Kipling 1960: 144–54.
16 Chevalier 1852 : 20, cited in Benjamin 1999: 598.
17 Davidson 1868: 27.
18 Andrew 1846: 86–7.
19 Thorner 1950: p. viii.
20 Richards and MacKenzie 1986: 68.
21 Ibid.
22 Davies 1987: 173.
23 Khilnani 1997: 110.
24 Davies 1987: 30–1.
25 De 1976: 124.
26 Ray 1995: 43–4.
27 Raychaudhuri 1995: 60.
28 Gandhi, cited in Erikson 1969: 259.
29 Gandhi 1997: 130–1.
30 Gandhi cited in Sankaran Nair 1922: 4–5.
31 Gandhi 1997: 132.
32 Lutgendorf 1995.
33 Allchin 1989.
34 For a detailed description of the Toyota 'chariot', see Davis 1996: 28. For context, see below, ch. 12.

Chapter Three: Hinduism Ancient and Modern

1   I follow Louis Renou in seeing the religion of the Vedas as 'ancient Hinduism' (Renou 1968: 19); ample iconographic proof of the unity of Vedism and early classical Hinduism is provided by Srinivasan 1997.

2   Jordens 1997: 56–7.
3   Halbfass 1988: 246.
4   Aurobindo 1955: 44–5.
5   Bryant 2001: 294–5.
6   Cited in Halbfass 1988: 199.
7   Hacker 1995: 233.
8   On the peripheral nature of Neo-Hinduism see Bharati 1970; Lutgendorf 1991: 360–7.
9   Rawson 1972: 5. On Tantra in the West, see Urban 2000.
10   Mukta 1994.
11   Ramanujan 1991: 53.
12   Kishwar 2000.
13   Narayana Rao 1992: 123.
14   Narayana Rao 1992: 126–7.
15   Omvedt 1997.

Chapter Four: Islam and Hinduism

1   Reported by the British administrator Malcolm Darling; cited in Hasan 1997: 128.
2   Indira Nehru married Feroze Gandhi, no relation in any way of M. K. Gandhi, the Mahatma, but her husband's name aided her political career.
3   Embree 1971: p. v.
4   Hardy 1960: 107.
5   Al-Biruni 1992: 1: 25.
6   Al-Biruni 1992: 1: 19–20.
7   Pines and Gelblum 1966: 309.
8   Nehru 1946: 213.
9   Babur 1969: 518.
10   Schimmel 1980: 75.
11   Babur 1969: 602.
12   Bakker 1986: 1: 134.
13   Babur 1969: appendix, p. lxxviii.
14   Ernst 2000: 116.
15   Nehru 1946: 214.
16   Richards 1998: 306.
17   Ziegler 1998: 269.
18   Bakker (1986: 1: 137 n. 9) gives the whereabouts of the three surviving coins, two gold, one silver.
19   Losty 1982: 76, 85.
20   Abu 'l-Fazl, A'in-Akari, cited in Welch 1973: 94.
21   Brend 1995: 62.
22   Ibid.
23   Nehru 1946: 216.
24   Barthes 1986: 139.

25 A fascinating account of Nur Jahan is given in Findly 1993, though her sugges-
    tions that Nur Jahan 'may have played Parvati to Jahangir's Shiva' and was also a
    Madonna figure seem unlikely (1993: 212–17).
26 Ettinghausen 1961: 99.
27 Sa'di n.d.: 124.
28 Losty 1982: 100.
29 Beach 1978: 167.
30 He continued the tradition established by his grandfather and great-grandfather.
    Such contacts arose not only from interest in religion, but also from the un-
    certainty of power. Advice from any source was welcome if it might reassure.
31 Shayegan 1997: 18.
32 Elliot 1964: 179.
33 Murr 1991.
34 Bernier 1934: 211–12.
35 Bernier 1934: 230–1.
36 Bernier 1934: 188.
37 Nehru 1946: 229.
38 Weber 1958: 65.
39 Bernier 1934: 276.
40 Eaton 2000a: 270.
41 Eaton 2000a: 267–8.

Chapter Five: The European Discovery of Hinduism

1   See above all Lach and Van Kley 1993 and Halbfass 1988.
2   Bouchon 1988: 74.
3   Bouchon 1988: 82.
4   *De open-deure tot het vorborgen heydendom.* There was no English version until the
    18th century.
5   Cited in Chandavarkar 1990: 368.
6   Filliozat 1983: 7.
7   Nilakantha Shastri 1955: 264.
8   Stein 1980: 392.
9   Wagoner 2000.
10 Stein 1980: 386.
11 Stein 1980: 388.
12 Mitter 1978: 51.
13 Lach and Van Kley 1993: 1044.
14 Roger 1915: 79.
15 Roger 1670: 156, 1915: 92–3. Roger's account follows the *Padma Purana.*
16 Baldaeus 1996: 814.
17 Bernier 1934: 318–19.
18 Bernier 1934: 345.
19 Bernier 1934: 347–8.
20 Bernier 1934: 323–5. Indeed, Bernier encouraged his patron to employ the pan-

dit in the first place. Bernier tells us that he collected materials on Hinduism, but abandoned them when he found that other Europeans had already done this.

21 Kopf's summary of Hastings's 'basic convictions' (Kopf 1969: 21).
22 Macaulay 1895: 646.
23 Cited in Trautman 1997: 72.
24 Trautman (1997) discusses Jones's statue and its pedestal. Paul Taylor points out that the square relief of the churning of the ocean seems to be a copy of the plate on the Tortoise incarnation of Vishnu in Baldaeus, and that the winged figure is the Genius of Jones (personal communication).
25 Wollstonecraft 1790.
26 Mill 1966: 19.
27 Mill 1826: 2: 434.
28 Mill 1968: p. xii.
29 *New York Daily Tribune*, 25 June 1853; Marx and Engels 1959: 20.
30 Ahmad 1992: 235.
31 A reference to thuggee. See below, ch. 8.
32 Marx and Engels 1959: 20.
33 An article on the 'freedom of the press' debates in the Rhineland province of Prussia. It appeared in *Rheinische Zeitung*, 125, on 5 May 1842, his twenty-fourth birthday.
34 Marx and Engels 1959: 14.
35 Pinch 1996: 7.
36 See below, p. 213 n. 4.
37 The title given to the English translation *The Religion of India* is misleading. The German title, translated, is *The Economic Ethics of World Religions: Hinduism and Buddhism*. The translation of the text by Gerth and Martindale is sometimes incomprehensible and sometimes completely wrong. See Kantowksy 1986.
38 Weber 1946: 267.
39 Kantowsky 1986: 38.
40 Weber 1958: 148–9.
41 Weber 1958: 122–3.
42 Weber 1958: 118, trans. revised in Gellner 2001.
43 Weber 1996: 520; Weber 1958: 325, trans revised in Gellner 2001.
44 Weber 1958: 328, trans. revised in Gellner 2001.
45 Bhattacharyya 1896: 36.
46 Weber 1958: 387 (the highly inauspicious vulture becomes by mistranslation a goose!); Weber 1996: 525.
47 Hodgson 1993.
48 Goody 1996.
49 Frank 1998: 336.
50 Weber 1930: 222.
51 Dumont 1980: 9–10.
52 Tocqueville, *Democracy in America*, quoted Dumont 1980: 18.
53 Dumont 1980: 43.
54 Dumont 1980: 50–1.
55 Dumont 1980: 276.
56 Dumont 1980: 286.

57   Dumont 1980: 275.
58   Dumont 1980: 293.

Chapter Six: Hinduism and Orientalism

1   Ahmad 1992: 168. Erich Auerbach is a literary critic often referred to by Said;
     Auerbach's *Mimesis* (Eng. trans. 1946) is 'one of the most admired and influen-
     tial books of literary criticism ever written' (Said 1984: 5).
2   Said 1978: 86.
3   Turner 1994: 183.
4   Prakash 1995: 200.
5   Rubies 2000: 287.
6   Rubies 2000: 286.
7   Kopf 1991: 21.
8   Kopf 1969.
9   Inden 1992: 1, 39.
10   Inden 1992: 39, 42.
11   Renou 1968: 30.
12   Renou 1968: 44.
13   Renou 1968: 35.
14   Renou 1968: 45.
15   Renou 1950: 46.
16   Malamoud 1978: 1.
17   Garbe 1925: 56.
18   Kejariwal's work establishes that 'the world of scholarship and the world of ad-
     ministration . . . were worlds apart' during the period he studies, 1784–1838
     (Kejariwal 1988: 226). Trautman notes, 'So far from there being a thick institu-
     tionalized connection between Orientalism and empire, as readers of Said might
     be led to imagine, one could say, roughly, that the study of Sanskrit varied *in-
     versely* with imperialism . . . It is as if the British had been persuaded by James
     Mill's preposterous argument that ignorance of Indian languages was a positive
     aid to the formation of unclouded views on imperial policy' (Trautman 1997:
     189).
19   See above, p. 74.
20   Feiling 1996: 105.
21   Anquetil-Duperron 1997: 75–7.
22   Said 1984: 252.
23   Inden 1992: 4.
24   Trautman 1997: 23.
25   Beames 1996: 64.
26   Pollock 1996: 198.
27   Pollock 1996: 241.
28   Aristotle, *Politics*, III. ix. 3, cited in Anderson 1974: 463.
29   Murr 1991.
30   Raynal 1820: 3: 187.

31 Lal 1997: 100.
32 Chaudhuri 1988: 775.
33 Raychaudhuri 1996: 358.
34 Kejariwal 1988: 233.
35 Chaudhuri 1988: 774.
36 Jaffrelot 1997: 331.
37 Pollock 1996: 233.
38 Pollock 1993: 115.
39 Pollock 1993: 116.
40 Toth 1988: 23.
41 Veer 2001: 49.
42 Deussen 1995.
43 Gilmour 1997: 35.
44 Geddes, cited in Nanda 1962: 95.
45 Lawrence 1928: 42–3.
46 The inner second panel of west pillar of north gate, the Great Stupa, Sanchi. The monkey's story is given in the *Dhammapadatthakattha*; see Sivaramamurti 1977: 190.
47 Risley 1915: 5.
48 Bayly 1997: 167.
49 Cannadine 2001: 4.
50 Cannadine 2001: 16.
51 Mason 1978: 80.
52 Letter to Engels (1867), cited in Wheen 2000: 298.
53 Girouard 1979: 28.
54 MacKenzie 1994: 16.
55 Bayly 1990a: 1313.
56 Lal 1996. In fact, Orme was only appropriating attitudes already expressed by the Mughals two centuries earlier (Eaton 2000b: 74–5).
57 Macaulay 1895: 611.
58 Tavernier 1925: 2: 141, 137.
59 McClintock 1995: 6–7.
60 Gauba 1930: 13.
61 Inden 1992: 86.
62 Inden 1992: 87.
63 Inden 1992: 88.
64 Inden 1992: 233–4.
65 Inden 1992: 96.
66 Inden 1992: 129.
67 Ibid.
68 Inden 1992: 120.
69 Inden 1992: 122.
70 Inden 1992: 123.
71 Padel 1995: 11.
72 Bayly 1990a: 1313.

Chapter Seven: 'Woman Caste' (*aurat jati*) and the Gender of Modernity

1 Mill 1826: 1: 383. See also Jose 2000.
2 It continues in psychoanalytical literature – see e.g. Ian 1993.
3 Butcher 1997: 17.
4 For the influence of India (amongst other Oriental sources) on European music and dance, see MacKenzie 1995. He notes, of a performance of *The Bayadères, or Priestesses of Pondicherry* in London in 1847, that it was reported by the press to have offered 'unalloyed, even uplifting pleasure' (1995: 194). Still famous today for her successes, the Dutch dancer Mata Hari, shot in France as a German spy in 1917, claimed to perform Hindu dance.
5 John 1998: 372.
6 There were several Indian rejoinders. Ernest Wood, educationist, theosophist and scholar, responded (see Wood 1929). See also Sinha 1994.
7 The West and modernity have many faults from the perspective, not just of Hindus, but of Indians in general. These faults include, along with general sexual immorality, neglect of the aged, cultural arrogance, gross materialism and exploitation of weaker nations.
8 See Thomas 1989; Roy 1998: 154–70.
9 Rajadhyaksha and Willemen 1999: 350.
10 Rushdie 1995: 138–9.
11 Das Gupta 1991: 119–20.
12 Tarlo 1996.
13 Nicholas 1995: 140–1.
14 Wadley 1995: 115.
15 Gellner 2001: 266.
16 Courtright 1995: 188.
17 See e.g. Hawley 1994; Mani 1998; Narasimhan 1990; Sharma 1988; Weinberger-Thomas 1999.
18 On the left, see Kumar 1993; on the right see Sarkar and Butalia 1995.
19 Ghosh 1995: 11.
20 She denied killing the thakurs herself (Sen 1991).
21 Hansen 1992: 192.
22 Nietzsche 1954: 544.
23 Nietzsche 1954: 547.
24 Dijkstra 1986.
25 Mukambika Bhagavati, in south Karnataka, is 'a naked, forest-dwelling goddess with a tiger's head in the place of her vagina' (Caldwell 1999: 148 and fig. 7, where she is shown clothed).
26 Geetha 1998: 320–1.
27 Speziale-Bagliacca 1991: 31.
28 Bhatt 2000: 156.
29 Clair 1989: 43.

Chapter Eight: Kali East and West

1   Smith 1996.
2   The son is necessary to feed his father after death in the *shraddha* ritual. The importance of boys is also demonstrated by the importance of boy gods, preeminently Krishna and Skanda. But girls are also ritually honoured. Hindu culture is exceptionally child-centred, as the corollary of being mother-centred.
3   Kakar 1978; see bibliography in Vaidyanathan 1999; and also Kakar 1996.
4   Interview in the *Hindustan Times*, 21 Nov. 1999. He reports that he felt much better after five sittings with Freud.
5   Kurtz 1992: 159.
6   Kripal 2000: 252.
7   Harlan 1992.
8   McDermott 1996a: 385. Gupta 2000 gives an account of relatively standard tantric worship of Kali.
9   The text leaves out this final detail of the formation of solid land, though this is implicit in the myth (Smith 1993b).
10   Clay idols of Phoolan were being sold, together with images of gods and goddesses, in local markets, according to a report in the *Times of India*, 24 Oct. 1984, cited in Hansen 1992: 196. This begs the question as to what is an idol and what is not.
11   Mankeka 1993.
12   Nuckolls 1993.
13   Nuckolls 1993: 215.
14   Heuzé 1989: 302.
15   Ramaswamy 1997.
16   Feldhaus 1995: 43, 46.
17   Erndl 1993: 102.
18   Macaulay 1900: Gates of Somnath speech.
19   Ibid.
20   Hardy 1994: 149.
21   Roy 1998: 50.
22   Roy 1998: 70.
23   Budhasvamin 1986: 130.
24   Hardy 1994: 148.
25   The book concludes with a section on the religious literature of the Hindus by one J. J. Weibrecht. Wright states that the lecture on the thugs is compiled from Sleeman, and the lecture on Durga and Kali festivals is compiled from the writings of Alexander Duff.
26   Woerkens: 1993.
27   Macmunn 1933: 199.
28   Macmunn 1933: 218.
29   Macmunn 1933: 219.
30   Merchant 1989: 4.
31   Kapur 1993: 38.
32   Melton 1992: 795.
33   Beth 1994. The prayer continues with the following words: 'Let us live purely in

love and by wisdom from now on. Transform unkindness and cruelty within us to compassion and courage. Bless all our passion for those we love, that new ways may arise and new works or new children': laudable, but unrelated to Kali.

34 Paglia 1992: 1.
35 Victoria of Luna Circa 1995.
36 McDermott 1996b: 288.
37 Alexandre 2001: 95.
38 Starhawk 1979: 95.
39 Gutschow 1996: 214.
40 Michaels 1996: 334. He points out, as we have already seen, that 'This power is, as Sudhir Kakar (1978: 20 *et passim*) has consistently analyzed, related to . . . mother experiences in early childhood and would thus explain why female goddesses tend to have such identities (while Western society is characterized by Oedipus myths).'

Chapter Nine: The Gods of Hinduism and the Idols of Modernity

1 The review in *Monthly Review* of *Asiatick Researches I–IV* (1789: 81: 653), cited in Cannon 1986: 234.
2 Mehta 1985: 127.
3 Mill 1826: 1: 285.
4 Cf. Lutgendorf's comment on Rama and Krishna, 'At the folk level, their characters, deeds, and even names bleed into one another' (1992: 218).
5 Lütt 1995: 152. Note that a tradition of an erotic Rama flourished in North India in the 18th and 19th centuries (Lutgendorf 1992).
6 Collins 1997: 138.
7 Collins 1997: 137.
8 Kakar 1981: 101–2, cited in Collins 1997: 137.
9 Obeyesekere 1978, 469–70, cited in Collins 1997: 137. Collins also refers to Ramanujan 1983.
10 Collins 1997: 137.
11 On Andhaka see Handelman and Shulman 1997: ch. 2.
12 Segal 2000.
13 Nehru 1946: 171.
14 Tagore 1935: 4–5.
15 Roy 1963: 149.
16 Weinberger-Thomas 1987: 173.
17 Gay 1997: 1: 3ff.; Despland 1973: 256.
18 Hume 1956: 49–50.
19 Solomon 1983: 610: 'Hegel, Hölderlin, and Schelling once tried to revive a religion with Zeus at its head'.
20 Nietzsche *Joyful Wisdom* no. 143, paraphrased in Steiner 1971: 37.
21 Weber 1946: 149, 152, 148, 147.
22 Le Rider 1993: 147–78.

23   Weber 1946: 154.
24   Vaidyanathan and Kripal 1999: 3.
25   Gamwell and Wells 1989: 110.
26   Brandt 1976: 52.
27   Bacon 1857–74: 3: 395.
28   *Novum Organum* (Bacon 1857–74: 1: 49), cited in Schopenhauer 1966: 2: 218.
29   Schopenhauer 1966: 2: 69.
30   Barth 1976: ch. 2.
31   Bhattacharyya 1896: 338.
32   Jairazbhoy 1991: p. viii. He quotes Wendy Doniger's remark that the Hindu myths are 'often intentionally hilarious' (O'Flaherty 1980).
33   Kipling 1898: 29.
34   Samuel Taylor Coleridge, cited in McClintock 1995: 181.
35   Marx 1970: 754.
36   Llobera 1994: pp. viii–ix.

Chapter Ten: The Image of the Self

1   Pinney 1997: 116. Pinney uses the Hindi spelling of the divine names, whereas elsewhere in this book the Sanskrit forms are used.
2   Siddhartha Ghosh, 'Early Photography in Calcutta' (*Marg* 41, 4), cited in Pinney 1997: 225.
3   Parry cited in Pinney 1997: 196.
4   Marriott 1976: 111.
5   Laws of Manu 6.90, trans. Bühler 1886: 214–15.
6   *Baudhayana Pitrimedha Sutra*.
7   Nicholas 1981: 187, 188.
8   Sivaramamurti 1978: 116.
9   Smith 1996.
10   Abbott 1932: ch. 4.
11   Lacan 1978: 128.
12   For an excellent account of trance in Hinduism, see Collins 1997: ch. 6; the author also mentions her own experiments in trance.
13   Kaelber 1989: 144.
14   From the psychoanalytical viewpoint, these powers, along with *tapas*, are an expression of infantile longings for omnipotence, themselves springing from the complete fulfilment of the foetus's needs within the womb.
15   Rawson 1972; see also Mookerjee 1975. Illustrated books on tantra appeared before Rawson, not least Tucci's *Rati–lila* (Eng. trans. 1969), but Rawson was the first to label tantric art as a specific form of art.
16   The long-lived and prolific French writer Alexandra David-Néel had that very image hanging on her study wall in Digne, but she was a Buddhist, and indeed a *yogini*!
17   Tonelli 1985, with an interesting essay by L. P. Sihare, who also refers to the work of Mondrian, Kandinsky and others. The artists in the catalogue are Biren De (b. 1926), K. V. Haridasan (b. 1938), Prafulla Mohanti (b. 1936), Om Prakash

(b. 1932), K. C. S. Paniker (1911–77), P. T. Reddy (b. 1915) and G. R. Santoshi (b. 1929).
18 Nikhilananda 1942: 197. Cf. *Chhandogya Upanishad* 6.10.13.
19 Freud 1982: 9.
20 Letter, 19 Jan. 1930, in Freud 1960: 392.
21 Freud 1982: 9–10.
22 Freud 1982: 27.

Chapter Eleven: Gurus

1   Kakar 1991: 52–60.
2   Chandrasekharendra 1991.
3   The valuable work of my former colleague at Lancaster Andrew Rawlinson (Rawlinson 1997) gives synoptic treatment of Western gurus of Eastern teachings. A parallel treatment of Indian gurus is needed. The topic aroused general interest in the 1970s (e.g. Bharati 1970; Brent 1972; Menen 1974; Singh 1975; Uban 1997). Steinmann 1986 is helpful; there is much more to be said today.
4   McKean 1996.
5   Jaffrelot 1996: 289.
6   Bhattacharyya 1896: 350.
7   Weber 1958: 325 (slightly altered); Weber 1996: 518.
8   His ninety-ninth birthday in Western reckoning: Hindus count time in the womb when calculating one's age.
9   Bhattacharyya 1896: 352.
10 For a reading of novel and film, see Mishra 1996.
11 Laws of Manu 2.142–50, trans. Bühler 1886, slightly altered.
12 Chandrasekharendra 1991: 207.
13 Social work by the Ramakrishna Mission and other Hindu religious organizations is often said to be based on Western influence in 19th-century India. See, however, Beckerlegge 2000; Tripathi 1997: 126.
14 Sil 1998.
15 Isherwood 1965: 124.
16 Isherwood 1965: 71.
17 Beckerlegge 2000: 129.
18 Virajaprana 1995: 16, cited in Beckerlegge 2000: 127.
19 Cited in Sil 1997: 158.
20 See Heehs 2000.
21 Minor 1999.
22 Ruhela 1993: 12.

Chapter Twelve: Modernity and Hindu Nationalism

1   *The Hindu*, 23 Aug. 1997, p. 10a.
2   Courtright 1992.

3   Sardar 1998: 69.
4   Derne 2000: 132.
5   Nandy 1998: 7.
6   Assayag 2001: 74–5.
7   Assayag 2001: 77.
8   Bayly 1998: 27.
9   Kedourie: 1993; Llobera 1994: p. xii: 'In the modern sense of the term, national consciousness has only existed since the French Revolution, since the time when in 1789 the Constituent Assembly equated the people of France with the French nation.'
10 Gellner 1998: 3.
11 Nairn 1977: 359.
12 Llobera 1994: 220.
13 Gandhi sought to serve all Indians, but at some point in time these images are provided with a snake's hood as parasol, as if Gandhi were an incarnation of Vishnu accompanied by Shesha the serpent, who is the remainder of the universe after its dissolution.
14 Swarup 1995.
15 Sinha 1998.
16 Parekh 1997: 5.
17 *Bharatuddhar* (Gandhi the Protector of India) by Prabhu Dayal, *c*.1930, in Bayly 1990b: 393.
18 Savarkar 1949: 41.
19 Savarkar n. d.: 374.
20 R. L. Dhooira, *I Was a Swayamsevak*, cited in Jaffrelot 1996: 70.
21 Sirsikar 1992: 201.
22 Jaffrelot 1996: 63–4.
23 Raychaudhuri 1999: 208.
24 *Constitution and Rules*, cited in Elst 1997: 5.
25 Upadhyaya 1992: 8.
26 Nandy et al.1995: 88.
27 *Organiser*, Diwali special issue (1964, p. 15), cited in Jaffrelot 1996: 197.
28 Frykenberg 1993: 245–6.
29 Nandy et al. 1995: 97.
30 *India Today*, 8 Feb. 1999, cited in Bhatt 2001: 199.
31 Hansen 2001.
32 Nandy 2000: 131.
33 Jaffrelot 1996: 42.
34 Kaviraj 1995: 309.
35 Pandey 1993: 242–3.
36 Details of the whole temple can be found in McKean 1996: 144–63.
37 Munshi 1957: 5.
38 Munshi 1976: 89.
39 Munshi 1976: 62.
40 See Veer 1992: 91.
41 Davis 1997: 217.
42 *The Hindu*, 2 Dec. 1995.

43   Jaffrelot 1996: 340.
44   *Organiser*, 12 Feb. 1984, p. 6, cited in Jaffrelot 1996: 361.
45   Frykenberg 1993: 246.
46   Rajagopal 2001: 72.
47   Ross 1998.
48   Oesterheld: 1998.
49   Veer 1994: 154–5. See also Bakker 1986: 2: 126.
50   Ambedkar 1989.
51   Tartakov 1990.
52   Jaffrelot 2000: 240.

Chapter Thirteen: Hinduism and the Global Future

1   Inden 1992: 55.
2   Another major lacuna in the history of India civilization should be mentioned here. 'The great library of the Mughals with its reputed 24,000 manuscripts, many of them illuminated, was sacked by the Afghan Nadir Shah in 1739 and many of its treasures carried off as booty to Iran. Little now survives to represent the achievements of the book-artists of the reigns of Akbar and Jahangir' (Losty 1982: 85).
3   From the *Balakanda* of the Jagat Singh *Ramayana*, painted by Manohar, 17th century.
4   The date of the test was that of the festival of the Buddha's birthday.
5   Some remarks on Hinduism and postmodernity are to be found in Smith 1993a.
6   Derrett 1986: 79, 88, 79.
7   Heuzé 1993: 169.

References

Films

1942–A Love Story. 1994, Hindi. Dir. Vidhu Vinod Chopra.
Ammoru. 1995, Telugu. Dir. Kodi Ramakrishna.
Ankur (The Seedling). 1973, Hindi. Dir. Shyam Benegal.
Apocalypse Now! 1979. Dir. Francis Ford Coppola.
Bandit Queen. 1994, Hindi. Dir. Shekar Kapur.
Bharat Mata (Mother India). 1957, Hindi. Dir. Mehboob Khan.
Bombay. 1995, Tamil/Hindi. Dir. Mani Rathnam.
The Deceivers. 1989. Dir. Nicholas Meyer.
Devi. 1960, Bengali. Dir. Satyajit Ray.
Devi. 1999, Telugu. Dir. Kodi Ramakrishna.
Gunga Din. 1939. Dir. George Stevens.
Indiana Jones and the Temple of Doom. 1984. Dir. Steven Spielberg
Jadugar (Magician). 1989, Hindi. Dir. Prakash Mehra.
Jai Santoshi Ma (In Praise of Mother Santoshi). 1975, Hindi. Dir. Vijay Sharma.
Meera. 1979, Hindi. Dir. Sampooran Singh Gulzar.
Sati. 1989, Bengali. Dir. Aparna Sen.
Satya (Truth). 1998, Hindi. Dir. Ramgopal Varma.

Books and Articles

Abbott, J. 1932: *The Keys of Power: A Study of Indian Ritual and Belief.* London: Methuen.
Ahmad, Aijaz. 1992: *In Theory: Classes, Nations, Literatures.* London: Verso.
Ahmad, Aijaz. 2000: *Lineages of the Present: Ideology and Politics in Contemporary South Asia.* London: Verso.
Al-Azmeh, Aziz. 1996: *Islams and Modernities.* London: Verso.

Al-Biruni [Alberuni]. 1992 [1910]: [*Al-Hind*] *Alberuni's India*, ed. and trans. Edward C. Sachau. Delhi: Munshiram Manoharlal.

Alexandre, Chandra. 2001: Through Vulture's Eye – With Peacock's Tail: A Western (Eco)Feminist Engagement with Kali and the Black Madonna as Antinomian Agents of Transformation in a Patriarchal World. Ph.D. thesis, California Institute of Integral Studies, UMI.

Allchin, F. R. 1989: City and State Formation in Early Historic South Asia. *South Asian Studies*, 5, 1–16.

Alter, Robert. 1991: *Necessary Angels: Tradition and Modernity in Kafka, Benjamin and Scholem*. Cambridge, MA: Harvard University Press.

Ambedkar, B. R. 1989: *Riddles in Hinduism*. In *Dr Babasaheb Ambedkar: Writings and Speeches*, vol. 4. Bombay: Government of Maharashtra.

Anderson, Perry. 1974: *Lineages of the Absolutist State*. London: NLB.

Andrew, W. P. 1846: *Indian Railways*. London: T. C. Newby.

Anquetil-Duperron, A. H. 1997 [1771]: *Voyage en Inde 1754–62*, ed. J. Deloche, M. Filliozat and P. S. Filliozat. Paris: EFEO.

Appadurai, A. 1996: *Modernity at Large: Cultural Dimensions of Globalization*. Minneapolis: University of Minnesota Press.

Appadurai, A. and Breckenridge, Carol A. 1998: Public Modernity in India. In Carol A. Breckenridge (ed.), *Consuming Modernity: Public Culture in a South Asian World*, 1–20. Minneapolis: University of Minnesota Press.

Assayag, Jackie. 2001: Nationalism: Imported or Invented Tradition? *Revue des Deux Mondes*, Sept./Oct.

Aurobindo [Ghose], Sri. 1955: *Bankim-Tilak-Dayanand*. Pondicherry: Sri Aurobindo Ashram.

Babb, L. 1975: *The Divine Hierarchy: Popular Hinduism in Central India*. New York: Columbia University Press.

Babur. 1969: *The Babur-nama in English (Memoirs of Babur)*, trans. Annette Susannah Beveridge. London: Luzac.

Bacon, Francis. 1857–74: *The Works of Francis Bacon*, 14 vols, ed. James Spedding, Robert Leslie Ellis and Douglas Denon Heath. London: Longman, Green, Longman & Roberts.

Bakker, Hans. 1986: *Ayodhya*, 2 vols in 1. Groningen Oriental Studies 1. Groningen: Egbert Forsten.

Baldaeus, Philip. 1996 [1672, 1703]: *A True and Exact Description of . . . Malabar and Coromandel*, trans. from the Dutch. New Delhi: Asian Educational Services.

Barth, Hans. 1976 [1945, 1961]: *Truth and Ideology*, trans. Frederic Lilge. Berkeley: University of California Press.

Barthes, Roland. 1986: The Discourse of History. In *The Rustle of Language*, trans. Richard Howard. New York: Hill & Wang.

Bayly, C. A., 1990a: Review of Inden, *Imagining India*, TLS, Dec., 7–13.

Bayly, C. A. (ed.). 1990b: *The Raj: India and the British 1600–1947*. London: Pearson.

Bayly, C. A. 1998: *Origins of Nationality in South Asia: Patriotism and Ethical Government in the Making of Modern India*. New Delhi: Oxford University Press.

Bayly, Susan. 1997: Caste and Race. In Peter Robb (ed.), *The Concept of Race in South Asia*, 165–218. Delhi: Oxford University Press.

Beach, Milo Cleveland. 1978: *The Grand Mogul: Imperial Painting in India 1600–*

1660. Williamstown: Sterling and Francine Clark Art Institute.

Beames, John. 1996: *Memoirs of a Bengal Civilian*. London: Eland.

Beckerlegge, Gwilym. 2000: *The Ramakrishna Mission: The Making of a Modern Hindu Movement*. New Delhi: Oxford University Press.

Benjamin, Andrew. 1991: *The Problems of Modernity: Adorno and Benjamin*. London: Routledge.

Benjamin, Walter. 1999: *The Arcades Project*, trans. Howard Eiland and Kevin McLaughlin. Cambridge, MA: Harvard University Press.

Bernier, François. 1934 [1670]: *Travels in the Mogul Empire*, trans. and annotated by Archibald Constable, rev. edn. by Vincent A. Smith. London: Oxford University Press.

Beth, Rae. 1994: *Reincarnation and the Dark Goddess: Lives and Teachings of a Priestess*. London: Robert Hale.

Bharati, Agehananda. 1970: The Hindu Renaissance and its Apologetic Patterns. *Journal of Asian Studies*, 29, 2, 267–88.

Bhatt, Chetan. 2001: *Hindu Nationalism: Origins, Ideologies and Modern Myths*. Oxford: Berg.

Bhatt, N. R. 2000: *La Religion de Siva d'après les sources sanskrites*, trans. P.-S. Filliozat [English original unpublished]. Palaiseau: Editions Agamat.

Bhattacharyya, J. N. 1896: *Hindu Castes and Sects*, Calcutta: Thacker, Spink.

Bouchon, Geneviève. 1988: L'Inde dans l'Europe de la Renaissance. In C. Weinberger-Thomas (ed.), *L'Inde et l'imaginaire*, 69–90. Paris: EHSS.

Brandt, Reinhardt. 1976: Über die vielfältige Bedeutung der baconschen Idole. *Philosophisches Jahrbuch der Görres-Gesellschaft*, 83, 42–70.

Brend, Barbara. 1995: *The Emperor Akbar's Khamsa of Nizami*. London: British Library.

Brent, Peter. 1972: *Godmen of India*, Harmondsworth: Penguin.

Brosius, Christiane. 1999: Empowering Visions: A Study on Videos and the Politics of Cultural Nationalism in India (1989–1998). Ph.D. dissertation, Kulturwissenschaftlichen Fakultät, Europa-Universität Viadrina, Frankfurt an der Oder.

Brownmiller, Susan. 1975: *Against Our Will: Men, Women and Rape*. New York: Bantam Books.

Bryant, Edwin. 2001: *The Quest for the Origins of Vedic Culture: The Indo-Aryan Migration Debate*. New York: Oxford University Press.

Budhasvamin. 1986: *Brihatkathaslokasamgraha*, ed. and trans Ram Prakash Poddar. Varanasi: Tara Printing Works.

Butcher, Melissa. 1997: Looking at Miss World. *SEMINAR*, 453, May, 16–20.

Cahoone, Lawrence E. 1988: *The Dilemma of Modernity: Philosophy, Culture, and Anti-Culture*. Albany: State University of New York.

Caldwell, Sarah. 1999: *O Terrifying Mother: Sexuality, Violence and Worship of the Goddess Kali*. New Delhi: Oxford University Press.

Cannadine, David. 2001: *Ornamentalism: How the British Saw their Empire*. London: Penguin.

Cannon, Garland. 1986. British Periodical Reaction to Sir William Jones's Introduction of Sanskrit Culture to the West. Proceedings of the fourth world Sanskrit conference, ed. W. Morgenroth. *Schriften zur Geschichte und Kultur des Altern Orients*, 18, 230–6.

Caplan, Lionel. 1997: Martial Gurkhas The Persistence of a British Military Discourse on 'Race'. In Peter Robb (ed.), *The Concept of Race in South Asia*, 260–81. Delhi: Oxford University Press.

Chandavarkar, Rajnarayan. 1990: 'Strangers in the Land': India and the British since the Late Nineteenth Century. In C. A. Bayly, (ed.), *The Raj: India and the British 1600–1947*, 368–79. London: Pearson.

Chandrasekharendra Sarasvati, Jagadguru. 1991: *The Guru Tradition*, trans. R. G. K. Bombay: Bharatiya Vidya Bhavan.

Chaudhuri, Nirad C. 1988: *Thy Hand, Great Anarch*. London: Chatto & Windus.

Chevalier, Michel. 1852: Chemins de fer. In *Dictionnaire de l'économie politique*. Paris.

Chomsky, Noam. 2001: Q and A after Public Lecture 'September 11th and its Aftermath: Where is the World Heading?' at the Music Academy, Chennai (Madras), India 10 Nov. 2001. *Frontline*, 18, 24, 24 Nov.–7 Dec.

Clair, Jean. 1989: *Méduse: Contribution à une anthropologie des arts du visuel*. Paris: Gallimard.

Clarke, T. J. 1999: *Farewell to an Idea*. New Haven and London: Yale University Press.

Coll, Steve. 1994: *On the Grand Trunk Road: A Journey into South Asia*. New York: Random House.

Collins, Elizabeth Fuller. 1997: *Pierced by Murugan's Lance: Ritual, Power, and Moral Redemption among Malaysian Hindus*. Dekalb: Northern Illinois University Press.

Conch, Marcel. 1997: *Nietzsche et le Bouddhisme*. Fougère: Encre Marin.

Courtright, Paul B. 1992: The Ganesh Festival in Maharastra: Some Observations. In E. Zelliot and M. Berntsen (eds), *The Experience of Hinduism: Essays on Religion in Maharashtra*, 76–94. Delhi: Sri Satguru Publications.

Courtright, Paul B. 1995: *Sati*, Sacrifice, and Marriage: The Modernity of Tradition. In Lindsey Harlan and Paul B. Courtright (eds.), *From the Margins of Hindu Marriage: Essays on Gender, Religion, and Culture*, 184–204. New York: Oxford University Press.

Daly, Mary. 1978: *Gyn/Ecology:The Metaethics of Radical Feminism*. Boston: Beacon Press.

Das Gupta, Chidananda. 1991: *The Painted Face*. New Delhi: Roli Books.

Davidson, Edward. 1868: *The Railways of India, with an Account of their Rise, Progress, and Construction*. London: E. & F. N. Spon.

Davies, Philip. 1987: *Splendours of the Raj: British Architecture in India*. Harmondsworth: Penguin.

Davis, Richard H. 1996: The Iconography of Ram's Chariot. In David Ludden (ed.), *Contesting the Nation: Religion, Community and the Politics of Democracy in India*, 27–54. Philadelphia: University of Pennsylvania Press.

Davis, Richard H. 1997: *Lives of Indian Images*. Princeton: Princeton University Press.

De, B. 1976: The Colonial Context of the Bengal Renaissance. In C. H. Philips and M. D. Wainwright (eds), *Indian Society and the Beginnings of Modernization, 1830–50*. London: University of London School of Oriental and African Studies.

De Beauvoir, Simone. 1968: *The Second Sex*, trans. H. M. Parshley. London: Jonathan Cape.

Derne, Steve. 2000: *Movies, Masculinity, and Modernity: An Ethnography of Men's Filmgoing in India*. Westport: Greenwood Press.

Derrett, J. Duncan M. 1986: A Post-Weberian Approach to Indian Social Organization. In *Max Weber e l'India. Atti del Convegno Internazionale su la tesi Weberiana della razionalizzazione in rapporto all'Induismo e al Buddhismo*, Turin 24–5 Nov. 1983, 79–97. Turin: CESMEO.

Despland, Michel. 1973: *Kant on History and Religion*. Montreal: McGill-Queen's University Press.

Deussen, Paul. 1995 [1904]: *My Indian Reminiscences*, trans. A. King. New Delhi: Asian Educational Services.

Dijkstra, Bram. 1986: *Idols of Perversity: Fantasies of Feminine Evil in Fin-de-Siècle Culture*. New York: Oxford University Press.

Droit, Roger-Pol. 1992: *L'Oubli de l'Inde: Une amnésie philosophique*. Paris: Livre de Poche.

Droit, Roger-Pol. 1997: *Le Culte du néant: Les Philosophes et le Bouddha*. Paris: Seuil.

Dubuisson, Daniel. 1986: *Le Légende royale dans l'Inde ancienne*. Paris: Economica.

Dumont, Louis. 1980: *Homo Hierarchicus: The Caste System and its Implications*, trans. Mark Sainsbury, Louis Dumont, and Basia Gulati. Chicago: University of Chicago Press.

Dworkin, Andrea. 1981: *Pornography: Men Possessing Women*. New York: Perigree Books.

Eaton, Richard M. 2000a: Temple Desecration and Indo-Muslim States. In David Gilmartin and Bruce B. Lawrence (eds), *Beyond Turk and Hindu: Rethinking Religious Identities in Islamicate South Asia*, 246–81. Gainsville: University of Florida Press.

Eaton, Richard M. 2000b: (Re)imagining Otherness: A Postmortem for the Postmodern in India. *Journal of World History*, 11, 1, 57–78.

Elliot, Sir H. M. 1964: *The History of India as Told by its Own Historians: The Muhammadan Period. The Posthumous Papers of Sir H. M. Elliot*, vol. 7, ed. and continued by John Dowson. Allahabad: Kitab Mahal.

Elst, K. 1997: *Bharatiya Janata Party vis-à-vis Hindu Resurgence*. New Delhi: Voice of India.

Embree, Ainslie T. (ed.). 1971: Introduction. In *Alberuni's India*, trans. Edward C. Sachau. New York: Norton.

Erikson, Erik H. 1969: *Gandhi's Truth: On the Origins of Militant Nonviolence*. New York: Norton.

Erndl, Kathleen M. 1993: *Victory to the Mother: The Hindu Goddess of Northwest India in Myth, Ritual, and Symbol*. New York: Oxford University Press.

Ernst, Carl W. 2000: Ellora Temples as Viewed by Indo-Muslim Authors. In David Gilmartin and Bruce B. Lawrence (eds), *Beyond Turk and Hindu: Rethinking Religious Identities in Islamicate South Asia*, 98–120. Gainsville: University of Florida Press.

Ettinghausen, Richard. 1961: The Emperor's Choice. In Millard Meiss (ed.), *De Artibus Opuscula XL: Essays in Honor of Erwin Panofsky*, 98–120. New York: New York University Press.

Ewing, Katherine Pratt. 1997: *Arguing Sainthood: Modernity, Psychoanalysis and Islam*. Durham, NC: Duke University Press.

Feiling, Keith. 1996: *Warren Hastings*. London: Macmillan.

Feldhaus, Anne. 1995: *Water and Womanhood: Religious Meanings of Rivers in Maharashtra*. New York: Oxford University Press.

Felski, Rita. 1995: *The Gender of Modernity*. Cambridge, MA: Harvard University Press.

Filliozat, Vasundhara. 1983: *Le Ramayana à Vijayanagara*. Paris: Publications Orientalistes de France.

Findly, Ellison Banks. 1993: *Nur Jahan: Empress of Mughal India*. New Delhi: Oxford University Press.

Firestone, Shulamith. 1979: *The Dialectic of Sex*. London: The Women's Press.

Forster, E. M. 1952: *A Passage to India*. London: Harcourt, Brace & Jovanovich.

Foucault, Michel. 1977: *Discipline and Punish*, trans. A.S. London: Allen Lane.

Frank, Andre Gunder. 1998: *ReOrient: Global Economy in the Asian Age*. Berkeley: University of California Press.

Freud, Sigmund. 1960: *The Letters of Sigmund Freud*, ed. E. Freud. New York: Basic Books.

Freud, Sigmund. 1982 [1930]: *Civilization and its Discontents*, trans. Joan Riviere, ed. James Strachey. London: Hogarth Press.

Friedan, Betty. 1963: *The Feminine Mystique*. New York: W. W. Norton.

Frisby, David. 1986: *Fragments of Modernity: Theories in the Work of Simmel, Kracauer and Benjamin*. Cambridge, MA: MIT.

Frykenberg, Robert Eric. 1993: Hindu Fundamentalism and the Structural Stability of India. In *The Fundamentalism Project*, vol. 3: *Fundamentalisms and the State: Remaking Polities, Economies, and Militance*. Chicago: University of Chicago Press.

Fuchs, Martin. 1994: India and Modernity: Towards Decentering Western Perspectives. *Thesis Eleven*, 39, v–xiii.

Gamwell, Lynn and Wells, Richard (eds). 1989: *Sigmund and Art: His Personal Collection of Antiquities*. London: Freud Museum.

Gandhi, M. K. 1997: *Hind Swaraj and Other Writings*, ed. Anthony J. Parel. Cambridge: Cambridge University Press.

Garbe, Richard. 1925: *Indische Reiseskizzen*, 2nd edn. Munich-Neubiberg: Oskar Schloss.

Gauba, Kanhayalal. 1930: *H. H., or the Pathology of Princes*. Lahore: Time Publishing.

Gay, P. 1997: *The Enlightenment: An Interpretation*, 2 vols. New York: W. W. Norton.

Geertz, Clifford. 1984: Anti Anti Relativism. *American Anthropologist*, 263–78.

Geetha, Veena. 1998: On Bodily Love and Hurt. In Mary E. John and Janaki Nair (eds), *A Question of Silence: The Sexual Economies of Modern India*, 304–31. New Delhi: Kali for Women.

Gellner, David N. 2001: *The Anthropology of Buddhism and Hinduism: Weberian Themes*. New Delhi: Oxford University Press.

Gellner, Ernest. 1985: *The Psychoanalytic Movement*. London: Paladin.

Gellner, Ernest. 1992a: *Reason and Culture*. Oxford: Blackwell.

Gellner, Ernest. 1992b: *Postmodernism, Reason and Religion*. London: Routledge.

Gellner, Ernest. 1998: *Nationalism*. London: Phoenix.

Gérard, René. 1963: *L'Orient et la pensée romantique*. Paris: Marcel Didier.

Ghosh, Pika. 1995: Introduction. In Michael W. Meister (ed.), *Cooking for the Gods: The Art of Home Ritual in Bengal*, 11–13. Newark: Newark Museum.

Giddens, Anthony. 1991: *Modernity and Self-Identity*. Cambridge: Polity.

Gilmour, David. 1997: The Ends of Empire. *Wilson Quarterly*, Spring, 32–40.

Girouard, Mark. 1979: *The Victorian Country House*. New Haven: Yale University Press.

Glasenapp, Helmuth von. 1973: *Image of India*, trans S. Ambike. New Delhi: Indian Council for Cultural Relations.

Gombrich, R. F. 1996: *How Buddhism Began: The Conditioned Genesis of the Early Teachings*. London: Athlone.

Goody, Jack. 1996: *The East in the West*. Cambridge: Cambridge University Press.

Gupta, Sanjukta. 2000: The Worship of Kali According to the *Todala Tantra*. In David Gordon White (ed.), *Tantra in Practice*, 463–88. Princeton: Princeton University Press.

Gutschow, Niels. 1996: The Astamatrika and Navadurga of Bhaktapur. In Axel Michaels et al. (eds), *Wild Goddesses in India and Nepal*, 191–216. Berne: Peter Lang.

Haafner, J. 1811: *Voyages dans la Péninsule Occidentale de l'Inde et dans l'Ile de Ceilan*, vol. 2, trans. J[ansen] Paris: Arthus-Bertrand.

Habermas, Jürgen. 1985: Modernity: An Incomplete Project. In Hal Foster (ed.), *Postmodern Culture*, 3–15. London: Pluto Press.

Habermas, Jürgen. 1987: *The Philosophical Discourse of Modernity*, trans. Frederick G. Lawrence. Cambridge: Polity.

Hacker, Paul. 1995: *Philology and Confrontation*, ed. Wilhelm Halbfass. Albany: State University of New York.

Halbfass, Wilhelm. 1988: *India and Europe: An Essay in Understanding*. Albany: State University of New York Press.

Handelman, Don and Shulman, David. 1997: *God Inside Out: Shiva's Game of Dice*. New York: Oxford University Press.

Hansen, Kathryn. 1992: *Grounds for Play: The Nautanki Theatre of North India*. Berkeley: University of California Press.

Hansen, Thomas Blom. 1999: *The Saffron Wave: Democracy and Hindu Nationalism in Modern India*. Princeton: Princeton University Press.

Hansen, Thomas Blom. 2001: *Wages of Violence: Naming and Identity in Postcolonial Bombay*. Princeton: Princeton University Press.

Hardy, Friedhelm. 1994: *The Religious Culture of India: Power, Love, and Wisdom*. Cambridge: Cambridge University Press.

Hardy, Peter. 1960: *Historians of Medieval India: Studies in Indo-Muslim Historical Writing*. London: Luzac.

Harlan, Lindsey. 1992: *Religion and Rajput Women: The Ethic of Protection in Contemporary Narratives*. Berkeley: University of California Press.

Harvey, David. 1985: *Consciousness and the Urban Experience*. Oxford: Blackwell.

Hasan, Mushirul. 1997: *Legacy of Divided Nation: India's Muslims since Independence*. London: Hurst.

Hawley, John Stratton (ed.). 1994: *Sati, the Blessing and the Curse: The Burning of Wives in India*. New York: Oxford University Press.

Hayek, F. A. 1978: *The Three Sources of Human Values*. London: London School of Economics and Political Science.

Hazard, Paul. 1964: *The European Mind 1680–1715*, trans. J. Lewis May. Harmondsworth: Penguin.

Heehs, Peter. 2000: 'The Error of All "Churches"': Religion and Spirituality in Communities Founded or 'Inspired' by Sri Aurobindo. In Antony Copley (ed.), *Gurus and their Followers: New Religious Reform Movements in Colonial India.* New Delhi: Oxford University Press.

Heelas, Paul (ed.). 1996: *Detraditionalization: Critical Reflections on Authority and Identity at a Time of Uncertainty.* Oxford: Blackwell.

Heelas, Paul (ed.). 1998: *Religion, Modernity and Postmodernity.* Oxford: Blackwell.

Hegel, G. W. F. 1975 [1837]: *Lectures on the Philosophy of World History,* trans. H. B. Nisbet. London: Cambridge University Press.

Herzog, Isaac. 1974: *Judaism – Law and Ethics: Essays by the Late Chief Rabbi Dr. Isaac Herzog,* selected by Chaim Herzog. London: Soncino Press.

Heuzé, Gérard. 1989: *Ouvriers d'un autre monde: L'Exemple des travailleurs de la mine en Inde contemporaine.* Paris: Maison des Sciences de l'Homme.

Heuzé, Gérard. 1993: *Ou va l'Inde moderne? L'Aggravation des crises politiques et sociales.* Paris: L'Harmattan.

Hodgson, Marshall G. S. 1993: *Rethinking World History: Essays on Europe, Islam, and World History.* Cambridge: Cambridge University Press.

Hulin, J. P. 1988: L'Inde dans les premiers ecrits de Kipling. In C. Weinberger-Thomas (ed.), *L'Inde et l'imaginaire.* Paris: EHSS.

Hulin, Michel. 1991: Nietzsche and the Suffering of the Indian Ascetic. In Graham Parkes (ed.), *Nietzsche and Asian Thought,* 64–75. Chicago: University of Chicago Press.

Hume, David. 1956 [1777]: *The Natural History of Religion,* ed. H. E. Root. London: Adam & Charles Black.

Ian, Marcia. 1993: *Remembering the Phallic Mother: Psychoanalysis, Modernism, and the Fetish.* Ithaca: Cornell University Press.

Inden, Ronald. 1992: *Imagining India.* Oxford: Blackwell.

Isherwood, Christopher. 1965: *Ramakrishna and his Disciples.* London: Methuen.

Jaffrelot, Christophe. 1996: *The Hindu Nationalist Movement and Indian Politics, 1925 to the 1990s.* London: Hurst.

Jaffrelot, Christophe. 1997: The Idea of the Human Race in the Writings of Hindu Nationalist Ideologues in the 1920s and 1930s: A Concept Between Two Cultures. In Peter Robb (ed.), *The Concept of Race in South Asia.* Delhi: Oxford University Press.

Jaffrelot, Christophe. 2000: *Dr Ambedkar: Leader intouchable et père de la constitution indienne.* Paris: Presses de Sciences Po.

Jairazbhoy, Nazir Ali. 1991: *Hi-Tech Shiva and Other Apocryphal Stories.* Van Nuys, CA: Apsara Media.

John, Mary E. 1998: Globalisation, Sexuality and the Visual Field. In Mary E. John and Janaki Nair (eds), *A Question of Silence: The Sexual Economies of Modern India.* New Delhi: Kali for Women.

Jordens, J. T. F. 1997: *Dayananda Sarasvati: His Life and Ideas.* Delhi: Oxford University Press.

Jose, Jim. 2000: Contesting Patrilineal Descent in Political Theory: James Mill and Nineteenth-Century Feminism. *Hypatia,* 15, 1, 151–74.

Kaelber, Walter O. 1989: *Tapta Marga: Asceticisim and Initiation in Vedic India.* Albany: State University of New York.

Kakar, S. 1978: *The Inner World: A Psychoanalytic Study of Childhood and Society in India.* New Delhi: Oxford University Press.

Kakar, S. 1991: *The Analyst and the Mystic: Psychoanalytic Reflections on Religion and Mysticism*. New Delhi: Viking.

Kakar, S. 1996: The Construction of a New Hindu Identity. In Kaushik Basu and Sanjay Subrahmanyam (eds), *Unravelling the Nation: Sectarian Conflict and India's Secular Identity*, 204–35. Delhi: Penguin.

Kant, Immanuel. 1983: *Perpetual Peace and Other Essays*, trans. T. Humphrey. Indianapolis, Ind.: Hackett.

Kant, Immanuel. 1996: *Religion and Rational Theology*, trans. and ed. Allen W. Wood and George di Giovanni. Cambridge Edition of the Works of Immanuel Kant. Cambridge: Cambridge University Press.

Kantowsky, Detlef. 1986: Max Weber on India and Indian Interpretations of Weber. In id. (ed.), *Recent Research on Max Weber's Studies of Hinduism*, 9–44. Munich: Weltforum Verlag.

Kapur, Geeta. 1993: Revelation and Doubt: *Sant Tukaram* and *Devi*. In Tejaswini Niranjana, P. Sudhir and Vivek Dhareshwar (eds), *Interrogating Modernity: Culture and Colonialism in India*. Calcutta: Seagull.

Kaviraj, Sudipta. 1995: Religion, Politics and Modernity. In Upendra Baxi and Bhikhu Parekh (eds), *Crisis and Change in Contemporary India*. New Delhi: Sage Publications.

Kedourie, E. 1993: *Nationalism*. Oxford: Blackwell.

Kejariwal, O. P. 1988: *The Asiatic Society of Bengal and the Discovery of India's Past 1784–1838*. Delhi: Oxford University Press.

Khilnani, Sunil. 1997: *The Idea of India*. London: Hamish Hamilton.

Kipling, Rudyard. 1898: *The Day's Work*. London: Macmillan.

Kipling, Rudyard. 1960: *Plain Tales from the Hills*. London: Macmillan.

Kishwar, Madhu. 2000: From *Manusmriti* to *Madhusmriti:* Flagellating a Mythical Enemy. *Manushi*, Mar.–Apr.

Kopf, David. 1969: *British Orientalism and the Bengal Renaissance: The Dynamics of Indian Modernization 1773–1835*. Berkeley and Los Angeles: University of California Press.

Kopf, David. 1991: European Enlightenment, Hindu Renaissance and the Enrichment of the Human Spirit: A History of Historical Writings on British Orientalism. In Nancy G. Cassels (ed.), *Orientalism, Evangelicalism and the Military Cantonment in Early Nineteenth-century India: A Historiographical Overview*, 19–53. Lampeter: Edwin Mellen.

Kripal, Jeffrey J. 2000: A Garland of Talking Heads for the Goddess. In Alf Hiltebeitel and Kathleen M. Erndl (eds), *Is the Goddess a Feminist?*, 239–68. Sheffield: Sheffield Academic Press.

Kumar, Radha. 1993: *The History of Doing: An Illustrated Account of Movements for Women's Rights and Feminism in India 1800–1990*. New Delhi: Kali for Women.

Kurtz, Stanley M. 1992: *All the Mothers are One: Hindu India and the Cultural Reshaping of Psychoanalysis*. New York: Columbia University Press.

Kuspit, Donald. 1993: *Signs of Psyche in Modern and Post-Modern Art*. Cambridge: Cambridge University Press.

Lacan, Jacques. 1978: *The Four Fundamental Concepts of Psychoanalysis*, trans. Alan Sheridan. New York: Norton.

Lach, Donald F. and Van Kley, Edwin J. 1993 [1965]: *Asia in the Making of Europe*,

3 vols. Chicago: University of Chicago Press.

Lal, Vinay. 1996: Masculinity and Femininity in *The Chess Players*. Sexual Moves, Colonial Manoeuvres, and an Indian Game. *Manushi: A Journal of Women and Society*, 92–3, 41–50.

Lal, Vinay. 1997: Good Nazis and Just Scholars: Much Ado About the British Empire, review of P. J. Marshall (ed.), *The Cambridge Illustrated History of the British Empire. Race and Class*, 38, 4, 89–101.

Lash, Scott (ed.). 1992: *Modernity and Identity*. Oxford: Blackwell.

Lash, Scott. 1998: *Another Modernity, a Different Rationality*. Oxford: Blackwell.

Lash, Scott and Whimster, Sam (eds). 1987: *Max Weber: Rationality and Modernity*. London: Allen & Unwin.

Lawrence, Sir Walter R. 1928: *The India We Served*. London: Cassell.

Le Rider, Jacques. 1993: *Modernity and Crises of Identity: Culture and Society in Fin-de-Siècle Vienna*, trans. Rosemary Morris. Cambridge: Polity.

Levinas, Emmanuel. 1988: The Paradox of Morality: An Interview with Emmanuel Levinas. In Robert Bernasconi and David Wood (eds), *The Provocation of Levinas: Rethinking the Other*. London: Routledge.

Levy, Robert I. 1990: *Mesocosm: Hinduism and the Organization of a Traditional and Newar City in Nepal*. Berkeley: University of California Press.

Llobera, Josen R. 1994: *The God of Modernity: The Development of Nationalism in Western Europe*. Oxford and Washington, DC: Berg.

Loomba, Ania. 1998: *Colonialism/Postcolonialism*. London: Routledge.

Losty, Jeremiah, P. 1982: *The Art of the Book in India*. London: British Library.

Ludden, David. 1999: *An Agrarian History of South Asia*, New Cambridge History of India, vol. 4. Cambridge: Cambridge University Press.

Lutgendorf, Philip. 1991: *The Life of a Text: Performing the Ramcaritmanas of Tulsidas*. Berkeley: University of California Press.

Lutgendorf, Philip. 1992: The Secret Life of Ramcandra. In Paula Richman (ed.), *Many Ramayanas: The Diversity of a Narrative Tradition in South Asia*, 217–34. Delhi: Oxford University Press.

Lutgendorf, Philip. 1995: Interpreting *Ramraj*: Reflections on the *Ramayana*, Bhakti and Hindu Nationalism. In David Lorenzen (ed.), *Bhakti Religion in North India*, 253–87. Delhi: Manohar.

Lütt, Jürgen. 1995. From Krishnalila to Ramarajya: A Court Case and its Consequences for the Reformation of Hinduism. In Vasudha Dalmia and Heinrich von Stietencron (eds), *Representing Hinduism: The Construction of Religious Traditions and National Identity*, 142–53. New Delhi and London: Sage.

Macaulay, T. B. 1895 [1841]: *Lord Macaulay's Essays and Lays of Ancient Rome*. London: Longmans Green and Co.

Macaulay, T. B. 1900 [1843]: *Miscellaneous Writings and Speeches*. London: Longmans.

MacKenzie, John M. 1994: Edward Said and the Historians. *Nineteenth Century Contexts*, 18, 1, 9–25.

MacKenzie, John M. 1995: *Orientalism: History, Theory and the Arts*. Manchester: Manchester University Press.

Macmunn, George. 1933: *The Underworld of India*. London: Jarrolds.

Malamoud, C. 1978: Preface to Louis Renou, *L'Inde fondamentale*. Paris: Herman.

Mani, Lata. 1998: *Contentious Traditions: The Debate on Sati in Colonial India*.

Berkeley: University of California Press.

Mankeka, Purnima. 1993: Television Tales and a Woman's Rage: A Nationalist Recasting of Draupadi's 'Disrobing'. *Public Culture*, 5, 469–92.

Marriott, McKim. 1976: Hindu Transactions: Diversity without Dualism. In B. Kapferer (ed.), *Transactions and Meaning*. Philadelphia: Institute for the Study of Human Issues.

Marx, Karl. 1970: *Capital: A Critique of Political Economy*, vol. 1, trans. from the 3rd German edn, ed. Samuel Moore and Edward Aveling. London: Lawrence & Wishart.

Marx, Karl. 1998: *Capital*, vol. 3, in *Collected Works of Karl Marx and Frederick Engels*, vol. 37. London: Lawrence & Wishart.

Marx, Karl and Engels, Friedrich. 1959: *The First Indian War of Independence: 1857–1859*. Moscow: Progress Publishers.

Mason, Philip. 1978: *Shaft of Sunlight: Memories of a Varied Life*. London: André Deutsch.

McClintock, Anne. 1995: *Imperial Leather: Race, Gender and Sexuality in the Imperial Contest*. London: Routledge.

McDermott, Rachel Fell. 1996a: Popular Attitudes to Kali and her Poetry Tradition. In Axel Michaels et al. (eds), *Wild Goddesses in India and Nepal*, 383–415. Bern: Peter Lang.

McDermott, Rachel Fell. 1996b: The Western Kali. In John S. Hawley and Donna M. Wulff (eds), *Devi: Goddesses of India*, 227–49. Berkeley: University of California Press.

McKean, Lise. 1996: *Spiritual Enterprise: Gurus and the Hindu Nationalist Movement*. Chicago: University of Chicago Press.

Mehta, J. L. 1985: *India and the West*. Chicago: Scholars Press.

Melton, J. Gordon. 1992: *The Encyclopedia of American Religions*, 3rd edn. Detroit: Gate Research.

Menen, Aubrey. 1974: *The New Mystics*. London: Thames & Hudson.

Merchant, Ismael. 1989: *Hullaballoo in Old Jeypore: The Making of* The Deceivers. New York: Doubleday.

Michaels, Axel. 1996: Goddess of the Secret. In Axel Michaels et al. (eds), *Wild Goddesses in India and Nepal*, 303–37. Berne: Peter Lang.

Mill, James. 1826: *The History of British India*, 6 vols. London: Baldwin, Cradock, & Joy.

Mill, James. 1966: *Selected Economic Writings*, ed. D. Winch. Edinburgh: Oliver & Boyd.

Mill, James. 1968: *The History of British India*, annotated by Horace Hayman Wilson, 6 vols in 4. New York: Chelsea House.

Miller, Daniel. 1994: *Modernity: An Ethnographic Approach, and Dualism and Mass Consumption in Trinidad*. Oxford: Berg.

Millet, Kate. 1971: *Sexual Politics*. London: Virago.

Minor, Robert N. 1999: *The Religious, the Spiritual, and the Secular: Auroville and Secular India*. Albany: State University of New York Press.

Mishra, Vijay. 1996: Defining the Self in Indian Literary and Filmic Texts. In Wimal Dissanayake (ed.), *Narratives of Agency: Self-Making in China, India, and Japan*. Minneapolis: University of Minnesota Press.

Mitter, Partha. 1978: *Much Maligned Monsters: History of European Reactions to In-*

dian Art. Oxford: Clarendon Press.

Mookerjee, Ajit. 1975: *Yoga Art*. London: Thames & Hudson.

Mukta, Parita. 1994: *Upholding the Common Life: The Community of Mirabai*. Delhi: Oxford University Press.

Mulvey, Laura. 1996: *Fetishism and Curiosity*. Bloomington: Indiana University Press.

Munshi, K. M. 1957: Preface. In *Ramayana*, trans. C. Rajagopala. Bombay: Bharatiya Vidya Bhavan.

Munshi, K. M. 1976: *Somanath: The Shrine Eternal*, 4th edn. Bombay: Bharatiya Vidya Bhavan.

Murr, Sylvia. 1991: Le Politique 'au Mogol' selon Bernier: Appareil conceptuel, rhétorique stratégique, philosophie morale. In J. Pouchepadass and H. Stern (eds), *De la royauté à l'état: Anthropologie et histoire du politique dans le monde indien*, 239–311. Paris: EHESS.

Nagele, Rainer. 1991: *Theater, Theory, Speculation: Walter Benjamin and the Scenes of Modernity*. Baltimore: Johns Hopkins University Press.

Nairn, Tom. 1977: *The Break-up of Britain: Crisis and New Nationalism*. London: New Left Books.

Nanda, B. R. 1962: *The Nehrus: Motilal and Jawaharlal*. London: George Allen & Unwin.

Nandy, Ashish (ed.). 1998: *Secret Politics of Our Desires*. New Delhi: Oxford University Press.

Nandy, Ashish. 2000: A Report on the Present State of Health of the Gods and Goddesses in South Asia. In Vinay Lal (ed.), *Dissenting Knowledges, Open Futures: The Multiple Selves and Strange Destinations of Ashish Nandy*, 127–50. New Delhi: Oxford University Press.

Nandy, Ashish et al. (eds). 1995: *Creating a Nationality: The Ramjanmabhumi Movement and Fear of the Self*. Delhi: Oxford University Press.

Narasimhan, Sakuntala. 1990: *Sati: A Study of Widow Burning in India*. New Delhi: Viking.

Narayana Rao, Velcheru. 1992: A *Ramayana* of their Own: Women's Oral Tradition in Telugu. In Paula Richman (ed.), *Many Ramayanas: The Diversity of a Narrative Tradition in South Asia*, 114–36. Delhi: Oxford University Press.

Nehru, Jawaharlal. 1946: *The Discovery of India*. London: Meridian Books.

Nicholas, Ralph W. 1981: Understanding a Hindu Temple in Bengal. In Adrian C. Meyer (ed.), *Culture and Morality*, 174–90. Delhi: Oxford University Press.

Nicholas, Ralph. 1995: The Effectiveness of the Hindu Sacrament (*Samskara*): Caste, Marriage and Divorce in Bengali Culture. In Lindsey Harlan and Paul B. Courtright (eds), *From the Margins of Hindu Marriage: Essays on Gender, Religion, and Culture*, 137–60. New York: Oxford University Press.

Nietzsche, Friedrich. 1954: *Beyond Good and Evil*, trans. Helen Zimmern. In *The Philosophy of Nietzsche*, ed. Willard Huntington Wright, 370–616. New York: The Modern Library.

Nikhilananda, Swami. 1942: *The Gospel of Sri Ramakrishna*. New York: Ramakrishna-Vivekananda Center.

Nilakantha Shastri, K. A. 1955: *A History of South India from Prehistoric Times to the Fall of Vijayanagar*. Madras: Oxford University Press.

Nuckolls, Charles W. (ed.). 1993: *Siblings in South Asia: Brothers and Sisters in Cul-*

tural Context. New York: Guilford Press.

Oesterheld, Christina. 1998: 'Ek Kahani, Ganga Jamni' Satirizing Secularity. In Vasudha Dalmia and Theo Damsteegt (eds), *Narrative Strategies: Essays on South Asian Literature and Film*. Leiden: CNWS Publications.

O'Flaherty [Doniger], Wendy. 1973: *Asceticism and Eroticism in the Mythology of Siva*. London: Oxford University Press.

O'Flaherty [Doniger], Wendy. 1980: *Sexual Metaphors and Animal Symbols in Indian Mythology*. Delhi: Motilal Banarsidas.

Olson, Alan M. 1992: *Hegel and the Spirit: Philosophy as Pneumatology*. Princeton: Princeton University Press.

Omvedt, Gail. 1997: The Death of a Poet. *The Hindu*, 14 Aug., 12.

Owen, David. 1994: *Maturity and Modernity: Nietzsche, Weber, Foucault and the Ambivalence of Reason*. London: Routledge.

Padel, Felix. 1995: *The Sacrifice of Human Being: British Rule and the Konds of Orissa*. Delhi: Oxford University Press.

Paglia, Camille. 1992: *Sexual Persona*. London: Penguin.

Pandey, Gyanendra. 1993: Which of us are Hindus? In G. Pandey (ed.), *Hindus and Others: The Question of Identity in India Today*, 238–73. New Delhi: Viking.

Parekh, Bhikhu. 1997: *Gandhi*. Oxford: Oxford University Press.

Parsons, William B. 1999: Freud's Encounter with Hinduism: An Historical-Textual Overview. In T. G. Vaidyanathan and Jeffrey J. Kripal (eds), *Vishnu on Freud's Desk*, 41–80. Delhi: Oxford University Press.

Pinch, William R. 1996: *Peasants and Monks in British India*. Berkeley: University of California Press.

Pines, Shlomo and Gelblum, Tuvia. 1966: Al-Biruni's Arabic Version of the Patanjali's *Yogasutra*: A Translation of his First Chapter and a Comparison with Related Sanskrit Texts. *Bulletin of School of Oriental and African Studies*, 29, 2, 302–25.

Pinney, Christopher. 1997: *Camera Indica: The Social Life of Indian Photographs*. London: Reaktion Books.

Pintard, René. 1983: *Le Libertinage érudit*. Geneva and Paris: Slatkine.

Pollock, Sheldon. 1993: Deep Orientalism? Notes on Sanskrit and Power beyond the Raj. In Carol A. Breckenridge and Peter van der Veer (eds), *Orientalism and the Postcolonial Predicament*, 76–133. Philadelphia: University of Pennsylvania Press.

Pollock, Sheldon. 1996: The Sanskrit Cosmopolis, AD 300–1300: Transculturation, Vernacularization, and the Question of Ideology. The Ideology and Status of Sanskrit in South and Southeast Asia. In J. E. M. Houben (ed.), *Ideology and Status of Sanskrit: Contributions to the History of the Sanskrit Language*. Leiden: Brill.

Pollock, Sheldon. 2001: The Death of Sanskrit. *Comparative Studies in Society and History*, 43, 2, 392–426.

Prakash, Gyan. 1995: *Orientalism* Now: A Review of Reviews. *History and Theory*, 34, 199–212.

Radhakrishnan, S. 1968: Hinduism and the West. In L. S. S. O'Malley (ed.), *Modern India and the West: A Study of the Interaction of their Civilization*, ch. 9. Oxford: Oxford University Press.

Raheja, Gloria Goodwin and Gold, Ann Grodzins. 1994: *Listen to the Heron's Words: Reimagining Gender and Kinship in North India*. Berkeley: University of California Press.

Rajadhyaksha, Ashish and Willemen, Paul. 1999: *Encyclopedia of Indian Cinema*, rev. edn. New Delhi: Oxford University Press.

Rajagopal, Arvind. 2001: *Politics after Television: Hindu Nationalism and the Reshaping of the Public in India*. Cambridge: Cambridge University Press.

Ramanujan, A. K. 1982: On Women Saints. In J. S. Hawley and D. M. Wulff (eds), *The Divine Consort*, 316–24. Berkeley: Graduate Theological Union.

Ramanujan, A. K. 1983: The Indian Oedipus. In Lowell Edmunds and Alan Dundes (eds), *Oedipus: A Folklore Casebook*. New York: Garland.

Ramanujan, A. K. 1991: Toward a Counter-System: Women's Tales. In Arjun Apadurai, Frank J. Korom, and Margaret A. Mills (eds), *Gender, Genre, and Power in South Asian Expressive Traditions*, 33–55. Philadelphia: University of Pennsylvania Press.

Ramaswamy, Sumathi. 1997: *Passions of the Tongue: Language Devotion in Tamil India, 1891–1970*. Berkeley: University of California Press.

Rawlinson, Andrew. 1997: *The Book of Enlightened Masters: Western Teachers in Eastern Traditions*. Chicago and La Salle: Open Court.

Rawson, P. 1972: *Tantra*, catalogue of an exhibition organized by Phillip S. Rawson and held at the Hayward Gallery, London, 30 Sept.–14 Nov. 1971; 2nd edn, revised and enlarged. London: Arts Council of Great Britain.

Ray, Rajat Kanta. 1995: Introduction. In Rajat Kanta Ray (ed.), *Mind Body and Society: Life and Mentality in Colonial Bengal*, 1–44. Calcutta: Oxford University Press.

Raychaudhuri, Tapan. 1995: The Pursuit of Reason in Nineteenth-Century Bengal. In Rajat Kanta Ray (ed.), *Mind Body and Society: Life and Mentality in Colonial Bengal*, 47–64. Calcutta: Oxford University Press.

Raychaudhuri, Tapan. 1996: British Rule in India: An Assessment. In P. J. Marshall (ed.), *The Cambridge Illustrated History of the British Empire*. Cambridge: Cambridge University Press.

Raychaudhuri, Tapan. 1999: *Perceptions, Emotions, Sensibilities: Essays on India's Colonial and Post-colonial Experiences*. New Delhi: Oxford University Press.

Raynal, Abbé G. T. 1781: *Histoire philosophique et politique des établissemens et du commerce des Européens dans les deux Indes*, 10 vols. Geneva: J.-L. Pellet.

Raynal, Abbé G. T. 1820: *Histoire philosophique et politique des établissements et du commerce des Européens dans les deux Indes*, 7 vols. Paris: Amable Costes.

Renou, Louis. 1950: *Sanskrit et culture: L'Apport de l'Inde à la civilisation humaine*. Paris: Payot.

Renou, Louis. 1961: *Hinduism*. New York.

Renou, Louis. 1968: *Religions of Ancient India*. New York: Schocken Books.

Rich, Adrienne. 1976: *Of Woman Born: Motherhood as Experience and Institution*. New York: W. W. Norton.

Richards, J. F. 1998 [1978]: The Formulation of Imperial Authority. In J. F. Richards (ed.), *Kingship and Authority in South Asia*, 285–326. Delhi: Oxford University Press.

Richards, Jeffrey and MacKenzie, John M. 1986: *The Railway Station: A Social History*. Oxford: Oxford University Press.

Richman, Paula (ed.). 1992: *Many Ramayanas: The Diversity of a Narrative Tradition in South Asia*. Delhi: Oxford University Press.

Risley, Herbert H. 1915: *The People of India*. Calcutta: Thacker, Spink.

Robb, Peter (ed.). 1997: *The Concept of Race in South Asia*. Delhi: Oxford University

Press.

Roger[ius], A. 1670: *La Porte ouverte*, trans. Thomas La Grue. Amsterdam: Jean Schipper.

Roger[ius], A. 1915 [1651]: *De Open-deure tot het Verborgen Heydendom*, ed. W. Caland. 's-Gravenhage: M. Nijhoff.

Rose, Gillian. 1993: *Judaism and Modernity: Philosophical Essays*. Oxford: Blackwell.

Ross, Barbara. 1998: *From the Ocean of Painting: India's Popular Paintings, 1589 to the Present*. New York: Oxford University Press.

Roy, Parama. 1998: *Indian Traffic: Identities in Question in Colonial and Postcolonial India*. Berkeley: University of California Press.

Roy, Rammohun. 1963: *Dialogue between a Theist and an Idolater: An 1820 Tract Probably by Rammohun Roy*, ed. Stephen N. Hay. Calcutta: K. L. Mukhopadhyay.

Rubies, Joan-Pau. 2000: *Travel and Ethnology in the Renaissance: South India through European Eyes, 1250–1625*. Cambridge: Cambridge University Press.

Ruhela, S. P. 1993: *Sri Sathya Sai Baba: His Life and Divine Role*. Delhi: Vikas Publishing House.

Rushdie, Salman. 1995: *The Moor's Last Sigh*. London: Jonathan Cape.

Sa'di n.d.: *The Bustan*, trans. A. Hart Edwards. Lahore: Ashraf.

Said, Edward W. 1978: *Orientalism*. London: Routledge & Kegan Paul.

Said, Edward W. 1984: *The World, the Text, and the Critic*. London: Faber & Faber.

Sankar Ray, Annada. 1968: A Note on Modernity. In Niharranjan Ray (ed.), *Modernity and Contemporay Indian Literature*, 62–6. Simla: Indian Institute of Advanced Study.

Sankaran Nair, Sir Chettur. 1922: *Gandhi and Anarchy*. Madras: Tagore & Co.

Sardar, Zaiuddin. 1998: Dilip Kumar Made Me Do It. In A. Nandy (ed.), *The Secret Politics of our Desires*. New Delhi: Oxford University Press.

Sarkar, Tanika and Butalia, Urvashi (eds). 1995: *Women and the Hindu Right: A Collection of Essays*. New Delhi: Kali for Women.

Savarkar, V. D. 1949: *Hindu Rashtra Darshan. A Collection of the Presidential Speeches Delivered from the Hindu Mahasabha Platform*. Bombay: L. G. Khare.

Savarkar, V. D. n.d.: *Hindudhwaj: Public Statements of the President of the Hindu Mahasabha, 1938–1941*. n.p.

Scaff, Lawrence A. 1989: *Fleeing the Iron Cage: Culture, Politics, and Modernity in the Thought of Max Weber*. Berkeley: University of California Press.

Schimmel, Annemarie. 1980: *Islam in the Indian Subcontinent*. Leiden and Cologne: E. J. Brill.

Schopenhauer, Arthur. 1966: *The World as Will and Representation*, trans. E. J. F. Payne, 2 vols. New York: Dover.

Schwab, Raymond. 1950: *La Renaissance orientale*. Paris: Payot.

Segal, Robert. 2000: Inaugural lecture. Lancaster: Lancaster University.

Sen, Mala. 1991: *India's Bandit Queen: The True Story of Phoolan Devi*. London: Pandora.

Sharma, Arvind. 1988: *Sati: Historical and Phenomenological Essays*. Delhi: Motilal Banarsidass.

Shayegan, Daryush. 1997: *Hindouisme et Soufisme: Une lecture du confluent des deux océans le Majma 'al-Bahrayn de Dara Shokuh*. Paris: Albin Michel.

Shih, H. 1937: The Indianization of China. In *Independence, Convergence, and Bor-*

rowing. Cambridge, MA: Harvard University Press.

Sil, Narasingha P. 1988a: The Troubled World of the Ananda Marg. *Quarterly Review of Historical Studies* (Calcutta), 27, 4, 3–19.

Sil, Narasingha P. 1988b: Anatomy of the Ananda Marga: Hindu Anabaptists, *Asian Culture Quarterly* (Taiwan), 16, 2 (Summer), 1–18.

Sil, Narasingha P. 1997: *Swami Vivekananda: A Reassessment*. Selinsgrove: Susquehanna University Press.

Sil, Narasingha P. 1998: *Ramakrishna Revisited: A New Biography*. Lanham: University Press of America.

Singh, Khushwant. 1975: *Gurus, Godmen, and Good People*. Bombay: Orient Longman.

Sinha, Mrinalini. 1994: Reading *Mother India*: Empire, Nation, and the Female Voice. *Journal of Women's History*, 6, 2 (Summer), 6–44.

Sinha, Rakesh. 1998: Secular Love for Macaulay. *Hindustan Times*, 3 Nov.

Sirsikar, V. M. 1992: My Years in the RSS. In E. Zelliot and M. Berntsen (eds), *The Experience of Hinduism: Essays on Religion in Maharashtra*. Delhi: Sri Satguru Publications

Sivaramamurti, C. 1977: *Amaravati Sculptures in the Madras Government Museum*. Madras: Madras Government Museum.

Sivaramamurti, C. 1978: *Chitrasutra of the Vishnudharmottara*. New Delhi: Kanak Publications.

Smith, David. 1993a: The Premodern and the Postmodern: Some Parallels. *Religion*, 23, 157–65.

Smith, David. 1993b: Violence and the Goddess. In Karel Werner (ed.), *Love Divine: Studies in Bhakti and Devotional Mysticism*, 193–206. Richmond: Curzon Press.

Smith, David. 1996: *The Dance of Siva*. Cambridge: Cambridge University Press.

Smith, David. 2002: Hinduism. In Linda Woodhead et al. (eds), *Religions in the Modern World*, 15–40. London: Routledge.

Smith, Frederick M. 1992: Indra's Curse, Varuna's Noose, and the Suppression of the Woman in the Vedic *Srauta* Ritual. In J. Leslie (ed.), *Roles and Rituals for Hindu Women*, 17–45. Delhi: Motilal Banarsidass.

Solomon, Robert C. 1983: *In the Spirit of Hegel: A Study of G. W. F. Hegel's Phenomenology of Spirit*. New York: Oxford University Press.

Speziale-Bagliacca, Roberto. 1991: *On the Shoulders of Freud: Freud, Lacan, and the Psychoanalysis of Phallic Ideology*, trans. D. E. W. Jones. New Brunswick: Transaction Publishers.

Spinoza, Baruch (attributed to) n.d. [*c*.1795]: *Traité des trois imposteurs*. No place of publication: Bibliothèque nationale de France N062998.

Sprung, G. M. C. 1983: Nietzsche's Interest in and Knowledge of Indian Thought. In David Goicoechea (ed.), *The Great Year of Zarathustra (1881–1981)*, 166–81. Lanham, Md.: University Press of America.

Srinivasan, Doris. 1997: *Many Heads, Arms and Eyes: Origin, Meaning and Form of Multiplicity in Indian Art*. Leiden: Brill.

Starhawk. 1979: *The Spiral Dance: A Rebirth of the Ancient Religion of the Great Goddess*, 10th anniversary edn. San Francisco: Harper.

Stein, Burton. 1980: *Peasant State and Society in Medieval South Inda*. Delhi: Oxford University Press.

Steiner, George. 1971: *In Bluebeard's Castle: Some Notes Towards the Re-definition of*

Culture. London: Faber & Faber.

Steinmann, Ralph Marc. 1986: *Guru-Sisya-Sambandha: Das Meister–Schüler Verhültnis im traditionellen und modernen Hinduismus.* Stuttgart: Steiner.

Swarup, Ram. 1995: Hindu Renaissance, *Organiser,* 10 Dec.

Tagore, Rabindranath. 1935: Inaugurator of the Modern Age in India. In *The Father of Modern India. Commemoration Volume of the Rammohun Roy Centenary Celebrations, 1933,* pt. 2, 4–5. Calcutta: Rammohun Roy Centenary Committee.

Tarlo, Emma. 1996: *Clothing Matters: Dress and Identity in India.* London: Hurst.

Tartakov, G. M. 1990: Art and Identity: The Rise of a New Buddhist Imagery. *Art Journal,* 49, 4 (Winter), 409–16.

Tavernier, JeanBaptiste. 1925 [1676]: *Travels in India,* trans. V. Ball, ed. William Crooke, 2nd edn, 2 vols. London: Oxford University Press.

Thomas, Rosie. 1989: Sanctity and Scandal: The Mythologization of Mother India. *Quarterly Review of Film and Video,* 11, 3, 11–30.

Thorner, Daniel. 1950: *Investment in Empire.* Philadelphia: University of Pennsylvania Press.

Tonelli, Edith A. 1985: *Neo-Tantra: Contemporary Indian Painting Inspired by Tradition.* Los Angeles: Frederick S. Wight Art Gallery.

Toth, Lazslo. 1988: Existe-t-il une doctrine traditionnelle de la race? *Politica Hermetica,* 2, 23.

Trautman, Thomas R. 1997: *Aryans and British India.* Berkeley: University of California Press.

Tripathi, Gaya Charan. 1997: Hinduism through Western Glasses. In G.-D. Sontheimer and H. Hulke (eds), *Hinduism Reconsidered,* 121–33. New Delhi: Manohar.

Tucci, Giuseppe. 1969: *Rati-lila: An Interpretation of the Tantric Imagery of the Temples of Nepal,* trans. James Hogarth. Geneva: Nagel.

Turner, Bryan S. 1992: *Max Weber: From History to Modernity.* London: Routledge.

Turner, Bryan S. 1994: *Orientalism Postmodernism and Globalism.* London: Routledge.

Twitchell, James B. 1999: *Lead Us Into Temptation.* New York: Columbia University Press.

Uban, Sujan Singh. 1997: *The Gurus of India.* London: Fine Books.

Upadhyaya, Deendayal. 1992: *Integral Hinduism.* New Delhi: Jagriti Prakashan.

Urban, Hugh B. 2000: The Cult of Ecstasy: Tantra, the New Age and the Spiritual Logic of Late Capitalism. *History of Religions,* 39, 268–304.

Vaidyanathan, T. G. and Kripal, Jeffrey J. 1999: *Vishnu on Freud's Desk: A Reader in Psychoanalysis and Hinduism.* Delhi: Oxford University Press.

Veer, Peter van der. 1988: *Gods on Earth: The Management of Religious Meaning and Identity in a North Indian Pilgrimage Centre.* New Delhi: Oxford University Press.

Veer, Peter van der. 1992: Ayodhya and Somnath: Eternal Shrines, Contested. *Social Research,* 59, 1 (Spring).

Veer, Peter van der. 1994: *Religious Nationalism: Hindus and Muslims in India.* Berkeley: University of California Press.

Veer, Peter van der. 1997: The Ideal Brahman as an Indological Construct. In G.-D. Sontheimer and H. Hulke (eds), *Hinduism Reconsidered,* 153–72. New Delhi: Manohar.

Veer, Peter van der. 2001: *Imperial Encounters.* Princeton: Princeton University Press.

Venn, Couze. 2000: *Occidentalism: Modernity and Subjectivity.* London: Sage.

Victoria of Luna Circa and the Rainbow Connection. 1995: *Kali! Death of the Ego*. <www.houseofkaos.abyss.com>.

Vidal, Denis. 1998: When the Gods Drink Milk! Empiricism and Belief in Contemporary Hinduism. *South Asia Research*, 18, 2, 149–71.

Wadley, Susan S. 1995: No Longer a Wife: Widows in Rural North India. In Lindsey Harlan and Paul B. Courtright (eds), *From the Margins of Hindu Marriage: Essays on Gender, Religion and Culture*. New York: Oxford University Press.

Waghorne, Joanne Punzo. 1999: The Divine Image in Contemporary South India: The Renaissance of a Once Maligned Tradtion. In Michael B. Dick (ed), *Born in Heaven, Made on Earth: The Making of the Cult Image in the Ancient Near East*, 211–43. Winona Lake, IN: Eisenbraun.

Wagoner, Phillip B. 2000: The Delhi Sultanate in the Political Imagination of Vijayanagara. In David Gilmartin and Bruce B. Lawrence (eds), *Beyond Turk and Hindu: Rethinking Religious Identities in Islamicate South Asia*. Gainsville: University of Florida Press.

Washbrook, D. A. 1997: From Comparative Sociology to Global History: Britain and India in the Prehistory of Modernity, *Journal of the Economic and Social History of the Orient*, 40, 4, 410–43.

Washbrook, D. A. 1999: Orients and Occidents: Colonial Discourse Theory and the Historiography of the British Empire. In Robin W. Winks (ed.), *Historiography*, Oxford History of the British Empire 5, 596–611. Oxford: Oxford University Press.

Weber, Max. 1930: *The Protestant Ethic*, trans. Talcott Parsons. London: Allen & Unwin.

Weber, Max. 1946: *From Max Weber: Essays in Sociology*, trans. Hans H. Gerth and C. Wright Mills. New York: Oxford University Press.

Weber, Max. 1958: *The Religion of India: The Sociology of Hinduism and Buddhism*, trans. Hans H. Gerth and Don Martindale. Glencoe: The Free Press.

Weber, Max. 1996 [1916]: *Max Weber Gesamtausgabe*, 20: *Wirtschaftsethik der Weltreligionen Hinduismus und Buddhismus*, ed. H. Schmidt-Glintzer and K.-H. Golzio. Tübingen: J. C. B. Mohr (Paul Siebeck).

Weinberger-Thomas, Catherine. 1987: Le Crépuscule des Dieux: Regards sur le polythéisme bouddhique (XVIIe–XIXe siècles). *History and Anthropology*, 3, 149–76.

Weinberger-Thomas, Catherine. 1999: *Ashes of Immortality: Widow-Burning in India*, trans. Jeffrey Mehlman and David Gordon White. Chicago: University of Chicago Press.

Welch, Stuart Cary. 1973: *A Flower from Every Meadow: Indian Paintings from American Collections*. New York: Asia Society.

Wheen, Francis. 2000: *Karl Marx*. London: Fourth Estate.

Wilson, H. H. 1958: *Religious Sects of the Hindus*. Calcutta: Susil Gupta (1st pub. in *Asiatic Researches*, 16 (1828) and 17 (1832)).

Woerkens, Martine van. 1993: Un Procès des thugs en 1877. In Denys Lombard et al. (eds), *Rêver l'Asie: Exoticisme et littérature coloniale aux Indes, en Indochine et en Insulinde*. Paris: EHESS.

Wokler, Robert. 1998: The Enlightenment Project as Betrayed by Modernity. *History of European Ideas*, 24, 4–5, 301–13.

Wolff, Janet. 1985: The Invisible Flâneuse: Women and the Literature of Modernity.

Theory, Culture and Society, 2, 3, 37–46.

Wollstonecraft, Mary. 1790: Review of *Sacontala, or, the Fatal Ring; An Indian Drama* by Câlidâs. *Analytical Review*, 7, 361–73.

Wood, Ernest. 1929: *An Englishman Defends Mother India: A Complete Constructive Reply to 'Mother India'*. Madras: Ganesh & Co.

Woodhead, Linda and Heelas, Paul (eds). 2000: *Religion in Modern Times: An Interpretive Anthology*. Oxford: Blackwell.

Wright, Caleb. 1851: *Lectures on India*, 5th edn. Boston: Caleb Wright.

Zelliot, E. and Berntsen, M. (eds). 1992: *The Experience of Hinduism: Essays on Religion in Maharashtra*. Delhi: Sri Satguru Publications.

Ziegler, Norman P. 1998 [1978]: Rajput Loyalties During the Mughal Period. In J. F. Richards (ed.), *Kingship and Authority in South Asia*, 242–84. Delhi: Oxford University Press.

Index